The Parlement of Paris,
1774–1789

BAILEY STONE

The Parlement of Paris, 1774–1789

The University of North Carolina Press

Chapel Hill

© 1981 The University of North Carolina Press

Manufactured in the United States of America

Library of Congress Cataloging in Publication Data

Stone, Bailey, 1946–
The Parlement of Paris, 1774–1789.

Bibliography: p.
Includes index.
1. France. Parlement (Paris) 2. France—Politics
and government—1774–1793.   I. Title.
JN2428.S86   328.44'36   79-27732
ISBN 0-8078-1442-3

To My Mother and

to the Memory of My Father

Contents

Acknowledgments

I owe a very special debt of gratitude to the late Jean Egret, eminent parlementary historian and former Professor of History at Poitiers, and to his widow, who resides in Paris. M. Egret's guidance immensely facilitated my initial research during 1970–71 on the Paris Parlement under Louis XVI. His erudition in eighteenth-century parlementary affairs suggested some of the principal lines of inquiry in my work, and his eagerness to advise me was a constant source of inspiration. Since his untimely death, Mme Egret has been so generous as to give me all the documentary material her husband had been collating in anticipation of writing a book on the parlementary opposition under Louis XVI. This material has aided significantly in the preparation of the present study. I can only hope that my book will in some measure justify the assistance, encouragement, and hospitality unfailingly tendered to me by M. and Mme Egret.

My work over the past eight years has also profited greatly from the encouragement and wise criticism of Professor Robert Darnton of Princeton University. Recognition is also due to Professors Lawrence Stone of Princeton and David Bien of the University of Michigan, who along with Professor Darnton read an earlier version of this book with critical eyes.

Thanks go also to Professors Pierre Goubert and François Furet of the Sixième Section de l'Ecole pratique des Hautes Etudes in Paris. Both men advised me and abetted my initial research in the Parisian archives. I should also acknowledge the counsel of J. François Bluche at an early point in my studies, as well as the more recent advice and guidance I have received from the professional staffs at many archives in the French capital.

I must also thank the comte and comtesse d'Eprémesnil of Paris for having allowed me to consult the private papers of Jean Jacques IV Duval d'Eprémesnil at the Archives nationales. I hope that my portrayal of this prominent junior *parlementaire* of the 1770s and 1780s will do him a fuller justice than has so far been accorded him in accounts of the politics of the period.

I should in addition mention the counsel given to me at various times by Professors Philip Dawson, Paul Lucas, and Gerald Cavanaugh of the United States, and Professor J. H. Shennan of England.

Three limited grants-in-aid from the University of Houston have provided substantial financial support for supplementary research in the Pa-

Acknowledgments

risian archives during the summers of 1976 and 1977 and for the writing of the final version of the manuscript during the past year.

Finally, I can never sufficiently thank my mother and father for their unfailing encouragement of my work during the past eight years. Their support has been crucial to me on more than one occasion since I first embarked upon this study.

Houston, September 1978

The Parlement of Paris,
1774–1789

The Parlement in Historiography

In late eighteenth-century France, the Parlement of Paris, while playing a vital role in royal justice and administration, helped frustrate critically needed reforms and thereby contributed to its own destruction and to that of the monarchy. There was an especially great irony in this situation, for, of the myriad institutions obstructing reform during those years, none stood closer to the crown or derived a higher prestige from French monarchical traditions than did this high court of law in the king's capital. The Paris Parlement could trace its origins far back into the medieval past and constituted, in the eighteenth century, the senior and most powerful tribunal in a network of parlements covering the entire kingdom. The parlements and other great law courts in the capital and the provinces dispensed royal justice and involved themselves in much public business of the realm, but it was above all the Parlement in Paris that by "remonstrating" against royal policies helped precipitate the final crisis leading to the Revolution of 1789.

Because the Parlement's clashes with the crown contributed to a political and social upheaval that eventually destroyed both adversaries, the clashes themselves have provoked much commentary over the years. Admirers of the enlightened ministers of Louis XV and Louis XVI have often condemned the parlementary opposition as negative and selfish, as stymieing the efforts of the Machaults and Turgots to doctor a sick ancien régime. Other historians, viewing the argument between the two sides with greater impartiality, have underscored crucial constitutional issues in the confrontation. Moreover, certain scholars from both of these traditions, along with other writers, have emphasized the aristocratic pedigree of the judges and assigned them a leading role in the aristocratic resurgence and revolution that supposedly preceded the middle-class and popular uprising of 1789. All of the Parlement's critics have decried the hypocrisy with which, they claim, the magistrates articulated popular grievances, and even advocates of the court's "constitutional" role have had to temper their respect for the Parlement's stand against Bourbon absolutism with recognition of the tribunal's defense of its own interests. It is true that accounts of the Parlement's behavior have seldom been purely positive or purely negative, and in any case they have often been developed with an eye to a broader consideration of the entire eighteenth-century judiciary or, indeed, of eighteenth-century society as a whole. Nevertheless, a brief review of the principal tendencies in the interpretation of parlementary activities will reveal the centrality of the Parisian magistrates to the long-standing debate over the collapse of the old regime. It will also reveal the failure of the participants in this debate to study the parlementary mentality carefully for its own sake and will suggest that there are benefits to be derived from such a study.

The French historian Marcel Marion exemplified a tendency, particularly prominent in twentieth-century historiography, to commend the expansion of the old regime's bureaucracy of ministers and intendants and to censure the irresponsibility of parlementary opposition to this development. In his studies of eighteenth-century finances and of Keeper of the Seals Lamoignon de Basville, Marion portrayed the men of the Paris Parlement as doggedly opposing the financial and judicial reforms of the enlightened servants of Louis XV and Louis XVI and thereby playing a significant role in the collapse of the Bourbon monarchy and in the convocation of the Estates General in 1789.[1] Although Marion had little more enthusiasm for Necker's first ministry than he had for the Parisian *parlementaires* of the 1770s and 1780s, he lauded Maupeou and Lamoignon as farsighted ex-magistrates determined to discipline their erstwhile colleagues of the Parlement, to streamline and modernize their judicial procedure, and to champion the prerogatives of the monarchy. Marion played down any role the magistrates might have assumed from time to time in tempering the arbitrary uses of royal power and treated all parlementary behavior in terms of the immediate confrontation between the monarchy and the magistracy.

Two of Marion's compatriots, the rather superficial Pierre Gaxotte and the eminent scholar Michel Antoine, have sustained this severe critique of the magistracy from a point of view predisposed in favor of Bourbon *raison d'état*. Gaxotte, in his history of the French Revolution and other works, excoriated the Parisian and provincial judges for sabotaging the reforms of the government and for disguising their reactionary ideas and selfish interests with humanitarian and "liberal" rhetoric.[2] Antoine, in a brief commentary upon judicial politics in the old regime and in a masterful study of the eighteenth-century Conseil du roi, approached these issues with a bit more subtlety.[3] He acknowledged the judges' custom of seeing themselves, in a misapplication of Montesquieu, as "intermediaries" between sovereign and subjects but nevertheless criticized the parlements for their corporate turbulence and vanity and accused them of having warred against legitimate monarchical prerogatives and policies throughout the eighteenth century. The parlementaires, asserted Antoine, were all too often impelled by irresponsible oratory into reckless sallies against the authority they had pledged themselves to uphold. They certainly did not evince the devotion to public interest and policies that, at least in part, characterized the viewpoint and behavior of the *conseillers du roi* under Louis XV.

Several writers in the English-speaking world have espoused this approach to the problem of the eighteenth-century monarchy and judiciary. In the first of three volumes on the history of France since 1715, the distinguished British historian Alfred Cobban castigated the Paris Parlement for its obstruction of enlightened royal policies in the "age of reform." The Parlement, said Cobban, was "the last relic of the medieval constitution left at the centre of government," and though appearing to itself— and to public opinion—as the defender of French constitutional liberties, the court was "no more in fact than a small, selfish, proud, and venal oligarchy." This self-styled palladium of the French "constitution" destroyed what it claimed to be defending by conducting "a running war with the Crown" that "brought the monarchy crashing down in a general destruction of the *ancien régime*."[4] That the parlementaires shared in the general havoc of 1789 and after in no way mitigated their folly in Cobban's eyes. Cobban's fellow countryman William Doyle, although somewhat more sympathetic toward the judges, has also minimized the constitutional significance of their oppositional role by viewing their prominence in political affairs in the 1770s and 1780s as little more than a function of passing intervals of weakness in the government—weak ministers, assertive parlements, and vice versa.[5] When the American historian John Gagliardo failed to find "enlightened despotism" in Bourbon France, he took the judiciary to task in a manner reminiscent of Cobban. Gagliardo summarily dismissed "the parlements' false propaganda that their opposition to the royal government stemmed from their concern for the public welfare." He also labeled the courts "one of the greatest obstructions to the progress of badly-needed reform" and characterized the Parlement in the capital as "particularly obnoxious."[6] Thus, one more historian had censured the judges for their benighted behavior in an age of Enlightenment.

But the strife between crown and judiciary in the old regime has also given rise to a significant historiography stressing constitutional issues and sympathizing to some extent with the judges' viewpoint in this strife. Alexis de Tocqueville, looking back at the old regime from the 1850s, noted the selfish interests and demagoguery of the parlementaires, but as always he was primarily concerned with the demagoguery and relentless growth of centralized government, in France and elsewhere. Hence, in Tocqueville's eyes, magisterial interference in eighteenth-century government only paralleled—and perhaps directly responded to—governmental encroachment upon domains of justice and administration traditionally entrusted to the men of the robe. Tocqueville was willing to acknowledge that at times "courts of law were allowed to make decisions on matters of public administration which were obviously outside their competence." But sometimes, he maintained, "they were debarred from hearing cases between private parties and thus excluded from their proper sphere." The French Parlement became "less and less an administrative and more and more a demagogic body"; but again, if this was primarily because of "the rising tide of popular feeling," it also reflected the monarchy's tendency to shoulder the judges out of traditional administrative roles. On the all-important issue of taxation, Tocqueville anticipated an argument of modern defenders of the Paris Parlement when he described the prerogative of taxing as "a power which, constitutionally, neither of the parties involved [i.e., neither the Parlement nor the crown] had any better right than the other to arrogate to itself."[7]

Toward the end of the nineteenth century, two other Frenchmen, Jules Flammermont and Hippolyte Monin, affirmed Tocqueville's thesis. In the introduction to the final volume of his edition of the Paris Parlement's eighteenth-century remonstrances, Flammermont conceded the judges' stubbornness in defending the parasitic interests of the old regime, but he added, in reference to the Parlement: "Without letting up, it continually criticized the prodigalities of the King and the Ministers, of the favorites at Court, as well as useless expenses, . . . secret depredations, the growth of the bureaucracy, and so on; it continually recommended economies and opposed the creation of new taxes and the borrowing policy that forced the Crown to declare bankruptcy; finally, it severely criticized at all times the *lettres de cachet* and championed the freedom of the individual, which it vigilantly guarded." Only the sovereign courts, claimed Flammermont, could exercise such a role under Bourbon absolutism and present to the Bourbon king "the confused plaints of his people."[8] Flammermont drove a similar point home in his study of Chancellor Maupeou and the lawcourts, insisting throughout that the parlementaires were essentially conservators of all the estates, corporations, privileges, and customs bequeathed by the past. Far from constituting a "new feudality" menacing royal authority in France, as their detractors had always alleged, the magistrates, said Flammermont, guarded the unwritten French "constitution" and were essential in that role to the continuance of legitimate, nondespotic monarchy.[9] Flammermont's contemporary Monin argued similarly in his survey of Parisian administrative and judicial institutions in 1789.[10] Monin detailed the Parlement's multifarious activities in administration and justice in the eighteenth-century capital and suggested that the tribunal's exercise of these functions, along with its strictures against despotism, had entitled it to something better than the condemnation of its many critics.

Twentieth-century historians in France have continued to wrestle with the problem of defining the magistracy's role in the "constitution" of the old regime—as well as with the problem of defining that nebulous constitution itself. Henri Carré, author of a book and of many articles on the parlements, pronounced a mixed judgment on the magistrates. On the one hand, he saw "ministerial despotism" as a very real issue in the France of Louis XV and Louis XVI and maintained that the perception of this issue had led a surprising number of "enlightened" Frenchmen to support the recall of the old judiciary after Maupeou's fall from power in 1774.[11] Moreover, Carré was convinced that the judges genuinely regarded themselves as mediating between the king and his subjects on many important political and social questions. Nonetheless, he conceded the zeal of the parlementaires to champion their own interests, noted that their agitation weakened the monarchy at a particularly dangerous time, and characterized them as an "aristocracy" of venal officeholders.[12] Elie Carcassonne, probing the relationship between Montesquieu and the eighteenth-century debate over the nature of the French constitution, felt that the parlements had by the 1780s passed far beyond the Master's definition of the magisterial role as one of tempering, not sharing, the royal prerogative.[13] Carcassonne's analysis of the parlementary remonstrances of this period suggested a judiciary with pretensions to an enlarged legislative role in the state. He saw the judges as starting to articulate the ideal of a constitutional monarch governing the realm in collaboration with the parlements and the Estates General. Carcassonne realized that the magistrates in broaching and popularizing such an idea were playing with fire. A similar realization influenced works by Roger Bickart and Daniel Mornet, which appeared shortly after Carcassonne's long study.[14] Bickart's analysis of parlementary propaganda pointed up its articulation of such potentially subversive concepts as "national sovereignty," "fatherland," and "individual rights." Mornet, for his part, mentioned the parlementary polemics of constitutional liberalism in his discussion of the Enlightenment and saw them as part of the Enlightenment's contribution to the Revolution of 1789.

Jean Egret, the preeminent twentieth-century historian of the parlementary opposition to Louis XV and Louis XVI, judiciously evaluated the arguments of both sides in this confrontation. Egret knew his parlementaires far too well to be able to gloss over their limitations. He admitted that the parlements often expended more energy in contesting each other's corporate pretensions than in dispensing their justice, and he agreed with the judges' critics that the remonstrances and rebellions of the courts were often maneuvers for popular favor. Again, he acknowledged the trouble that magisterial agitation frequently spelled for humanitarian ministers combating the prejudices, privileges, and inequities that were rotting the ancien régime. At the same time, however, Egret underscored the complexity of the issues raised in the course of the long struggle between the monarchy and the magistrates. In his study of the parlementary opposition under Louis XV, for example, he cited reactions to Maupeou's *coup de force* of 1771 to show that thoughtful men were as disturbed by the Bourbon ministers' high-handed uses of royal power as they were by the narrow motivation and political irresponsibility of the high magistracy.[15] To be sure, Egret conceded, Maupeou was able for the time being to quash the refractory behavior of the courts, but he was less successful in finding a legitimate and enduring solution to the problems posed by the ill-defined powers and relationships of judicial and political institutions in France. Again, in his remarkable study of the "pre-Revolution" of 1787–88, Egret showed how the Paris Parlement's defiant stance, however selfishly motivated at specific points during 1787 and 1788, awoke within the French people a more resounding defiance of arbitrary government.[16]

But if the Parisian judges and their provincial counterparts have appeared on some pages of history as antigovernment incorrigibles or as witnesses to the lack of a well-defined constitution in France, they have appeared on other pages as leaders of an aristocratic resurgence in prerevolutionary French society. All commentators upon the parlementaires have noted their aristocratic affiliations, but those stressing social or "class" dynamics in the ancien régime and in the onset of the Revolution have naturally concerned themselves the most with the magistrates' social origins and orientation.

Jules Michelet heralded this approach as far back as the 1840s. His emotional history of the Revolution celebrated the "act of faith" of 1789 in which the masses rose up against and overthrew their oppressors. In the introduction to his apocalyptic account, Michelet paused upon the parlementaires just long enough to lump them together with the reactionary nobility of the 1780s.[17] Some later French historians, influenced in their view of eighteenth-century France by Marx as well as by Michelet, have retained something of both men's apocalyptic vision as well as their suspicion of the classes and sympathy for the masses. In their work, the theme of a reactionary aristocracy has served as prologue to the central drama of a successful bourgeois, capitalist revolution and abortive popular revolution. Needless to say, the parlementaires have figured as prominent villains in that prologue of the reactionary aristocracy.

Albert Mathiez, for example, had no doubt that the Parisian judges led an "aristocratic revolution" whose central goal was a return to the "feudality" of the past—that is, the aristocracy's resumption of political power taken from it by the crown over the centuries.[18] Georges Lefebvre was more subtle in portraying the relationship between robe and sword in the ancien régime, but he, too, underscored the judiciary's alliance with the sword. "The nobility," he claimed, "no longer thought of recouping power through armed force: it now challenged and undermined the king's rule with bourgeois methods, opposing him through sovereign courts and appeals to public opinion."[19] Albert Soboul maintains this interpretation today. In his own history of the Revolution, Soboul speaks of the convergence of interests of robe and sword in the course of the eighteenth century and asserts that in the 1780s the nobility "firmly controlled" the parlements and relied upon these "bastions of aristocratic power" in its "violent" assault upon the crown.[20]

This rendition of the magistracy's role has also attracted the support of some non-Marxist historians on both sides of the Atlantic. The American scholar Franklin Ford has restated the *thèse nobiliaire* in his study of robe and sword after the death of Louis XIV. Ford postulates a "regrouping" of the aristocracy behind the leadership of the magisterial nobility during those years. The parlements, he says, having already won their spurs of caste, used their political role to champion the "feudal" values they had adopted from the ancient military nobility. Ford's analysis ends with midcentury, but his thesis is clearly designed to explain the subsequent behavior of the high courts of law. Ford concedes the persistence, in the eighteenth century, of traits differentiating robe from sword but still insists that "in the very process of conquering the feudal nobility, the robe had succumbed to the standards of the older status group."[21] Ford's illustrious contemporary Robert R. Palmer has adopted this perspective in toto in his survey of the "Atlantic" revolution of the eighteenth century.[22]

Back in France, meanwhile, the exhaustive prosopographical research of François Bluche has seemed to given another boost to the thèse nobiliaire as applied to the magistracy.[23] After analyzing the pedigree of 590 families supplying magistrates to the eighteenth-century Paris Parlement, Bluche concludes that this tribunal participated fully in the century's aristocratic resurgence. For one thing, it was practically impossible for commoners to enter the court during this period. Although his genealogical labors terminate with the Maupeou years, Bluche suggests that not much changed in this regard after 1774. He is not unduly impressed by evidence Jean Egret had advanced a few years earlier showing a slightly larger percentage of *roturiers* admitted to the sovereign courts at Paris and elsewhere during the last fifteen years of the old regime.[24] Like Ford, Bluche acknowledges some of the aristocracy's internal divisions, stressing, for example, the differences between the world of the Parisian Palais de Justice and that of the sword noble on his rural *seigneurie*. Still, he draws what might appear to be facile conclusions about parlementary motivation from statistics of social provenance. The Paris Parlement, states Bluche, was distinguished primarily by the "violence of its demonstrations" against the crown, by the "lack of lucidity and absence of altruism in its antireformist position," and by its demagogic appeals to a public it did not truly represent or understand. The judges "practiced the different forms of 'noble reaction'" and faithfully watched over those aristocratic privileges they so fully shared with their cousins of the sword. As far as any "constitutional" role of the jurists was concerned,

Bluche asserts categorically that the parlementary opposition "was liberal only in its language, constructive only in appearance."[25] The parlementaires before all else were aristocrats taking care of their own, and that is that.

Or is it? Not necessarily, according to yet another participant in the debate. J. H. Shennan, a British scholar, has conceded the plausibility of this kind of argument but has offered an alternative interpretation of parlementary behavior.[26] Shennan acknowledges the noble life-style of the eighteenth-century parlementaires, the elements of aristocratic education and training in social deportment they often received, and the many familial alliances linking robe and sword. Still, he claims, the eighteenth century witnessed only the culmination of such tendencies: they had been present in the preceding century as well. Shennan also stresses the legal education required in most cases for membership in the sovereign courts and the respect for the legal profession inculcated by the daily routine in the Palais de Justice. These were important factors in the formation of a judicial and narrowly professional viewpoint quite different from the perspective of the sword nobility. Again, he emphasizes the fact that in the last analysis the judges depended upon their profession, and not upon their nobility, for what was in effect an ultraprivileged status *within* the second estate.[27] Shennan furthermore points to the pride evinced by the magistrates in their precedence over nobles of the sword at various public events such as religious festivals and royal marriages and funerals, and he recalls the carping esprit de corps that the Parisian justices repeatedly displayed—often in reaction against pretensions of the sword.[28]

Shennan therefore argues that the judges were precluded by the very nature of their training and experience from espousing (let alone leading) the alleged feudal resurgence in the eighteenth century: "The eighteenth-century magistrates made no break with the past, neither by developing into a narrowly exclusive caste, nor by taking over the leadership of the second estate. They maintained traditional social patterns, accepted traditional judicial obligations and, until the last years of the *ancien régime*, retained their traditional political relationship with the crown."[29] But during those "last years of the *ancien régime*," Shennan admits, the judges' "traditional political relationship with the crown" was in jeopardy. Upon occasion the Parlement, like the crown, was tempted by the aggravated crisis of the royal finances, and by the conflicts stemming from that crisis, to claim exorbitant powers and thus to stray outside the customary crown-Parlement relationship. The judges, therefore, did not deliberately spark an aristocratic rebellion, but they did at times overestimate their political-administrative role in matters affecting Louis XVI and his government.

This latest interpretation of the parlementaires' conduct, though certainly plausible, is raised upon secondary rather than primary sources and so remains (like all previous hypotheses) unproven. Professor Shennan, to do him credit, is more interested in presenting an English-language discussion of the Parlement's history and functions than in focusing upon the perilous subject of magisterial motivation in the twilight of the ancien régime. It remains nonetheless true that a thorough study of parlementary attitudes and behavior in the closing years of the old regime, utilizing all surviving parlementary records, has yet to be written. This is surprising in one sense and yet not, perhaps, in another. It is surprising in the sense that the Paris Parlement *was* so important in the governmental and judicial operations of Bourbon France and in the breakdown of the Bourbon regime. Yet this last event—the collapse of the monarchy in eighteenth-century France—reminds us that the overwhelming reality of the French Revolution has enthralled historical judgment and cast a long shadow back over the historiography of that traditional society the Revolution largely destroyed. Many specialists on eighteenth-century France either have been attracted directly to research upon the upheaval of the late 1780s and 1790s or have spent their time rummaging through the old regime for the causes of that upheaval. Consequently, the parlementaires, playing as they did an obstructionist political role during the crisis-ridden 1780s, have usually been resurrected by such specialists only to be incorporated into their explanations of the Great Revolution's origins.

Hence, on the one hand, those historians viewing the Revolution essentially as a consummation of the "ministerial Enlightenment" of the eighteenth century have scored the judges for their opposition to the government's policies without bothering to explore the judges' own perception of those policies and of the institutional forces behind them. On the other hand, those accentuating the social or "class" dynamics of the Revolution and of the preceding decades have hastened to assume that the magistrates' aristocratic origins and defense of aristocratic interests destined them for a leading role in an aristocratic resurgence, revolt, and revolution. Even those scholars such as Flammermont and Egret who have played up the constitutional element in the Revolution's causation have been compelled by their relative impartiality toward the conflicting theses of crown and judiciary to spend as much time poring over ministerial papers as analyzing parlementary documents. Nevertheless, although it is possible to suggest some reasons for the insufficiency of scholarship upon the parlementary mentality in the late eighteenth century, the need for research in this area should be obvious.

It should be all the more obvious in light of recent developments in the historiography of the causes of the French Revolution. During the past twenty-five years, historians on both sides of the Atlantic have become increasingly critical of attempts to explain the genesis of the Revolution primarily in terms of "aristocratic" and "bourgeois" class revolts.[30] Because this revisionism has had to come to grips with the notion that the Parisian magistrates participated in (and perhaps even initiated) an aristocratic revolt against the monarchy, it has dramatized the importance of a thorough understanding of parlementary attitudes and activities for any satisfactory explanation of the causes of the Revolution. This study may not be able in itself to suggest such an explanation, but it will lend new support to the suspicion that the Revolution of 1789 cannot be regarded as having resulted primarily from class consciousness and class revolts sharply defined in a Marxian sense.

The chapters that follow will attempt to provide an understanding of parlementary attitudes and behavior during the last fifteen years of the ancien régime. The first five chapters will cover the years from 1774 to 1786: the period from the accession of Louis XVI and his reinstatement of the old magistracy to the onset of the immediate prerevolutionary crisis. Chapter 1 will discuss the Paris Parlement's functions and the personnel of its several constituent chambers. Chapter 2 will consider judicial politics in the court and weigh some of the achievements and limitations of parlementary justice. Chapter 3 will examine the jurists' conception of kingship and their political relationship with Louis XVI and his ministers. Chapter 4 will explore the magistrates' conception of the aristocratic elite to which nearly all of them belonged. And Chapter 5 will study parlementary attitudes toward "corporations" and commoners within the third estate. Finally, the sixth chapter will consider the Parlement's attitudes toward the most important issues of the prerevolutionary crisis of 1787–88 and assess the degree of continuity in parlementary attitudes over the last fifteen years of the ancien régime.

The central argument of this study will be that the Parisian parlementaires, although eager at all times to augment their corporate privileges and powers, sought with equal zeal to articulate and balance the interests of all other groups in state and society. Such a balance of monarchical, aristocratic, judicial, and third estate interests, however precariously maintained, would have preserved the old regime essentially in its eighteenth-century condition—and simultaneously would have continued to maximize the influence and prestige of the parlementaires themselves. This study will also show, however, that in endeavoring to maintain this precarious balance of interests and champion its own corporate pretensions the Parlement in this period came increasingly into conflict with Bourbon *raison d'état* and as a result came increasingly to invoke the arguments of constitutional liberalism. Thus, by the time of the prerevolutionary crisis of 1787–88, the magistrates of the Paris Parlement were attempting to fulfill and reconcile a multiplicity of roles but were finding the task increasingly difficult. The ultimate failure of the judges to fulfill and reconcile their many roles, as they reaped the whirlwind of constitutional liberalism, should only further dramatize our need for a more sophisticated understanding of the parlementaires in the years after 1774.

◆❦ CHAPTER ONE **❧◆**

The Parlement and Its
Parlementaires, 1774–1786

As the preceding pages indicated, a number of historians have in recent years recapitulated the history and functions and investigated the personnel of the Paris Parlement. The present chapter, drawing upon this scholarship as well as upon some eighteenth-century sources, will briefly discuss the roles, internal organization, and personnel of the Parlement during the period from 1774 to the onset of the prerevolutionary crisis of 1787–88. The initial section of the chapter will review the principal responsibilities and prerogatives of the tribunal as a whole and mention some of the traditional attributes of its membership. The subsequent sections will deal more specifically with the chambers within the Parlement, detailing their functions and introducing their outstanding personalities. This closer look at the court's constituent chambers will also reveal differing perspectives among the membership regarding questions of precedence and discipline and the apportionment of responsibilities within the Parlement and will consequently suggest the possibility of future discord on such questions (as well as on others) that could threaten the unity of the court.

A Quick Sketch of the Parlement

The word "parlement" (or *pallamentum*) for a long time denoted imposing convocations of various kinds held under the aegis of the Capetian monarchs of medieval France.[1] By the end of the thirteenth century, however, a sedentary tribunal called the Parlement was emerging at Paris from the curia regis to hear the oral pleadings of cases that the monarch, though supreme magistrate of his realm, had progressively less time to adjudicate in person. In a strict sense, the corporation of legal specialists that developed from these beginnings only "represented" the magistrate-kings, who, down to the very end of the old regime, reserved and occasionally exercised their right to pronounce upon judicial affairs in their chief parlement. Nevertheless, in their more customary absence, the Parlement of Paris, followed later by provincial counterparts, continued to settle litigation and render decrees in the name of the monarch and his expanding royal law, thus bearing witness over the centuries to the slow expansion of France under her kings.

In the eighteenth century the Paris Parlement, despite the development of provincial parlements and of other high courts throughout the realm, retained supremacy in many judicial matters over a huge area of central and northern France. This jurisdiction included the Ile-de-France, Picardy, Champagne, Brie, Anjou and Maine, the Orléanais and Touraine, Auvergne, Saintonge, and Poitou, as well as Dunkirk and parts of Burgundy. A bewildering variety of civil and criminal litigation was appealed to the Paris Parlement from the lower courts in these provinces—from the provost and seigneurial courts at the bottom of the judicial hierarchy and the *bailliages, sénéchaussées* and *présidiaux* at the intermediate level. Highlighting this litigation were the so-called *cas royaux* which the bailliages judged in first instance. These cases involved alleged crimes against the person or prerogatives of the king or the peace of his realm: for instance, lèse majesté, the forgery of the royal seal, and debasement of the king's currency. The cas royaux also "came to include all instances of private war, of usury, of highway robbery, all matters pertaining to ennoblement or legitimization, to trade or to the peace of the realm."[2] Furthermore, by the theory of *prévention*, which emphasized the subordination of seigneurial justice to royal justice, increasing numbers of local disputes were taken out of seigneurial courts and tried by royal magistrates in the provost courts at the same level; and the Paris Parlement of course had cognizance of such litigation on highest appeal. Again, the Parlement's appellate jurisdiction embraced the famous *appels comme d'abus* from ecclesiastical courts that had allegedly exceeded their competence, transgressed against the forms of French justice, or violated the liberties of the Gallican church. The Parlement often capitalized upon such cases to champion secular and royal justice against ecclesiastical and seigneurial pretensions. Ordinarily the parlementaires' decisions in all these matters were final, although the king reserved (and at times exercised) the right to quash the judges' decrees and "evoke" such litigation to his own Council.

At the same time, the Parlement heard a variety of momentous cases in first instance. These included affairs involving the personnel and management of the royal household, the management of the royal domain, and the monarch's right of *régale*, that is, his right to administer and draw revenues from vacant bishoprics. The parlementaires also pronounced in first instance upon civil and criminal cases involving princes of the blood, dukes and peers, and great officers of the crown; criminal lawsuits involving lesser nobles, clerics, and officers of justice; and the civil disputes of those *privilégiés* whose royal letters of *committimus* entitled them to immediate parlementary justice. To be sure, the tribunal's competence was circumscribed by the jurisdiction of other courts at Paris, just as it was limited by the will of the magistrate-king sitting in his Council. Nevertheless, the Parlement ranked first among the regular courts of the realm in real judicial power as well as in prestige. Its unique stature was underscored on those solemn occasions when, with the princes of the blood, the peers, the councilors of the king, and perhaps the king himself in attendance, it deliberated as the Cour des Pairs and thus recalled its medieval origins in the curia regis.

The Parlement's judicial role implied an administrative role as well in a society whose justice and administration were often inextricably intertwined. It is true that during the eighteenth century the *lieutenant-général de police* in Paris and the intendants of the capital and the surrounding regions increasingly shared this administrative function with the Parlement. Nonetheless, the magistrates continued to have their fingers in a thousand and one administrative pies. The court could on the spur of the moment arrest or detain individuals, ban public gatherings in the streets of the capital, and impose curfews through its chief officers and their agents. More pervasive on a day-to-day basis was the influence of its *arrêts de règlement*. Such decrees lent a practical interpretation to the Parlement's own judicial pronouncements and to laws promulgated by the government, and the sovereign tolerated these interpretive arrêts so long as the magistrates did not attempt to seize a legislative initiative that belonged to the crown alone. By means of such decrees, the Parlement helped to insure the provisioning of foodstuffs and firewood to the capital, maintain the hygiene of its streets and the sound condition of its bridges and buildings, and regulate its hospitals, religious foundations, and prisons. Through its supervision of merchants, butchers, bakers, and a myriad of guilds the court had much to say about commerce, wages, and working conditions in Paris. The magistrates exercised a supervisory role over the University of Paris and other educational institutions in the capital and charged judicial officers of lower courts with the supervision of universities, religious chapters, and other corporations in the cities and towns of the jurisdiction. Again, the Parlement, always in conjunction with the police, acted as censor of public morals and literature in Paris, investigating the conduct of many a public official and ceremoniously burning many a condemned text at the Palais de Justice. From time to time the court also launched full-scale investigations of provincial administration. Its chief officers would, upon orders of the tribunal, instruct their counterparts in subordinate courts to follow up reports of malfeasance and abuses within the jurisdiction, and the Parlement often conveyed the findings of such inquests to the king himself. The tribunal's administrative activities were inseparable from its judicial function and augmented the influence it wielded in society.

But in a sense the Parlement's most critical role in the later years of the eighteenth century was legislative and, hence, political. By tradition, it legalized all royal acts bearing on taxation and on other matters affecting the kingdom as a whole; it did so by recording these acts upon its registers in formal plenary sessions. This ceremony of *enregistrement* was essential to the legitimization of the monarch's edicts, for it made them enforceable at law throughout the kingdom and simultaneously reaffirmed the "legality" of French kingship itself. On the other hand, the parlementaires could formally remonstrate against legislation they deemed illegal and/or harmful to the king and his subjects. The procedures of registration and remonstration, and the ritual by which the monarch on occasion enforced his supreme legislative prerogative in the Parlement, are discussed at greater length below in connection with the functions of the court's senior chamber.

It can come as no surprise that the magistrates who wielded such formidable influence in so many spheres of their contemporary society were privileged and prominent men.[3] Right down to 1789, the vast majority of parlementaires were full-fledged nobles; the few who were not were assured eventual ennoblement for themselves or for their sons through service in the court. As nobles, therefore, the men of the robe shared the standard privileges of their aristocratic cousins of the sword: a varying degree of exemption from the *taille*; exemption from the *corvée*, militia service, and the necessity of quartering royal troops; freedom from the *franc-fief* payments on the purchase and transferral of fiefs; *préséance* and *prééminence* in public convocations; and so on. Significantly, however, the parlementaire enjoyed additional rights denied to most aristocrats of the sword. For example, he was free from a variety of feudal dues still ordinarily paid to the crown by the sword nobility in transactions involving their fiefs, and he likewise profited from a host of tax, land, and commercial privileges granted in the course of the eighteenth century. Again, the robe noble as a royal counselor in the Paris Parlement could carry personal litigation directly to the king's privy council, whereas most of his counterparts of the sword had to initiate personal suits in the bailliages and sénéchaussées. Furthermore, after twenty years of service in his company, the parlementaire could acquire *lettres d'honoriat*, which would enable him to attend parlementary deliberations and retain his professional titles and honors even after his retirement from service in the tribunal. Finally, the parlementaire found that his participation in the great events of the capital, his proximity to the king and his government, conferred upon him an intangible but immensely important advantage over most nonrobe nobles. Clearly the Parisian parlementaire inhabited an ultraprivileged, ultraprestigious world within the privileged and prestigious *monde* of the nobility.

Nevertheless, as the arduous research of François Bluche has demonstrated, the typical eighteenth-century counselor of the Parlement enjoyed that wider monde as well.[4] If his professional duties kept him in

Paris ten months of the year, his family origins, friendships, and proprietary interests drew him back to the countryside during the annual vacations of September and October. If he maintained an adequate residence (or even, perhaps, a luxurious *hôtel*) in the Marais, the Ile Saint-Louis, or one of the fashionable *faubourgs* of the capital, he was likely as well to be seigneur of ancestral or acquired lands in the country and returned to the management and enjoyment of these lands in the Septembers and Octobers of his life. If the parlementaire derived some proportion of his usually considerable wealth from payments incidental to his office (such as the *gages, épices,* and *vacations*),[5] he likely derived a greater proportion from a variety of rents and annuities and from his own lands. True, he might be fortunate enough to inherit a handsome legacy from forebears who had enriched themselves in finance or commerce, or he might dabble in entrepreneurial activities himself; moreover, as a justice of the kingdom's greatest tribunal he might receive a royal pension, serve on a special royal committee looking into provincial *coutumes,* or counsel a prince of the blood. Still, the majority of magistrates, like many an aristocrat of the sword, secured their present and their future through accumulation of landed rents and annuities, careful estate management, and calculated marriage alliances. They were not for the most part as opulent as some *grands bourgeois, gens de finance,* or the wealthiest *noblesse de la cour,* but for that matter neither were the great majority of nonrobe nobles in France; and in any case the parlementaires eclipsed all these other groups in prestige and power. They truly enjoyed the best of both worlds, Parisian and provincial, and, along with their wives and children, mixed with the "best" people within each of those worlds.

Yet it is well to restate the importance for the magistrates of that Parisian world, that ultraprivileged milieu within which they thought and functioned as officers of the monarchy. If most of them were nobles, this was usually due to prior purchase of a charge such as *secrétaire du roi* or to long years of service in the Parlement rather than to an immemorial pedigree. If some of the judges improved their fortunes and enhanced their status through familial alliances with the sword, there was an equally significant tendency in the eighteenth century toward familial alliances within the robe itself. Such alliances made for a formidable solidarity of interests among the great robe families of the century: the Le Peletiers, Joly de Fleurys, Lamoignons, Séguiers, Gilbert de Voisins, and so on. Such families might assume an aristocratic life-style, defend aristocratic interests in parlementary remonstrances to the government, and bequeath certain values of the social elite to succeeding generations, but at the same time the vocation of justice left its imprimatur upon these families of the robe. A certain sense of public service, a tradition of moral severity deriving in some cases from Jansenism, a training in French jurisprudence, the ideal of the *parfait magistrat,* and above all the pride of participation in great political events—these were the distinguishing characteristics of the robe vocation and mentality. A final and momentous point is that membership in the Paris Parlement offered to the politically ambitious jurist something that few courtiers or rustic seigneurs could ever have: a natural springboard for advancement into the highest posts of the government. There was to be a sinister irony in this fact for most of the parlementaires dispensing justice in the waning years of the ancien régime, for just as Maupeou had risen out of parlementary ranks to become the reforming scourge of his ex-colleagues in the last years of Louis XV's reign, so Chrétien François de Lamoignon de Basville was to move from the Parlement to the government and attempt judicial reform under Louis XV's grandson and successor.

This cursory description of the eighteenth-century Parlement and its membership has suggested some of the reasons for the importance of this institution in the closing years of the ancien régime. A more careful examination of the court's functions and personnel during the reign of Louis XVI entails consideration of the several chambers within the Parlement. The following sections will therefore trace the evolution and discuss the roles of these constituent chambers and introduce some of their outstanding personalities in the years from 1774 to 1786.

The Grand' Chambre and Some Grand' Chambriers

The Parlement of Paris had scarcely emerged as a distinct institution from the medieval curia regis when its multiplying judicial duties necessitated the development of separate chambers within the tribunal to handle those duties.[6] Indeed, as early as 1278 Philip III issued a series of procedural regulations prescribing the activities of the tribunal's central Chambre pour pledier. It was here, in the original chamber of the Parlement, that all litigation was introduced, pleaded, and judged definitively in the earliest times, with the magistrates' judgments published in official decrees or *arrêts*. During the early fourteenth century, however, new chambers materialized within the company to lighten the workload of the magistrates in the central chamber and to provide a more careful examination of the legalities involved in the suits to be judged in the Chambre pour pledier. The Chambres des Requêtes approved or rejected the original requests for parlementary consideration of cases, and the Chambres des Enquêtes investigated the written evidence of parties to the disputes admitted to the court by the Requêtes and often conducted further inquests to ascertain other points in these cases. There were to be other specialized chambers within the Parlement at future junctures, but the primal Chambre pour pledier, known in later centuries as the Grand' Chambre, never relinquished its preeminence within the court: it retained its original title for a long time, because it long remained the sole chamber in which cases were decided upon oral as well as written evidence.

It is true that the subordinate Chambres des Enquêtes and Requêtes came to judge a variety of litigation on the basis of written evidence, but the Grand' Chambre always kept exclusive cognizance of the most important cases. It pronounced upon disputes involving the vital interests of the crown and settled civil cases involving the princes of the blood, the dukes and peers, the great officers of the crown, and such privileged corporations as the University of Paris, the Hôtel-Dieu, and other hospitals in the court's jurisdiction. The Grand' Chambre also judged on appeal the suits of privileged holders of royal letters of committimus who had applied in first instance to the Chambre des Requêtes, and indeed it had to corroborate *all* judgments rendered in the lower chambers. The senior chamber also received the *appels comme d'abus* in cases involving alleged abuses by ecclesiastical tribunals. Finally, it was the Grand' Chambre, convened with the much smaller chamber of criminal law within the Parlement known as the Tournelle, that pronounced in criminal proceedings upon the fate of all princes, peers, and lords within the realm as well as officers of the Parlement itself and members of other tribunals upon petition. In these crucial areas of litigation, the court's senior chamber seemed almost synonymous with the court itself.

However, although the preeminent judicial role of the Grand' Chambre engaged its members in many celebrated trials right down to the Diamond Necklace affair of 1785–86, this central chamber of the Parlement gained its greatest prestige from the fact that it accommodated all plenary sessions of the court called to debate public affairs.[7]

When, for example, the government submitted legislation to the Parlement, the Grand' Chambre immediately assembled with the Tournelle (two-thirds of whose members were grand' chambriers) to consider this legislation. The senior chamber debated measures concerning its own prerogatives and certain other questions without even consulting the lower chambers. In all cases involving taxation and other public issues, the Grand' Chambre convoked a plenary session of all chambers to consider the crown's proposed legislation. In most cases the court, by majority vote, approved the legislation and formally "registered" it by transcribing it upon its registers and enjoining subordinate courts in the jurisdiction to do likewise. If, however, objections arose to what the government was proposing, the court could order "remonstrances" or slightly less formal "representations" to be made to the king, explaining why the court found the legislation in question to be "unconstitutional" and/or potentially harmful to sovereign and subjects. In such circumstances the first president of the Parlement appointed a committee to draw up the formal protests, which a subsequent plenary session would debate and ordinarily approve by majority vote. (Because the first president chose mostly grand' chambriers to staff the committee drafting the protests, the resultant remonstrances or representations bore from the start the imprimatur of the senior judges.)[8] The first president and several other senior parlementaires then presented these protests to the king at Versailles; if, as usually happened, he rejected them, the Parlement could (and often did) draft additional protests. The magistrates could also pass ad hoc resolutions called *arrêtés* to signify their displeasure with government policies and announce their own stance on the pending public question. If the tribunal persisted in opposing the royal will in legislative matters, the magistrate-king could always return to his primal parlement in the Palais de Justice at Paris, accompanied by his chancellor or keeper of the seals and other great personages, and impose his will in a *lit de justice*. This ceremony, highly formalized and impressively staged, recalled at least two continuities in French legal history: the primal magisterial quality of kingship and the priority of the Grand' Chambre within the king's oldest and most prestigious parlement.

The Grand' Chambre had additional (if less spectacular) ways to assert its supremacy within the Parlement. The senior chamber could by itself or in session with the lower chambers admit new personnel into the court, confer special honors upon those of its members who had distinguished themselves, and accord special *lettres de grâce* and *lettres de pardon* to disgraced individuals petitioning for them. It often received delegations from subordinate tribunals or from privileged associations imploring the Parlement's protection. Finally, it was in the senior chamber that the judges especially charged with representing the monarch's interests—the first president, the *procureur-général*, and the two or three *avocats-généraux*—cooperated with a small number of subordinate presidents and untitled but influential counselors in distributing royal favors and lucrative judicial assignments among the members of the Parlement. The senior grand' chambriers thereby maintained the discipline within the court and harmony between court and crown necessary for the dispensation of royal justice and the registration of royal legislation.

As the foregoing discussion probably implies, the typical parlementaire could achieve the envied status of the grand' chambrier only through a long apprenticeship in one or more of the lower chambers and a slow advancement up the ladder of seniority. An eighteenth-century contemporary aptly characterized the Enquêtes and Requêtes as "the novitiate of the Grand' Chambre" and asserted that promotion by seniority guaranteed for the most part that the senior chamber "was composed of weightier dispositions, of more rational minds susceptible to the coolness and moderation that long reflection and experience produce." Somewhat equivocally, however, this observer conceded that although the Grand' Chambre had "the useful attributes of old age," it was accused by some of harboring "the vices of old age" as well.[9] The novices of the Enquêtes and Requêtes would probably have endorsed the last observation, for they were constrained to take a back seat to their older colleagues in prestige and power within the court, and certain zealots among their number were always eager to assail the "vices" of their seniors. Not surprisingly, few of the grand' chambriers were willing to engage in professional self-criticism: as far as they were concerned, their juniors should be content to serve their apprenticeship in the Enquêtes and Requêtes, as most parlementaires had since time out of mind, and defer to the veterans of the company in all matters. The younger judges' turn would come later; in the meantime, what better schooling for the responsibilities of the Grand' Chambre than patient service in the lower chambers?

The next chapter will show how these opposing attitudes sparked controversies within the Parlement during the 1770s and 1780s. For the moment it is more important to note that the men who led the Grand' Chambre in the closing years of the old regime had additional reasons for defending their status against would-be reformers within the tribunal. For men such as First President d'Aligre, President Joly de Fleury, and Counselor Lefebvre d'Amécourt, enjoyment of the senior chamber's prestige and prerogatives had been bought at the additional price of exile from Paris during the confrontation between crown and robe in the 1750s and professional nonexistence from 1771 to 1774 under the chancellorship of Maupeou. As they resumed their duties under the youthful Louis XVI, these leaders of the Parlement drew together instinctively to protect their chamber's status. At the same time, they brandished the pretensions of their company as a whole—while striving to dispense the king's justice and register most if not all of his laws.

Historians of this period have understandably suggested the existence in the court of a *parti ministériel*, including the most influential grand' chambriers and maintaining that rapport between crown and Parlement requisite for the prompt approval of the government's legislation.[10] Such a "ministerial party" seems indeed to have existed in the court. Though it cannot be defined with any precision, the attributes of several grand' chambriers suggest that they belonged to such a party and were thus most influential after 1774 in directing the Parlement and in managing its relations with the government. Among these definitional attributes were official positions within the court, royal pensions, and the elusive factor of personal influence.

The first president had always been the chief officer of the Parlement; theoretically appointed by the king, his ownership of his office and the normal workings of promotion made that appointment a mere formality in most cases.[11] Etienne François d'Aligre, who counted many prominent officers of the robe among his forebears, had held this post since 1768, though the exile of the Maupeou years had temporarily deprived him of it.[12] D'Aligre presided over the deliberations of the Grand' Chambre and over the Parlement as a whole when it convened in plenary session. In conjunction with several subordinate presidents of the senior chamber, he distributed among the court's membership special judicial assignments that often involved generous honoraria. Moreover, d'Aligre acted as intermediary between court and crown by presenting his company's remonstrances to the king at Versailles and by relaying the king's responses back to his confreres. Despite frequent allegations that d'Aligre was an inferior magistrate milking his office for all it was worth,[13] and despite various ailments, he managed relations between the Parlement and the crown well enough to retain the king's confidence for a long time. "He was," admitted one observer, "singularly skillful at managing his company" and, after 1774, "constantly assured himself of majority support in the court."[14] Tangible signs of the king's satisfaction were forthcoming. D'Aligre received 80,000 *livres* from Louis XV in 1768 to defray the considerable expenses of his position,[15] a pension of 20,000 livres in 1775, another of 8,000 livres for his wife four years later, and exemptions from the *vingtièmes* in 1777 and 1785.[16] The first president was hardly in desperate need of such royal largesse—like all the other leading parlementaires, he held extensive lands—but the king and his ministers left nothing to chance in cultivating the support of the key magistrates.

Several of the subordinate *présidents à mortier* who sat on the Grand Banc in the senior chamber during this final period of the Parlement's existence seem to have been similarly influential. The second president and successor apparent to d'Aligre was Louis François de Paule Lefevre d'Ormesson de Noyseau, member of one of the most illustrious robe families of France.[17] A memoirist of the day expressed an almost universal opinion in characterizing Lefevre d'Ormesson as "an inflexibly honest and severe individual, unsympathetic to the courtier class, strongly attached to the old ways of doing things, and entirely devoted to parlementary pretensions."[18] The government, apparently recognizing his stature among his colleagues and the general public, accorded him a pension of 15,000 livres at an early point in his parlementary career.[19] During the late 1770s and the 1780s Lefevre d'Ormesson often presided over the court in the absence of the chronically ailing d'Aligre, and his elevation to the first presidency following the latter's resignation in 1788 was widely applauded. Another influential président à mortier was Jean Omer Joly de Fleury, member of another famous robe family.[20] He profited from no less than three pensions: one of 7,080 livres granted in 1755, another of 6,000 livres granted in 1767, and yet another of 4,000 livres rewarding him in 1769 for his services as a president in the Grand' Chambre.[21] Joly de Fleury cooperated with d'Aligre, Lefevre d'Ormesson, and the other six presidents of the Grand' Chambre in directing the affairs of the tribunal, but he was also singled out by some observers for his unrelenting ambitions. One contemporary noted that President Joly de Fleury "was intelligent, knowledgeable, and talented" and asserted that he coveted d'Aligre's position.[22] Another memorialist saw this magistrate's ambitions as extending far beyond the Parlement and recalled that as late as 1789 Jean Omer Joly de Fleury was angling for a post in the government.[23] That the Grand Banc harbored political ambition as well as professional sentiments and talents was most dramatically illustrated by the case of the future keeper of the seals Lamoignon de Basville, who is discussed in a slightly different context below.

Those three or four parlementaires known as the "king's men" were also, by their functions, natural members of the "ministerial party" within the court. The *gens du roi* were the *procureur-général* and the two or three *avocats-généraux*: these royal attorneys, special pleaders for royal and public interests, comprised the *parquet*, a term that also designated the spot on the floor of the Grand' Chambre where these jurists stood when addressing their fellows. As procureur-général, Guillaume François Louis Joly de Fleury, older brother of the president, functioned as the king's chief solicitor.[24] He oversaw the pleading by the avocat-général of the royal side in any litigation involving the crown's interests and, as *trésorier garde des chartes et papiers de la couronne*, championed the inalienability of the royal domain and of all royal prerogatives. The procureur-général also maintained order within his tribunal and exercised an analogous role outside the court in concert with the lieutenant-général de police at Paris and with his own substitutes in the local bailliages. He furthermore presented the king's legislation to the Parlement; sent the court's decrees to subordinate tribunals to be read, registered, and published; and supervised various investigations of administrative and judicial affairs mandated by his company. In all these activities, Joly de Fleury was seconded by his associates of the parquet, especially the senior avocat-général Antoine Louis Séguier.[25] Séguier had the additional task of responding after First President d'Aligre to the compulsory registration of royal acts in the lits de justice of Louis XVI's reign, and on these solemn occasions—as in the regular course of parlementary business—used the Grand' Chambre as a sounding board for his grievances against philosophes, monopolists, and "ministerial despotism." Indeed, Séguier, though subordinated by function to Guillaume François Louis Joly de Fleury, excelled in his oral pleading of cases in the Grand' Chambre and far outshone his superior in most contemporaries' eyes. The procureur-général never escaped from the shadow of his father and celebrated predecessor, Guillaume François Joly de Fleury: many an observer contrasted the plodding conscientiousness or mediocrity of the son to the brilliance of the father.[26] Séguier, on the other hand, articulated parlementary concerns in a style of oratory celebrated among his colleagues and well becoming one whose family had given France a chancellor, seven *maîtres des requêtes,* and many parlementaires over the years.[27] Despite his frequent opposition to measures sponsored by the government, Séguier's role in the parquet warranted special notice from the crown, for he received a pension of 10,000 livres as early as 1767 "in consideration of his services and to favor his marriage" and additional largesse of 6,000 livres nine years later.[28]

The king also conferred the position of *rapporteur* upon one of the regular counselors of the Grand' Chambre. It was the duty of this magistrate to support royal legislation in the court and in particular to argue for its registration in plenary session. Three men held this commission in succession after 1774: the abbé Sahuguet d'Espagnac until 1781, Adrien Lefebvre d'Amécourt from 1781 to 1785, and the abbé Tandeau during 1786 and most of 1787.[29] The attributes of office, pension, and personal influence combined strikingly in the person of Lefebvre d'Amécourt. Son of a barrister in the Paris Parlement, aspiring toward noble status, seigneur of vast estates near Lisieux in Normandy, and accomplished jurist, Lefebvre d'Amécourt seems to have been one of the tribunal's most influential spirits during this final phase of its existence. Indeed, one contemporary termed him "the eagle and oracle of the Grand' Chambre" and asserted that his pleasing appearance, companionable ways, bounteous hospitality, *esprit cultivé,* and "manner of clearly presenting and analyzing what he had to say in court" accorded him "a great influence in his company."[30] Another memorialist commented in a similar vein but added cautiously that "persons who claimed to know him well accorded him less than their full confidence; they suspected him to be just as smooth and ambitious as President Joly de Fleury, with whom he appeared to be closely allied."[31] As a matter of fact, Lefebvre d'Amécourt, like Jean Omer Joly de Fleury and many another grand' chambrier in the past, found ministerial ambitions as well as ingrained professionalism orienting him toward the government. His long acquaintance over five decades of parlementary service with ministers such as Bertin and Maurepas, his alleged intriguing against Turgot and Necker, and his eleventh-hour attempt to enter the government with President Joly de Fleury in 1789 tailored him well for membership in any "ministerial party" in the Grand' Chambre.[32] Even before d'Amécourt succeeded the abbé d'Espagnac as king's rapporteur in the Parlement, First President d'Aligre was appointing him to every commission of parlementaires charged with drawing up remonstrances to the king; after 1781, rapporteur Lefebvre d'Amécourt became more influential than ever in this key political role of the tribunal.[33] The government was aware of his influence among his colleagues. It violated the customary procedure of naming a cleric as rapporteur in the Parlement when it chose him for that position in 1781, and two years later it granted him a yearly pension of 6,000 livres "in consideration of his services" in the Parlement's senior chamber.[34] Lefebvre d'Amécourt would still be playing a significant role in the court during the crisis that was to shatter all in 1787–88.

Several other parlementaires were regular members of the committees that hammered out the company's remonstrances during the later 1770s and 1780s and may have thereby wielded influence within the court. For example, Denis Louis Pasquier had been a parlementaire since 1718 and a grand' chambrier since 1754; he drew a royal pension of 2,000 livres until his death in 1783.[35] Again, Jean-Baptiste Joseph Sauveur, parlementaire since 1739 and grand' chambrier since 1766, drew a pension of 1,800 livres.[36] Other magistrates' names—Jacques de Chavannes, Titon de Villotran, Boula de Montgodefroy, Berthelot de Saint-Alban—appear in the papers of the Joly de Fleury brothers, the abbé d'Espagnac, and Lefebvre d'Amécourt with such frequency as to suggest the involvement of these additional senior judges in the direction of the court's business. Nevertheless, these same papers indicate, as do a plethora of contemporary memoirs, that d'Aligre, Lefevre d'Ormesson, the Joly de Fleury brothers, Séguier, the abbé d'Espagnac, and Lefebvre d'Amécourt were the magistrates who counted for the most in the direction of the Parlement and its relations with the crown. Louis XVI's government as much as admitted this (and therefore the existence of a parti ministériel in the court) when in 1784 it submitted President Lamoignon's clandestine memorandum on judicial reform to the consideration of five specified judges in this select group.[37]

That the Parlement possessed some natural leaders among its seniors did not, however, guarantee an untroubled harmony within the company. Not even the "ministerial" clique sketched above acted in a monolithic fashion upon all occasions. No doubt the government regarded the grand' chambriers (and a few younger jurists) whom it pensioned as forming the nucleus of support within the Parlement for royal initiatives, and it is true that the magistrates discussed above usually collaborated to obtain the registration of important legislation. Still, the king and his ministers had to reckon with the rumored political ambitions of President Joly de Fleury and Lefebvre d'Amécourt, with the unbending allegiance of Lefevre d'Ormesson and Séguier to their company's proud traditions, and with First President d'Aligre's grasping ways.[38] Given such differing concerns of the leading parlementaires, perfect consensus on all issues—and monolithic support for the government at all times—was impossible. But the government had also to reckon with the fact that the Parlement's leaders, even when united among themselves, could encounter opposition from certain grand' chambriers attuned less to ministerial wishes than to mutterings of discontent from the court's lower chambers.

Outstanding among these fractious grand' chambriers was a magistrate already alluded to, the future keeper of the seals Lamoignon.[39] Member of one of the great families of the French magistracy, Chrétien François II de

Lamoignon de Basville had been a parlementaire since 1755, a président à mortier in the Grand' Chambre since 1758. Like Maupeou before him, Lamoignon found his original métier unsatisfactory: his surviving papers attest to a long-germinating desire to reform French justice and administration, and he allegedly intrigued for a ministerial portfolio during the Maupeou years.[40] After the chancellor's disgrace in 1774, Lamoignon returned to the Parlement as fourth president in the senior chamber (after d'Aligre, Lefevre d'Ormesson, and Bochard de Saron), but he continued to find his charge unfulfilling. Although Lamoignon shared the fundamentally royalist orientation of his fellows in the Grand' Chambre, he was soon to spark a controversy over judicial reform in alliance with some of the court's rebellious juniors in the Enquêtes and Requêtes.

Several other grand' chambriers could trouble the tribunal's leaders from time to time, though they were especially to do so during the political crisis of 1787–88. Prominent among them were: Robert de Saint-Vincent, a parlementaire since 1748 who was renowned for his Jansenist austerity and opposition to "ministerial despotism" and who would eloquently champion a degree of toleration for Protestants in 1787; Fréteau de Saint-Just, a parlementaire since 1764 who was famed for his eloquence, integrity, and defiance of government dictates; and two clerical magistrates recently admitted to the Grand' Chambre and similarly prepared to defy "ministerial despotism," Abbé Le Coigneux de Bélabre and Abbé Sabatier de Cabre.[41] The presence of such individuals in the court's senior chamber (and of a few like-minded jurists in the Enquêtes and Requêtes) meant that the Parlement, even before the crisis of 1787–88, would find its consensus occasionally tested.

Nevertheless, down to 1787, the court's traditional leaders, even when challenged on some particular issue such as judicial reform by the Lamoignons of their company, successfully managed the majority of their associates in all chambers and profited from their special working relationship with the crown to preserve their own prerogatives and gratuities. Furthermore (and perhaps of greatest significance), the majority of parlementaires, seniors and juniors alike, seem to have shared basically similar viewpoints on the great social and political questions of the day.

However, the subordination of the lower chambers to the Grand' Chambre remained a cardinal fact of intraparlementary life. And by and large the grand' chambriers had been conditioned by their lifelong service in the Paris Parlement to defend that subordination, and the other traditions of their corporation and métier, with zeal. Statistics tell much of the story. In 1775, the court's first full year after its restoration by Louis XVI, 52 of the 139 parlementaires—10 présidents à mortier, 4 members of the parquet, 27 lay counselors, and 11 clerical magistrates—were members of the senior chamber. All 38 regular counselors, lay and clerical, had been parlementaires since 1750 or before, and 27 of the 38, since 1740 or before; 27 of these 38 magistrates had served in the Grand' Chambre before Maupeou's coup de force of 1771, many having been there during the great confrontations between Louis XV and the magistracy in the 1750s and 1760s. The dean of the senior chamber in 1775 was Etienne Vincent Lemée, ninety-four years of age and a parlementaire since 1711! A number of other grand' chambriers were octogenarians; the youngest were in their fifties. The active leaders of the court were all full-fledged veterans of their profession. First President d'Aligre, forty-eight in 1775, had served in the Parlement since 1745. As of 1775, the procureur-général and his brother, President Joly de Fleury, were sixty-six and sixty, respectively; the former had served in the court for forty-six years, the latter for forty years. Antoine Louis Séguier had been an avocat-général since 1755, and Lefevre d'Ormesson's parlementary career spanned five decades. The abbé d'Espagnac was to die in 1781 after forty-four years as a parlementaire. As for the influential Lefebvre d'Amécourt, fifty-five in 1775, his career had been interrupted at a significant juncture by Maupeou's coup de force of 1771: he had just become the dean of the third chamber of Enquêtes after thirty-one years of service in that chamber and was anticipating elevation into the prestigious Grand' Chambre. He returned to the Palais de Justice as a junior grand' chambrier at the end of 1774 and was to rank fourth in seniority among the regular counselors of that chamber before his company's revolutionary demise.[42]

Heredity of office meant that there was a certain inequality among the parlementaires when it came to their advancement in the court. Those benefiting from an illustrious magisterial parentage often started in the Parlement as members of the parquet or even as présidents à mortier; they seldom knew the years of apprenticeship in the Enquêtes or Requêtes that were put in by the d'Espagnacs and Lefebvre d'Amécourts. Still, what the grand' chambriers held and experienced in common was more significant than what divided them. Above all, the sheer duration of their service in this most prestigious of French tribunals goes far toward explaining the conservatism of their political and social orientation. It helps also to explain the tenacity with which they defended their company's supremacy in French justice, their chamber's preeminence within the company, and the traditions of their profession.

Apprenticeship in the Lower Chambers

While the grand' chambriers lorded it over the Parlement, their juniors served their apprenticeship in the three chambers of Enquêtes and one chamber of Requêtes that were reestablished after Louis XVI's accession. As has already been said, these subordinate chambers had started to emerge during the early fourteenth century as adjuncts to the court's embryonic Grand' Chambre. While the Enquêtes and Requêtes eventually acquired the power to judge a variety of litigation themselves, they were to remain firmly subordinated to the Grand' Chambre throughout the Parlement's existence.

This subordination manifested itself in a number of ways.[43] For instance, the presidents of these chambers, rather than being styled présidents à mortier or "presidents of the court," were merely "presidents in the Enquêtes" or "presidents in the Requêtes." They were counselors charged with disciplining and overseeing the business of their respective chambers, not executives of the whole Parlement. They, and the junior magistrates over whom they presided, knew that the senior chamber (together with the Tournelle) determined when the full court should convene to discuss controversial affairs and who should sit on committees to draw up remonstrances. As far as the daily function of justice was concerned, every junior parlementaire knew that his chamber's judgments required the approbation of the Grand' Chambre before they could actually become "law." Furthermore, although the Enquêtes might have appellate jurisdiction over *petit-criminel* transgressions punishable by fines, the Grand' Chambre and Tournelle judged on appeal the more serious criminal suits that could involve physical punishment. As for the chamber of Requêtes, it might pronounce in first instance upon the civil litigation of those *privilégiés* holding letters of committimus, but all dissatisfied parties to such cases could appeal the decisions of the Requêtes to the Grand' Chambre. Moreover, due to the fact that the chamber of Requêtes had something of a special status, never having been, like the chambers of Enquêtes, totally integrated into the court, its members, should they desire elevation into the Grand' Chambre some day, would ordinarily have to enter one of the chambers of Enquêtes and endure the standard apprenticeship there.[44] Small wonder, then, if service in the Enquêtes and Requêtes, the "novitiate of the Grand' Chambre," engendered frustration, impatience, and what an eighteenth-century observer called "the high-spiritedness which makes youth dangerous."[45]

Some standard sources, along with more recent archival labors, permit a closer look at the personnel in the Parlement's lower chambers.[46] In 1775 these junior magistrates outnumbered the grand' chambriers by eighty-seven to fifty-two. The three chambers of Enquêtes fairly evenly shared seventy-one of these parlementaires, while the one chamber of Requêtes claimed the remaining sixteen. The ages and duration of service of these judges marked them off quite sharply from their seniors in the Grand' Chambre. Whereas the grand' chambriers were mainly in their fifties and sixties, with a few much older than that, the men dispensing justice in the lower chambers were for the most part in their thirties and forties. The youth of the Enquêtes and Requêtes became, if anything, more pronounced during the fifteen years after 1775: at least fifty-nine of the seventy-one lay counselors admitted to the court in this period were thirty-five or less as of 1790. As for those junior magistrates in office in 1775, few could claim a parlementary tenure antedating the decade of the 1760s. Of sixty-five regular counselors of the Enquêtes, fifty-one had been admitted to the Parlement after 1759, and some of these as late as 1774. None of the regular counselors of the Requêtes had been parlementaires before 1759. In some ways, then, the judges of the lower chambers were a far cry from the battle-scarred deans of the Grand' Chambre.

That is, they were a far cry in terms of age and professional tenure but not in terms of social origins. Most of the younger judges serving in the tribunal in 1775 had had some brief parlementary experience prior to Maupeou's drastic reforms and so were included in François Bluche's portrayal of the eighteenth-century Parlement's relatively stable patterns of social recruitment. Little seems to have changed in this regard after the reinstatement of the old magistracy. Nearly 90 percent of the magistrates admitted to the Enquêtes and Requêtes after 1775 were lay as opposed to clerical counselors, and their social provenance is known. Of these seventy-one magistrates, twenty-seven issued from families of the parlementary aristocracy, eight were *gentilshommes* whose families had been of the military noblesse for a century or more, and at least twenty-eight others came from families ennobled in the course of the eighteenth century by other means—service in the Parisian Chambre des Comptes or Cour des Aides, purchases of the post of secrétaire du roi, and so on. Finally, eight of these junior parlementaires seem to have been commoners or, at most, in the process of acquiring nobility through parlementary service or some other means. None of these tendencies marked a significant break with the past. True, there may have been a few more commoners in the court at the end of its existence than at earlier points in the eighteenth century, but not markedly more. The presence of a few judges of "ancient" aristocratic extraction, the variety of other backgrounds outside the parlementary aristocracy, the prominence of secrétaires du roi in a number of youthful jurists' families—these traits were all very much part of the traditional picture.

Basically, then, the younger parlementaires of the 1770s and 1780s reveal backgrounds similar to those of their seniors in the Grand' Chambre. To be sure, the Grand Banc and parquet of the court's central chamber boasted the majority of magistrates of illustrious robe lineage, but this had long been the case and resulted naturally from the workings of venality and heredity in office. That the judges of the Enquêtes and Requêtes lacked the age, experience, and perhaps the maturity of the grand' chambriers was equally traditional. The tension between two different generations within the Parlement could acquire a new significance only in the event of a severe crisis external to the court—such as government bankruptcy.

Yet there were some potential leaders of rebellion in the lower chambers, most of whom entered the Parlement after its reinstatement in 1774. Outstanding among these insubordinates was Jean Jacques IV Duval d'Eprémesnil.[47] Born in 1746 at Pondichéry in French India, son and grandson of officers of the Compagnie des Indes, Duval d'Eprémesnil was educated for a legal career in France. After serving for a brief period as avocat du roi in the Châtelet, the provost court at Paris, he entered the first chamber of Enquêtes in the Paris Parlement in 1775 and speedily achieved a reputation as one of the most active and eloquent of the junior magistrates. Reportedly an admirer of Montesquieu and the British constitution,[48] ardent foe of "ministerial despotism," and champion of France's traditional society of estates, privileges, and corporations, Duval d'Eprémesnil was simultaneously in touch with some of the most unorthodox cults and currents of thought in prerevolutionary Paris.[49] In the years to come, he was to fan the embers of revolt in the Enquêtes over issues of court discipline and procedure, champion Cagliostro during the latter's involvement in the Diamond Necklace affair, defend the privileges of the aristocracy whose ranks he had himself but recently entered, and, even before the political crisis of 1787–88, offend the government with his stinging denunciations of ministerial abuse of power.[50] Although some observers saw Duval d'Eprémesnil as little more than a mischiefmaker profiting from controversial times, others admired him, and all agreed that the influence he wielded among the younger jurists of the Parlement on a wide variety of issues made him a force to be reckoned with—both by his elders of the Grand' Chambre and by the government.[51]

Of similarly turbulent disposition in the court's lower chambers were Charles-Louis Huguet de Sémonville and (in the late 1780s) Anne Louis Goislard de Montsabert. Huguet de Sémonville, member of the second chamber of Enquêtes from 1777 until his company's demise, struck one contemporary as being "of ardent and restless character, desiring a role of political intrigue even more than professional success, and sacrificing all to the wish to make a noise for himself and be counted for something."[52] Goislard de Montsabert, son of a long-time counselor in the Parlement, entered the third chamber of Enquêtes in 1785 and was to join the eleventh-hour campaigns of Duval d'Eprémesnil, Huguet de Sémonville, and like-minded parlementaires against Louis XVI's government.[53]

Several other members of the lower chambers, though admiring and indeed concurring in Duval d'Eprémesnil's resolute opposition to "ministerial despotism," nevertheless followed their own counsel and, at least to some extent, steered independent courses in parlementary affairs. Antoine François Claude de Ferrand, member of a distinguished aristocratic and parlementary family, entered the second chamber of Enquêtes in 1769, just in time to experience along with his colleagues the professional nonexistence of the Maupeou years. Though surviving documents suggest that Ferrand had no more say in the determination of court policy during the years from 1774 to 1786 than did most of the junior magistrates, he was to play a significant role in the confrontation between crown and parlement during the summer of 1787. In his *Mémoires*, published only toward the end of the nineteenth century, he portrayed himself as a constitutional monarchist and social conservative striving to moderate the antigovernment campaign of Duval d'Eprémesnil and his turbulent allies and thus facilitate a compromise with the government men over its financial legislation.[54]

If the differences between Duval d'Eprémesnil and Ferrand were primarily temperamental, those between Adrien Jean François Duport de Prélaville and the majority of parlementaires were far more substantial. This future tribune of the Revolution, son and grandson of aristocratic counselors in the Paris Parlement, had been received in the third chamber of Enquêtes in 1778 at the age of nineteen.[55] Disciple of philosophes and physiocrats, friend to Lafayette, and patron of the radical "Committee of Thirty" in 1788 and 1789, Adrien Duport found his dissatisfaction with Bourbon absolutism allying him at an early date with Duval d'Eprémesnil and other parlementaires. The young liberal nobles of the day lionized him as they lionized his associate d'Eprémesnil. As one memorialist recalled, Duport's parlementary speeches made him "one of our premier orators, if this rank was accorded with justice to elevation of sentiment, form of dialectical expression, clarity of style, and a true sense of justice."[56] According to another contemporary, Duport's fellows at the Palais de Justice, concurring with opinion outside the court, saw him "as a good judge, very enlightened . . . eminently fair-minded and industrious in the extreme."[57] Yet, with the collapse of Bourbon absolutism in 1789, this magistrate's convictions were to lead him along a path radically different from that of his erstwhile companion Duval d'Eprémesnil. For the latter, defiance of ministerial despotism masked a fundamental acceptance of France's traditional society; for Adrien Duport, similar defiance betokened a readiness to dispense with all or at least much of the ancien régime. Prior to 1789, however, the two men shared an idealism and discontent that can only have been reinforced by their chambers' subordination within the Parlement. An influx of like-minded and extremely youthful judges into the Enquêtes and Requêtes in 1786 and 1787 was to augment that idealism and discontent at the hour of the crown's supreme peril.

In concluding this brief discussion of the prerogatives and personnel of the Paris Parlement during the years from 1774 to 1786, it seems advisable to underscore once more the domination of the grand' chambriers within their company. Admittedly, the impression of such a predominance is enhanced by the fact that the senior grand' chambriers—men like the Joly de Fleury brothers, the abbé d'Espagnac, and Lefebvre d'A-mécourt—left an abundance of parlementary papers behind them. Yet, that they did so reflects in large measure their seniority of service and consequent ascendancy within the Parlement. They were the ones who had to negotiate with the king's agents on a regular basis; they were the ones whom the king expected to discipline his most important court of law so that his edicts might be legitimized, his justice dispensed, and his order maintained. From time to time during these years, one of the junior magistrates of the lower chambers (usually Duval d'Eprémesnil) might challenge the leadership on some particular issue, might insist that the first president appoint *commissaires* to look into this or that administrative scandal or judicial abuse. The younger parlementaires might even manage to stir up a minor tempest within the court should they find allies within the Grand' Chambre—as they did in 1783–84 when President Lamoignon challenged his fellow grand' chambriers over the question of judicial reform. For the most part, however, the Enquêtes and Requêtes deferred to the senior chamber. In the final analysis, such deference reflected much more than the apportionment of responsibility and power within the court. It reflected the fact that the parlementaires, young and old, novices and veterans alike, issued from the ranks of the privileged in French society, followed a common profession, and in most cases held similar views of the monarchy and social order of the ancien régime. Come the political crisis of 1787–88, this situation might in some respects change, but not before.

❧ CHAPTER TWO ❧

The Politics, Achievements, and Limitations of Parlementary Justice, 1774–1786

The eighteenth-century Parlement of Paris was a political as well as judicial institution, but its registrations and remonstrances should not obscure the fact that its members spent most of their time administering royal justice. The immense collections of judicial documents in the Parisian archives testify eloquently to that fact. Although this study cannot possibly come to grips with these archival treasures, it will occasionally look at the judges' professional work as it attempts to portray the parlementary state of mind under Louis XVI. This chapter will examine professional attitudes within the Parlement and discuss some of the achievements and problems in parlementary justice deriving from those attitudes. It will first of all explain how the Parlement reasserted its supremacy in the hierarchy of French courts in the years after 1774. It will then show how tenaciously the leading grand' chambriers defended the special privileges of their chamber against efforts at reform by a minority of parlementaires. Finally, it will examine the Parlement's ingrained professional conservatism and show how this adherence to the severe and sometimes inhumane ways of French justice joined with other magisterial considerations to counterbalance the judges' genuine solicitude for the king's subjects and thus mar the justice these parlementaires meted out. Such a discussion should yield a fuller appreciation of the ways in which the parlementaires viewed and exercised their profession on the eve of the Revolution in France—and suggest how closely the crown and the Parlement were linked in this critical period.

The Reassertion of the Parlement's Supremacy (1774–1777)

Memories of professional nonexistence during the Maupeou years rankled in the magistrates' minds long after their reinstatement in 1774. Sometime in the late 1780s, Lefebvre d'Amécourt recalled the confrontation between Maupeou and the magistracy. Maupeou, he alleged, had exiled most of the parlementaires to "uninhabitable places," had flooded the press with propaganda extolling his various "operations" and smearing the judges, and had left all decent folk wondering "when the true Magistrates would be reinstated."[1] Lefebvre d'Amécourt's colleague, President Joly de Fleury, similarly denounced Maupeou's reforms in a memorandum he circulated among his associates in 1784. The former chancellor had, according to this parlementaire, first attempted to blacken his enemies' reputations with a flurry of scurrilous pamphlets: he meant to dishonor the judges before he destroyed them. Soon they had been exiled, "proscribed like criminals," and in their absence Maupeou had perpetrated all kinds of outrages upon the defenseless kingdom.[2] Yet, long after the fact, both Lefebvre d'Amécourt and Jean Omer Joly de Fleury treated the restoration of the old magistracy as an event bound to have occurred sooner or later. In past times, they commented, innovations in the natural order of things had come and gone, along with their unscrupulous sponsors: the "true magistrates" had unfailingly reemerged triumphantly from such crises.

Long before Lefebvre d'Amécourt and President Joly de Fleury penned these words, however, the Parlement's leaders had voiced their indignation before Louis XVI himself. They did so at the *lit de justice* of 12 November 1774, which ceremoniously reinstated the Parlement and other tribunals of the old magistracy.[3] When the king and his new keeper of the seals, Hue de Miromesnil, exhorted the judges to greater obedience in the future, First President d'Aligre and senior Avocat-Général Séguier responded with a standard encomium of their company that belittled the significance of the last four years under the chancellorship of Maupeou. The first president spoke of the Parlement as being composed of jurists "whose entire lives are continually sacrificed to law, whose entire glory consists in safeguarding law, whose entire ambition is to merit the confidence and esteem of their sovereigns." Glossing over the controversy of the preceding four years, d'Aligre assured Louis XVI that he and his fellows would continue to discharge their sacred duties to the crown and display "on all occasions the same fidelity that we have always shown the kings who preceded you."[4] Séguier, for his part, glibly assumed that the recently deceased Louis XV had been inveigled into sanctioning Maupeou's schemes against his better judgment and against the sentiments of his heart. No doubt the chancellor had induced the late sovereign to envisage his so-called reforms "under the appearance of the general weal." Such innovations had always been but brief aberrations, brief departures from the natural order of things in France. Self-styled reformers might tamper with institutions like the Parlement, but sooner or later "the public interest, the fairness of our sovereigns, and love for the common welfare have always returned the constitution of the Parlement to its former condition." Now, continued the avocat-général, "functions so long suspended" were to be reassumed by magistrates whose only crime had been that "they did not want to consent to being dishonored," magistrates who

35

were "treated like criminals, because the forces of intrigue and ambition had good reason to calumniate their attachment to the ancient laws."[5]

But Séguier was not content with citing alleged outrages against the magistracy in the past. He wanted to drive certain points home for the present and future as well. For example, he seized upon the solemnity of the lit de justice to glorify age-old parlementary prerogatives such as the tenure and venality of office. As far as Séguier was concerned, the display and pomp surrounding the sovereign in his lit de justice "could only add a new sanction to the immutable law of property and to the political law of irremovability from office." Furthermore, the avocat-général, after having spoken in this vein of the continuity of the magistracy and its prerogatives, respectfully but firmly subordinated the youthful king and his ministers to that parallel continuity of French law that the magistracy upheld in its daily judicial role. "In a word, it is not for the sole duration of a sovereign's life that the destiny of his state is confined to him; he must aspire to rule in concert with all the laws, even in centuries when he will continue to exist only in the memory of his wisdom and his virtue."[6] This assertion, if paradoxical in the literal sense, reflected a key motif in parlementary doctrine, the idea that the rule of law had always restrained the king and his servants and must continue to do so. Séguier was lecturing Louis XVI on the constitutional quality of his power.

The redoubtable avocat-général, speaking for his company, also reacted in a predictable manner against the edicts, registered at this lit de justice, that increased the competence of the presidial courts and restored the Grand Conseil at Paris. The quality of *présidialité* had been conferred by the Valois kings of the sixteenth century upon a number of the principal *bailliage* and *sénéchaussée* courts in France.[7] These tribunals, forty-three of which existed in the Paris Parlement's jurisdiction as of 1764, judged most criminal cases appealed from the inferior provost and seigneurial courts and from the lesser bailliages, as well as civil lawsuits appealed from these lower courts. Since the sixteenth century, though with occasional modifications of this general rule, the presidial courts had judged in last resort litigation not involving more than 250 livres in capital or 10 livres in annual income, and lawsuits appealable to the Parlement not involving more than 500 livres in capital or 20 livres in annual income. Hence, the presidials frequently intervened in the otherwise straight line of appeal from the nonpresidial bailliages to the Parlement and were resented by bailliages and Parlement alike. The edict of November 1774 sharpened this resentment by increasing presidial competence in final judgments to 2,000 livres in capital or 80 livres in annual income and in appealable judgments to 4,000 livres in capital or 160 livres in annual income. The legislation thus compensated to some degree for the inflation of the seventeenth and early eighteenth centuries and brought more justice within the reach of the inhabitants of the presidial jurisdictions.

The Grand Conseil had functioned at various times since the late fifteenth century.[8] It had incurred the enmity of the parlementaires at Paris for three primary reasons. First, it considered a variety of lawsuits involving royal interests but denied to the Parlement's cognizance for political reasons. Second, it settled some jurisdictional conflicts between the Parlement and the presidial courts. Third, it had replaced the Parlement on those occasions when the parlementaires had been exiled or had suspended justice in protest over government policies. Just recently, the personnel of the Grand Conseil had staffed the much-derided "Maupeou Parlement." Now, in November 1774, this tribunal was reinstated in its traditional functions and was expressly promised the functions of the Paris Parlement in the event of another judicial strike by the parlementaires.

At the lit de justice of 12 November, Antoine Louis Séguier immediately set the tone of his company's hostility toward the Grand Conseil and the presidial courts. The increase in presidial competence elicited from him this defense of a strictly graded hierarchy of tribunals subordinating the presidials and all other inferior courts to the "sovereign courts" of France: "The Sovereign Courts, depositories of the authority of our kings in the administration of justice, are in a sense invested with the plenitude of power. The inferior tribunals have been restrained within more or less circumscribed limits, according to the nature of affairs and the quality of persons. These differences form, so to speak, so many stages on the approach toward the Throne, from which justice, issuing from such a fertile source, penetrates into all parts of the Realm."[9] The implications for the presidials were clear. It could be dangerous, admonished Séguier, to give inferior jurists so much control over the fortunes of litigants and thus reduce their right of appeal, "which could be a valuable resource, given the extent of enlightenment that one finds in the magistrates who are charged with reforming the judgments of inferior jurisdictions."[10] As for the Grand Conseil, Séguier anticipated his colleagues' campaign against that rival tribunal by asserting tersely that "the jurisdiction established under the name Grand Conseil" owed its existence to certain requests made by members of a past assembly of the Estates General—and had later been condemned by another convocation of the Estates.[11] Séguier also responded to the compulsory registration of the edict reestablishing the Parisian Cour des Aides by emphasizing that this court must confine its activities in justice to its traditional (and relatively narrow) areas of competence.[12]

The first president and senior avocat-général of the Parlement were sufficiently circumspect to acknowledge the young king's beneficence in recalling the old magistracy, as well as to do homage to his ultimate supremacy in the affairs of justice. Still, the general tenor of their remarks revealed how little the years of exile had affected their corporate sentiments. That the legislation they had criticized was intended, at least in part, to facilitate justice for the king's subjects was of little import to them. That it reinstated and strengthened tribunals rivaling their own was what really mattered—though it might be unfair not to suggest that veterans like d'Aligre and Séguier, steeped in the traditions of their company, had long convinced themselves that it dispensed the best justice available. In any case, the Parlement through Séguier went on to notify Louis XVI that it would be further reviewing his November edicts in its own assemblies. The king's pessimistic brother, the comte de Provence, had not been entirely amiss in warning that the magistrates "will return as meekly as lambs; once back, they will be lions."[13]

Indeed, the parlementaires wasted little time in inviting the princes of the blood and the peers of France to join them in the Grand' Chambre of the Palais de Justice to examine the edicts of November 1774.[14] The resultant sessions of the Cour des Pairs debated several royal acts in addition to those that had already drawn the criticisms of Séguier. Most controversial of these was the Ordinance on Discipline, designed in part to reinforce the control exercised by the Grand' Chambre over the whole court, thus curbing the restlessness of the Enquêtes and Requêtes.[15] The ordinance confirmed the senior chamber's procedural and jurisdictional supremacy over the other chambers. The first president was invested with almost total authority to convoke (or to refuse to convoke) plenary sessions for the purpose of judicial or political deliberations. He could be overruled only by a plurality of his fellow grand' chambriers. Individual members of the Enquêtes and Requêtes could call for such deliberative sessions only through the recommendations of their chamber's presidents to the senior chamber. Only the procureur-général could denounce public abuses in the court's deliberative assemblies, and no magistrate, not even an officer of the court, could introduce a controversial public issue in an assembly called ostensibly for other reasons. Finally, no deliberative voice in parlementary affairs was to be granted to judges under the age of twenty-five save in cases where such judges acted as rapporteurs presenting evidence in litigation.

Some of the grand' chambriers might have welcomed legislation fortifying their chamber's position within the Parlement; unfortunately, there were two other stipulations involved that they must have perceived as attacking their company as a whole. First, the ordinance stated that, henceforth, remonstrances against royal edicts must come within a month of the government's submission of the edicts to the Parlement. Reiterated remonstrances could be made, but the registration of the legislation in question was to proceed automatically after the king had received the *first* remonstrances. Second, the ordinance forbade judicial strikes or collective resignations by the magistrates in the future. Those defying such a prohibition would be judged by a special "Plenary Court" composed of various "Notables" of the realm, and would forfeit their offices.

There was plenty of grist in these measures for the mill of parlementary opposition, and the magistrates decided almost immediately to register a protest. At the plenary assembly of 2 December, several of the présidents à mortier of the Grand' Chambre reportedly led the way in calling for a rejoinder to the legislation of November 1774.[16] Although Second President Lefevre d'Ormesson reportedly advised the usual procedure of appointing a committee of judges to work on formal protests to Louis XVI, one of his associates went further, demanding the convocation of the Cour des Pairs. The latter course of action was adopted by a nearly unanimous vote.

After sessions of the Cour des Pairs on 9 and 30 December, three men— the prince de Conti, First President d'Aligre, and Procureur-Général Joly de Fleury—drew up representations on the November edicts, which d'Aligre presented to Louis XVI on 8 January 1775.[17] The corporate jealousies of the Parlement and its leaders vented themselves in these protests against the "Plenary Court," the Grand Conseil, and the crown's attempt to tighten parlementary discipline and curb parlementary politics. The judges and their aristocratic allies derided the Plenary Court as a mere "commission," a congeries of various "officers," "great and notable personages," and just plain "men of the Council," which would have nothing of the Parlement's integrity, nothing of its professional experience, and nothing of its prestige. How could such an arbitrary creation, unsanctified by tradition, resist the whims of the ministry? "It would in essence be nothing but a commission controlled in advance, ready to be summoned and used as a tool for all the purposes determined by powerful ministers."[18] In any case, because it was inconceivable that the parlementaires should ever defy the crown, there could be no justification for such a body. Again, the Grand Conseil, that "extraordinary judicial bureau" deriving its whole existence from the government's whim, could under no circumstances whatsoever exercise the functions of the Paris Parlement, let alone debate the great issues of the realm, which the Cour des Pairs alone could ponder. Nothing more strikingly indicates the jurists' bitter contempt for the Grand Conseil than the use of the term "bureau," which like "commission" connoted everything illegal, arbitrary, and impermanent in what the judges conceived as an ageless and unchanging order of justice.

The magistrates also lashed out at the Ordinance on Discipline. The provision concerning remonstrances and the registration of royal acts was a standing invitation to the king's agents to abuse their powers. Now, the parlementaires correctly stated, the government knew that its future legislation would become operable in spite of all magisterial protests against it. From this fact they inferred, rightly or wrongly, that France must prepare herself once more for the possibility of those traditional scourges, "ministerial despotism" and heavier taxation. The magistrates also championed the right of any member of the court to raise public issues in its plenary sessions. Was there not an ancient maxim stating that all members of the Parlement were in a sense procureurs-généraux? Therefore every one of these magistrates had "an indestructible right . . . to promote deliberations that the public welfare and service to the State demanded."[19] The discussion of public affairs in the Parlement required the concentrated *lumières* of all its members, not just the grand' chambriers. So spoke the senior judges, junior parlementaires, and a scattering of allies from the high aristocracy in a display of corporate spirit that some of the court's seniors may have endorsed with private reservations.

Louis XVI responded ten days later by denying the validity of these assertions, but the Cour des Pairs insisted upon having the last word. At the session of 20 January, the duc d'Orléans reportedly called for further action in defense of the assembly's pretensions, but Lefevre d'Ormesson and his fellow presidents seemingly persuaded the majority that the assemblage should content itself with a vague rejoinder to the king.[20] Accordingly, a resolution carried contending that the November edicts had been published prematurely, as the magistrates and their allies had not had sufficient time to examine them and as certain individuals had attended the November lit de justice "who have neither right of attendance nor right of deliberation" in the Parlement.[21] The resolution also stated grandly that the court was not to be understood as having consented to anything in the edicts that could be "prejudicial to the Laws, Maxims, and customs of the Kingdom, to the service of our Lord the King, and to the essential rights of his subjects." This last statement was simply the formula customarily employed by the parlementaires to record their displeasure with royal legislation they had been compelled to register. The king and his ministers chose to ignore the judges' allegations concerning irregularities at the lit de justice, and so another chapter in the old story of sparring between crown and Parlement had closed. Clearly, however, the parlementaires had abandoned nothing of their corporate exclusiveness. In fact, they continued tacitly to signify this by ignoring some of the provisions of the Ordinance on Discipline.[22] Parlementary procedure remained after 1774 pretty much as it had been before the dark days of 1771.

The parlementaires never forgave the members of the Grand Conseil for having filled their professional shoes during the Maupeou years. When, in early 1776, Keeper of the Seals Miromesnil requested from Procureur-Général Joly de Fleury an opinion on the demands of the *procureurs* (proctors) of the Grand Conseil to be compensated for various services rendered in the "Maupeou Parlement," he only succeeded in stirring up old resentments. Joly de Fleury, First President d'Aligre, and the king's rapporteur, Abbé d'Espagnac, concocted a tart reply expressing their company's position: "If there is any Tribunal justified in complaining, it is certainly the Parlement. . . . the Grand Conseil, having been in a sense abolished in 1771 but simultaneously authorized somehow to usurp the title and the prerogatives of the Parlement, ought not, strictly speaking, to recover its former existence, or at the very least should lose all cognizance of affairs it never had the right to consider in the first place."[23] The magistrates politely refused to cooperate in compensating the claimants for any services other than those strictly defined as germane to the Grand Conseil.

But the Parlement's veterans wished to do more than harbor old grudges against rival jurisdictions such as the Grand Conseil and the presidials: they wished to cripple them. This resolution can only have strengthened immediately after the reinstatement of the old magistracy. The Grand Conseil, which as a "sovereign court" had registered the edicts returning it to its old functions and augmenting the powers of the presidial courts, sent copies of the edicts and a circular letter dated 21 December 1774 to all the presidials of the kingdom, instructing these courts to register and publish the edicts.[24] During the following months, the Parlement received a flood of complaints from the inferior tribunals in its jurisdiction: a number of the presidials protested to the procureur-général that they were not in the habit of taking orders from the Grand Conseil concerning its registered edicts, and many of the nonpresidial bailliages assailed the recent increase in jurisdiction accorded to the presidials![25] The charges and countercharges that the tribunals at all levels hurled at each other testified eloquently to the confusions and internecine jealousies riddling the judicial system in France on the eve of the Revolution.

The Parlement entered the fray with a will. President Joly de Fleury reacted to the Grand Conseil's circular instruction of 21 December 1774 by fashioning a memorandum that excoriated the activities of this rival court and suggested that its continued existence was still an open question.[26] During the following two years, the quarrel between the two courts at Paris developed into an exchange of decrees between the Grand Conseil and parlements all over the kingdom.[27] The Grand Conseil contended that it was the original "sovereign court" of the realm, antedating by centuries the oldest of the parlements, and it continued to defend its right to arbitrate between the parlements and the presidials. These claims involved all of the parlements, for the Grand Conseil's jurisdiction covered the entire realm. Not surprisingly, the parlementaires at Paris, Toulouse, Metz, Dijon, Rouen, and Nancy counterattacked vigorously.

The parlementaires in the capital were apparently meditating a revenge that would encompass Grand Conseil and presidials alike. When, in March 1777, the officers of the bailliage of La Fère complained to First President d'Aligre that the presidial court at Laon was receiving and judging appeals from their sentences in matters outside presidial competence, d'Aligre seized the occasion to demand of Miromesnil legislation that would curb the presidials and the Grand Conseil. At this point, the keeper of the seals refused, finding the current arrangements adequate, but in reporting this to his colleagues the First President seemed to augur a new initiative on the matter.[28] The next time the Parlement's leaders discussed the question with Miromesnil, they must have found him more amenable to their views, for it was soon being bruited about that he was allowing the grand' chambriers to devise a new edict on the presidials.[29] The Grand Conseil got wind of these rumors, for it sent its first president, de Nicolae, to Versailles to ask that "a certain regulation fixing the relative jurisdictions of the Grand Conseil and the Parlement, which the Keeper of the Seals is currently working at, not be published" before the king and his Council had the chance to "examine it, Article by Article."[30] These apprehensions were confirmed in August 1777 by the appearance of an edict on the presidials, which the parlementaires promptly registered on 12 August.[31] The edict circumscribed the jurisdiction of the presidial courts in several ways and emphasized their incompetence to issue regulatory decrees or to require other courts within their jurisdictions to register and publish royal acts. Moreover, the edict integrated the presidials more thoroughly into the network of bailliages and sénéchaussées at the intermediate level of the judicial hierarchy. As a result of these provisions, the presidials were subordinated even more than they had been previously to the parlements, and the scope for intervention by the Grand Conseil between parlements and presidial courts was correspondingly reduced. The Grand Conseil and some of the presidials protested this legislation bitterly,[32] but in spite of a royal declaration a year later that modified some points of the edict in favor of the presidials, the situation remained substantially unchanged.

Whether or not the grand' chambriers themselves helped draft the edict of August 1777, it marked an undeniable if ultimately short-lived victory for their company in its skirmishing with rival jurisdictions. In the waning years of the old regime, the parlementaires would remain zealous guardians of their corporate supremacy, though there would be no more general campaigns against rival courts. In the early 1780s, the king's most prestigious tribunal found judicial controversy to be more an internal preoccupation than an external distraction.

A Defense of Precedence within the Parlement

If upon some occasions the members of the *parti ministériel* flaunted their company's pretensions before the king or squabbled with other tribunals, at other times they defended their ultraprivileged status as grand' chambriers in a manner defining them as stubborn and grasping old men. The ascendancy of the Grand' Chambre within the Parlement already assured them cognizance of the most important litigation, and still they were quick to extend their chamber's jurisdiction. They were immensely rich from their estates and their *rentes*, and yet they clung to their judicial fees with a tenacity belying their wealth. When some of their juniors from the Enquêtes and Requêtes allied with several "renegade" grand' chambriers to question the older magistrates' prerogatives and urge judicial reforms, the court's leaders resisted. They resisted in part as veteran professionals, but also in part as old men saying to their juniors: you, too, shall enjoy in your turn what we enjoy in ours. The intraparlementary tensions of the early 1780s further complicated the Parlement's administration of justice and anticipated the more significant divisions of 1787–88.

An episode of 1780 illustrated the readiness of the senior parlementaires to extend their chamber's jurisdiction. In December the Grand' Chambre obtained from the government a decree according it exclusive cognizance of certain types of litigation susceptible of summary judgment upon appeal.[33] The first president would appoint rapporteurs to weigh the evidence of the parties to such cases, and because these relatively uncomplicated lawsuits would require no consultation between rapporteurs and judges prior to final judgment in the Grand' Chambre, they could be settled quickly on Tuesdays and Fridays after the regular morning or afternoon audiences of the Grand' Chambre. This legislation was submitted by the *gens du roi* to the Grand' Chambre and Tournelle on 12 December and registered immediately. Needless to say, the court's junior chambers were not consulted on the matter.

President Joly de Fleury had suggested such an act the previous summer. In late July he had sent a preliminary draft of such legislation to an acquaintance who had returned it with praise and suggested that Lefebvre d'Amécourt also read it.[34] Joly de Fleury no doubt followed this advice, for Lefebvre d'Amécourt recorded his own thoughts on the need for such a measure. He referred to unsuccessful attempts in the past to handle the flood of cases appealed to the Parlement, cases susceptible of summary procedure but delayed for months by the perpetual backlog of pending litigation. At times, these suits had even had to be judged by senior barristers in the court. This was doubly unfortunate for the parties involved: it forced them to pay the stiff fees of these *avocats*, and it deprived the litigants of "their natural judges, in whom they have confidence, submitting arbitration of their interests to a single barrister, whose judgment is never as sure as that of a magistrate." The remedy, said d'Amécourt, was "to find a way to expedite these summary cases, without charging the litigants, and without depriving them of their natural judges."[35] Of course, "their natural judges" could only mean the jurists of the Grand' Chambre.

President Joly de Fleury and Lefebvre d'Amécourt undoubtedly cooperated with the gens du roi of the parquet and with the king's rapporteur d'Espagnac in securing this legislation from the government. But apparently the news of the upcoming reform was common currency during the summer of 1780, for an anonymous pamphleteer lampooned the scheme in August, predicting that it would only burden the litigants in the Grand' Chambre with heavier charges.[36] More significantly, he detailed an offer that some of the junior magistrates in the Enquêtes were allegedly making to lighten their seniors' responsibilities by judging the appeals the Grand' Chambre wished to arrogate to itself. The pamphleteer lauded this offer and reminded the grand' chambriers that the 1599 Ordinance of Blois had declared the Enquêtes competent to judge cases for which their seniors had no time. Not only would this expedite justice and relieve the overcharged clients—the younger parlementaires were supposedly volunteering to judge the overflow of cases for nothing—but it would also challenge and mature young men whose dissipation was notorious.

The members of the lower chambers could hardly have concurred in this allusion to their profligacy, but it was reliably reported that some of them were anxious to wrest the consideration of various appeals from their seniors.[37] Moreover, one of the Joly de Fleury brothers took the alleged offer seriously enough to reject it in a lengthy memorandum. The older parlementaires probably would have corroborated reports of dissipation among their juniors, but for them this was all the more reason to stand firm. Predictably, the Joly de Fleury memorandum stressed the experience and maturity of the grand' chambriers: "It is necessary that the magistrates who judge these kinds of affairs have a consummate experience, that they be thoroughly familiar with the judicial principles involved, and that a wise uniformity reign in their decisions. . . . the gentlemen of the Enquêtes cannot have the qualities requisite for the expedition of these kinds of matters, and intelligence and zeal are no substitute for the experience that is the fruit of long years."[38]

True, the Ordinance of Blois had authorized the Grand' Chambre to assign certain types of litigation to the lower chambers, but it had left such a decision squarely in the hands of the courts' seniors. To have done otherwise would have been to undermine the authority of the Grand' Chambre and tamper with the essential distinctions among the several chambers of the Parlement. Hence, the senior judges were perfectly justified in claiming this litigation in summary procedure, and, indeed, they ought to in view of their experience and maturity.[39] So spoke one of the court's seniors, and his colleagues' prompt registration of the legislation of December 1780 emphatically seconded his views.

Thus, the Parlement's elders in 1780 denied to the Enquêtes what the court as a whole had helped deny to the presidials several years before: an additional area of jurisdiction. On both occasions the magistrates' motives seem to have been compounded of professionalism—that is, the sense that precedence reflected superior ability and experience—and of something less than professionalism—the insistence upon precedence as a reward and end in itself.

Another observation in the Joly de Fleury memorandum of 1780 foreshadowed the tactics the Parlement's deans would adopt in the coming controversy over their judicial fees. The memorandum proclaimed that the real culprit in the matter of litigants' expenses was the crown's taxation of justice, not the allegedly excessive honoraria of the judges.[40] As a matter of fact, claimed the memorandum, taxes victimized the judges and the judged alike, for the magistrates found their own "salaries" practically nullified by the bite of tributes to the state—a point that was perfectly true but that conveniently ignored more fruitful sources of magisterial wealth. In any case, one of the leading grand' chambriers may have been implying here that he and his colleagues would defend their fees as they had defended their jurisdictional ascendancy and would, if menaced by reformers, link their own finances to those of their royal master.

What were these perquisites that were to embroil the leaders and rebels of the Parlement during 1783–84? In addition to his annual *gage*, which represented the interest on the value of his office but which in practice was severely reduced by *capitation* and *dixième*, the magistrate could earn fees known as *épices* and *vacations*.[41] Whereas the gages compensated the judges' traditional function of hearing oral testimony and pronouncing decisions in the audiences of the court's chambers, the vacations and épices remunerated consideration of the written evidence in cases (*appointements*) that were too complex to be settled in the regular audiences. The vacations went to the presidents and counselors appointed by the court's leadership to unravel the issues in such cases; the épices went to the rapporteurs and ordinary counselors who in concert judged such cases definitively. Because the épices were evaluated on the basis of the number of vacations earned in each chamber, and because the latter fee was calculated in a more freehanded fashion in the Grand' Chambre than it was in the lower chambers, abuses often resulted—or, at least, so claimed the many detractors of the grand' chambriers.[42] These honoraria were to be the primary bone of contention in the reform controversy of 1783–84.[43]

But the fees of the parlementaires were not the only abuses alleged against parlementary justice in the 1780s. One contemporary who knew the lawcourts very well was Félix Faulcon, who came to Paris from Poitiers and, as law student, barrister, and judge, gained an insider's view of justice in the capital. Faulcon filled his letters to friends with complaints about the administration of justice and, above all, the justice of the Parisian parlementaires.[44] The judges, he lamented, exacted enormous fees from their luckless litigants, failed to restrain the cupidity of their secretaries and the depredations of clerks, ushers, and proctors in the various chambers, and profited, as did their underlings, from the slowness and complexities of judicial procedure. With good reason he feared that the magistrates were too entrenched in their ways, too wedded to the system, to be able even to conceive of basic reform, let alone sponsor it. Faulcon prescribed uniform laws and procedures, more tribunals with smaller areas of jurisdiction, and numerous other reforms as timely medicines for a failing system of justice. Not all of the Parlement's critics took such a drastic view of the situation, but the debates that erupted in the Palais de Justice in 1783 and 1784 did raise some of the same points that appear and reappear throughout the Faulcon correspondence.

Actually, rumors of impending trouble over the judges' fees circulated from the time the parlementaires were reinstated. One fairly reliable source reported parlementary debate over the épices and vacations as early as 16 December 1774. The same source reiterated on 2 February 1775 that the issue was being hotly discussed: the Enquêtes were demanding that the grand' chambriers lead the way in reform, while the court's seniors stubbornly clung to the perquisites, regarding them "as legitimate honoraria of their place, as overdue compensation for their labors," which the youth of the Enquêtes would themselves want to enjoy later on.[45] Despite corroborating reports from the bookseller and memorialist S.-P. Hardy, who usually had an ear to the ground for news from the Palais de Justice, the issue was temporarily shelved; but it was not too long before he and other observers had more substantial news to report.[46]

It was, somewhat ironically, an officer of the privileged Grand' Chambre, President Lamoignon, who touched off a full-scale debate over this issue early in 1783. The fourth president of the Parlement had long been disgusted with the chaotic state of justice and apparently coveted a reformer's role in the state. In the early months of 1783, Lamoignon voiced his dissatisfaction to his close friend the baron de Bésenval and signaled his intention to rekindle the controversy over the épices among his parlementary associates.[47] Evidently, he saw in this issue a vehicle both for wide-ranging judicial reform and for his own ambitions, but because of a lack of natural allies in the Grand' Chambre, save possibly for three fellow presidents, he was forced to seek his army among the younger magistrates of the lower chambers.[48] Not surprisingly, Duval d'Eprémesnil and several other junior counselors agreed to precipitate the matter in alliance with Lamoignon at the plenary session already called for 11 March.

The court's leaders had called for an assembly of chambers on that date to deliberate upon alleged royal abuses of "evocations" of cases from the Parlement to the King's Council and of nullifications of parlementary decrees.[49] But S.-P. Hardy reported that the younger magistrates were still seething over the December 1780 legislation on summary procedure. Some of their more vocal spokesmen had been demanding cognizance of these summary appointements for their own chambers and had accused their elders of turning these lawsuits into "an abominable source of rapine." Similar charges were allegedly made by Duval d'Eprémesnil and several other judges at the plenary session of 11 March.[50] Temporarily, the reform forces won the day, for the Parlement voted to establish a commission to consider the abuses that had crept into the administration of justice, from the royal taxes levied upon every act in litigation to the perquisites of the magistrates and the mercenary practices of their secretaries.

The weekly sessions of the commission at the first president's residence drew the attention of the polemicists and gossips of the capital and stimulated some unflattering portrayals of the senior magistrates. Lamoignon and his allies circulated a pamphlet ridiculing the grand' chambriers as grasping parasites: even Second President Lefevre d'Ormesson had his reputation for austere magisterial mores thrown in his teeth.[51] First President d'Aligre was especially pilloried by several anonymous hacks, one of whom portrayed him as a "cannibal" devouring unfortunate litigants in court.[52] The grand' chambriers, or someone favorable to their cause, countered with a lengthy polemic that attempted unconvincingly to shift the blame from their alleged cupidity to the government's taxation policies.[53] It was not likely that the younger parlementaires, or the public at large, would accept the plaints of privileged old men who had in the past clung to emoluments of which they had no real need.

But the leaders of the Parlement were resourceful and found ways to frustrate the zealots of their company. To begin with, d'Aligre exercised his prerogative as first president to establish the usual safe majority of grand' chambriers on the reform commission. Lamoignon, Duval d'Eprémesnil, and Fréteau de Saint-Just might be members, but how could they make any headway against a coalition of *épiciers* such as d'Aligre, President Joly de Fleury, and Lefebvre d'Amécourt and hidebound conservatives such as Séguier, Procureur-Général Joly de Fleury, and Lefevre d'Ormesson?[54] Séguier in particular did his part to delay affairs: whenever the commission solicited his advice on how to streamline procedures in the audiences of the Grand' Chambre, he pleaded the necessity to confer on the matter with the proctors and barristers of the court, thus putting off any definitive pronouncements on the question.[55] An observer also reported that the épiciers of the senior chamber labored to persuade the "zélantis" of the Enquêtes that they were being duped by "a few ambitious characters" who were using the issue of reform to further their own political careers.[56] Given Lamoignon's apparent state of mind, such an assertion was not altogether wrong.

The older magistrates' counterattack was temporarily blunted by disquieting news from Versailles. The king, whether influenced by partisans of the *zélantis* or acting upon his own initiative, took notice of what was transpiring in Paris at the Palais de Justice. On 20 July he ordered d'Aligre to have concrete proposals for judicial reform before him by the following Easter.[57]

Yet, once again, the épiciers, led by the resourceful Lefebvre d'Amécourt, were equal to the occasion. One observer reported soon thereafter that d'Amécourt, now king's rapporteur in the court, was urging his colleagues to define two main types of abuses: those deriving "from lax enforcement of existing laws" and those resulting "from wrongly administered or poorly conceived laws." Abuses of the first category could be remedied simply by "reviving the old laws," while those of the second kind would have to be dealt with by the king himself, acting as sovereign legislator to change existing court procedures.[58] This stratagem, reported during the summer of 1783, actually anticipated the memoir on judicial reform that Lefebvre d'Amécourt was to write for his company the following year. The intention behind it clearly was to criticize (as an example of "wrongly administered or poorly conceived laws") the bite of royal taxation in litigation, thus discouraging the hard-pressed government from implementing any reforms that might conceivably threaten a source of revenue. Yet, even with this stratagem in hand, the Parlement's leaders dragged their heels. The sessions of the reform commission became mired in the minutiae of a review of past ordinances, and, despite a flurry of proposals from Lamoignon and other judges for a complete overhauling of fees and procedures in the royal tribunals, nothing concrete resulted from the conferences during the remainder of 1783.[59]

Lamoignon's frustration in these circumstances was understandable, and he sought to improve the situation by linking events in the Parlement with ministerial politics at Versailles. According to Bésenval, both Controller-General Calonne and the baron de Breteuil, secretary for the royal household, would have liked to see Lamoignon replace the ailing and unassertive Miromesnil as keeper of the seals.[60] However, Miromesnil tenaciously hung on to his post and retained Louis XVI's confidence, and Lamoignon had no choice but to bide his time. He nevertheless insisted upon relaying his private views on the administration of justice to Miromesnil or to Louis himself, thus bypassing his stalling colleagues of the Grand' Chambre.

When, however, Miromesnil was informed through an intermediary that the Parlement's fourth president wished to see him or at least to send him a memorandum on the judicial question, he refused both requests. His suggestion that Lamoignon submit his ideas to the conferences at the Parlement could hardly satisfy the president, because the conferences were controlled by those adamantly opposed to reform. Lamoignon therefore persisted, endeavoring without success to see Miromesnil during February 1784. Finally, Lamoignon, having been rebuffed by the keeper of the seals in a letter of 10 February, got Breteuil to convey his judicial memorandum directly to the king.[61] He did not hear from Breteuil again until the end of February, when he received from the minister a formal letter instructing him to refer any future proposals for reform to his associates in the Parlement. Breteuil did not return Lamoignon's memoir, but its author learned from Calonne several days later that Miromesnil had prevailed upon Louis not to accord the memoir any special treatment. The implication was that Miromesnil had sent Lamoignon's confidential memoir to the commission in the Parlement—an implication that turned out to be true.

Lamoignon wrote his memoir under uncertain circumstances, and he can hardly have envisioned at this point all the drastic judicial measures he would implement four years later as keeper of the seals.[62] All the same, his imperious will to ameliorate French justice evidenced itself in this clandestine memorandum. Lamoignon celebrated the king's justice as the emanation of royal authority over the French people and declared the highest duty of His Majesty's magistrates to be the prompt and honest discharge of that justice. The president attacked the increasing tendency of the parlementaires, especially the grand' chambriers, to collect exorbitant épices and vacations from the luckless people they were supposed to be aiding. Furthermore, he condemned the increasing recurrence to the appointements, which yielded written judgments rendered out of audience and which were used as an additional pretext for overcharging litigants. He went on to suggest that the magistrates conspired with their secretaries and with barristers and proctors to fleece the parties by multiplying the documents in their lawsuits, thereby dragging out trial procedure and maximizing its expense. Lamoignon proposed that all abusive perquisites be abolished and replaced by a fixed and reasonable retribution for the judges based at least in part on a uniform taxation of the litigants. He also recommended a strict control over the number of secretaries working for officials in all royal tribunals and suggested that they henceforth be paid directly by the judges in these courts. Finally, he urged a drastic simplification of the procedures for preparing, pleading, and judging all lawsuits and assured the king of his readiness to supply exact details on all these points.

First President d'Aligre received this memoir from the government in March, with orders that he make it available to the Joly de Fleury brothers, Lefevre d'Ormesson, and rapporteur Lefebvre d'Amécourt—four members of the parti ministériel and four champions of both Parlement and Grand' Chambre. Predictably, the judges were infuriated by Lamoignon's initiative, and President Joly de Fleury swiftly drafted a counter-memoir attacking both the motives and the substantive proposals of the fourth president.[63] "Certain restless, intriguing, and ambitious spirits," claimed Joly de Fleury, "see with chagrin the working relationship that has developed between Your Majesty's Ministers and the principal Magistrates of your Parlement of Paris." Immediately, the old resentment of the senior counselor toward his juniors reappeared as Joly de Fleury accused unnamed renegade grand' chambriers of rekindling the fires of insubordination in the Enquêtes: "They attempt to incite the young Magistrates, who are talented but still inexperienced, to do as youth often does, to throw off all subordination. They turn them against the preponderance of the Grand' Chambre; they stir them up and win them for their cause by inflaming them with sentiments of glory and selflessness, and they achieve all this by following the tactics of 1770. Defamation, calumny, libels . . ."[64] These individuals, warned Joly de Fleury, were trying to worm their way into the royal confidence, trying to usurp the faithful magistrates who had served king and Parlement so well and so long.

Jean Omer Joly de Fleury went on to cite statutes and ordinances authorizing the épices and vacations and claimed that the litigants were better off paying such fees than having to contend with Lamoignon's uniform tax, which he portrayed as exorbitant and, unlike the épices, affecting even the poorest clients in the most minor cases. As for the allegation of conspiracy among judges, proctors, and secretaries, that was an insult to the magistracy. So was the assertion that the parlementaires disliked hearing cases in the audiences of the senior chamber because such cases brought them less money than did the appointements: were there not already too many audiences every week, taking their valuable time away from the private consideration of more difficult lawsuits? Joly de Fleury then returned to the old strategy of associating the judges' fees with the king's taxes: "It would certainly be better if there were neither épices nor taxes in justice, and if Your Majesty's finances could allow you to increase the gages of all judicial officers throughout the Kingdom, and to endure the diminution of revenues from judicial taxes."[65] The message was clear: either the government must augment the gages (and forfeit some revenue) or the judges' fees must remain.

Perhaps the message was a bit too clear. Although Joly de Fleury circulated this polemic among his confidants and won their unanimous praise for what d'Amécourt called "your excellent memoir," he never submitted it to Louis.[66] But in the meantime the king had once again prodded d'Aligre on the judicial question, and his peremptory command on 2 May 1784 that a comprehensive plan for reform of the judiciary be presented to him in a week spurred a newly designated commission of parlementaires to draw up two memoirs on the subject and submit them to the full Parlement.[67] At the plenary session of 7 May the memoir that Lefebvre d'Amécourt had drafted for the commission was approved over an alternative document from Lamoignon's and d'Eprémesnil's faction.[68] It would seem that substantial solidarity within the Grand' Chambre, and substantial division among the more numerous judges of the junior chambers, assured the passage of the d'Amécourt memoir over the strenuous objections of the reforming zélantis. First President d'Aligre presented the d'Amécourt memoir to Louis XVI two days later.

In this ingenious document, Lefebvre d'Amécourt, following up his earlier stategy, distinguished between the "particular causes" and the "general causes" of abuses in justice.[69] The "particular causes" in most cases meant the malpractices of subordinate officials such as proctors, barristers, secretaries, and notaries. The king could trust to the surveillance of his faithful magistrates to check such abuses. But the "general causes" were another matter altogether. They were far more injurious to litigants—and for the most part they derived from royal finances. For instance, observed d'Amécourt, the *droit de révision* gave the proctors twenty sous for each roll of testimony or evidence prepared by the barristers in a given case—a paradox unfair to the litigant who had to pay this fee, because by law the proctors were declared incompetent to prepare the rolls upon which they pocketed a fee! D'Amécourt then quickly pointed out the origin of this fee. A government declaration had established it in 1693 to compensate twenty proctors who had been forced to pay 100,000 livres to the royal treasury for the creation of their offices. Again, d'Amécourt in his memoir cited the stamp tax levied on so many documents drawn up in the course of litigation and recalled the declarations of June and July 1691, which, in order to increase the number of taxable pages in such documents, strictly prescribed the number of lines allowable per page and words allowable per line. It was to be hoped, declared this memoir piously, that the government could now see fit to abolish such sources of income.

Small wonder that Lefebvre d'Amécourt could then announce grandly that he and his colleagues were prepared to relinquish their well-earned perquisites and thus deprive the enemies of the magistracy of all pretext for slandering it. For in addition to suggesting that the king review the taxes that he assessed in his courts, d'Amécourt intimated that the judges ought to be compensated for their loss of perquisites such as the épices—compensated, that is, from the royal treasury. It is not hard to see why one contemporary referred to the Parlement's memorandum on justice as "a minor masterpiece in its own genre" whose author had artfully disguised greed "under the appearances of zeal and selflessness" and had, "in blaming the king for the vast majority of these costs in justice, [linked] the Magistrates' cause to that of His Majesty."[70]

At this point Louis XVI merely replied that he would study these proposals and subsequently announce his intentions to the Parlement. But the members of the court's parti ministériel left nothing to chance. On 20 May the ever-resourceful President Joly de Fleury submitted to d'Aligre the draft of a royal "response" he had been concocting. Predictably, it exonerated the Parlement's leaders from the allegedly libelous charges of their enemies and cited the difficulties of the royal finances as reason for not abolishing the épices, because to do so would naturally mean increasing the judges' gages in compensation.[71] The first president endorsed this "response" and sent it on to Miromesnil. The correspondence of Miromesnil with the king reveals that the former accepted Joly de Fleury's response as quickly as had d'Aligre—and subtly reminded the king of his dependence upon the senior magistrates for the easy registration of his edicts.[72] As a result, the king's definitive reaction to the d'Amécourt memoir, which came on 18 July, echoed the surreptitious response of Joly de Fleury and the corroborative sentiments of the keeper of the seals.[73] Louis XVI lauded the "purity of views of the magistrates of the Grand' Chambre" and enjoined the younger judges of the Enquêtes and Requêtes to continue to follow the sterling examples of their seniors. Louis was diplomatic enough to express his confidence in the younger parlementaires, but this can hardly have begun to mollify Lamoignon and those allied with him in the lower chambers.

Yet this petty victory for the leaders of the tribunal proved as ephemeral as their earlier triumph over the Grand Conseil and the presidial courts. No comments by any of the would-be reformers in the Parlement upon the affair of 1783–84 have survived, but it must have left a residue of bitterness in the court. After all, here were the most influential grand' chambriers profiting from their special relationship with the government to aggrandize a jurisdiction that was already supreme within the tribunal and to defend perquisites of which they could have no real need. But soon Lamoignon would indeed hold the seals, in place of Miromesnil, and then the Parlement's leaders would have to reckon with him.

The Inadequate Benison of Parlementary Justice

The Parlement's tenacious defense of its corporate supremacy and its quashing of efforts at internal reform complicated its exercise of justice and implied something about the conservative nature of that justice. It is true, and significant, that the magistrates occasionally spoke out on behalf of individuals, humble as well as great folk, who had been victimized by *lettres de cachet* or by other abuses of power. Furthermore, the magistrates could display a genuine concern for litigants caught up in the bickering among rival tribunals or injured by the malfeasance of subordinate officers within the Parlement itself. Nevertheless, the benison of parlementary justice in these areas and others was limited by the judges' own prejudices and corporate pretensions and by their overall adherence to the severe and mechanistic procedures of French justice.

Allegations of judicial abuse occasionally provoked indignation at the Palais de Justice and in so doing reflected political and constitutional tensions between crown and Parlement as well as the confusion of justice and administration characterizing the ancien régime. For example, on 24 July 1778 someone from the Enquêtes reported to his assembled colleagues that an artisan and grocer named Jean-Baptiste Favriot had been arrested the month before at the town of Montgeron, dragged away to a prison, and incarcerated for over a month under inhuman conditions. Apparently, Favriot had incurred the enmity of the priest at Montgeron, who had secured his arrest as a vagabond disturbing the peace. But the speaker in the Enquêtes claimed to have the true story of the affair from another source and in his denunciation distinguished explicitly between the legitimate operations of law and order (as in the suppression of beggars and vagabonds) and the illegal use of force: "If a private resentment or some other passion . . . by itself determined this vexatious act, which is what the Company has just learned from the judicial officers and principal inhabitants at Montgeron, it is all the more necessary to utilize the most severe precautions to stop such an abuse of an authority irregular in its principle and use, which, under the pretext of delivering society from the burden of beggars and vagabonds, becomes a means of oppression and an instrument of private vengeance."[74] That the Parlement voted to refer this matter to the *gens du roi* shows among other things that its advocacy of stern measures of social control (which included judicial torture) failed to blunt its awareness of the individual's basic insecurity in a regime lacking explicit constitutional guarantees of personal freedom.

A week later, Avocat-Général Séguier was unable to report to his associates anything definite regarding the case of Favriot, other than that he had been "arrested by orders of the King," but he was able to reveal "some long and very curious details on the suppression of mendicity, at Paris as well as in the other towns and rural areas of the jurisdiction."[75] This revelation of additional abuses by agents of the government in the suppression of beggary spurred the court to investigate the Favriot case more thoroughly and to follow up Séguier's findings on general administrative abuse within the jurisdiction. On 21 August, the parlementaires directed First President d'Aligre to present the findings of these investigations to the king and at the same time to protest against the alleged infringements of individual freedom. On 25 August, d'Aligre went to Versailles and in the royal presence voiced his associates' concern: "Obliged by duty to watch over the security and liberty of your subjects, especially those who by their inferior fortune and standing in society have no other protectors than the magistrates, your parlement feels itself obligated to implore Your Majesty to contain within the limits of indispensable necessity or of obvious usefulness the dispensing of orders emanating from the supreme power."[76] In response to this plea Louis stated that he was well acquainted with the case of Jean-Baptiste Favriot and had had every reason to issue his orders in the affair; however, he assured the first president that such orders would be given only when judged absolutely necessary.

Louis had nothing more to say on the subject, but it was not long before the parlementaires were again clamoring over judicial abuses involving crown and commoners.

On 21 January 1779, one of the judges denounced to his associates a case involving the principle of double jeopardy.[77] A fire of suspicious origins at the town of Marseillan in southeastern France in March 1774 had resulted in the arrest of thirteen residents of the town. The "sieur Rigault," a former mayor of Marseillan whose storehouse had been destroyed by the conflagration, had secured the arrest of these individuals as "seditious persons." In February 1775, the tribunal at Marseillan had passed sentences of varying severity against six in this group: a former constable, a wholesale merchant, a fisherman, a son of a captain in the army's Piedmont regiment, and two "bourgeois de Marseillan." All six had appealed the sentences handed down at Marseillan to the Parlement of Toulouse, which had overturned the convictions and ordered the original plaintiff Rigault to pay the damages it awarded to the vindicated parties. Two others originally accused by Rigault at Marseillan but subsequently acquitted by the lower court were also awarded damages by the Toulouse parlementaires.

However, Rigault had managed to have the ruling of the Toulouse Parlement quashed by a royal decree of cassation. The same decree had "evoked" the case from Toulouse to the Requêtes de l'Hôtel at Paris and ordered the incarceration of the formerly acquitted defendants in the Conciergerie, the prison at the Palais de Justice.[78] This was the way the situation stood in January 1779, and the judge denouncing the whole procedure in the Paris Parlement urged his company to protest without delay a long list of procedural irregularities he had enumerated in his address.

The court settled upon two courses of action. First, it charged Lefebvre d'Amécourt and some other parlementaires with the task of preparing a report on the crown's increasing recurrence to cassation, or nullification, of rulings in the royal tribunals. Second, it deputized the first president to warn Louis XVI again about dangerous irregularities in the administration of justice. D'Aligre went out to Versailles that very evening and in his remarks to the king bore down hard upon the theme of double jeopardy and its implications for all Frenchmen:

> Your parlement cries out against the injuries done to the order of justice and to these individuals, whose misfortune menaces the security of all your subjects. . . . it is unprecedented that an accused person who has been exculpated by the legal judgment of his natural judges should again run the risk of examination in court. The accuser has no right to call for corporal punishment and the prosecuting magistrate can have no more to say once sovereign justice has

pronounced in favor of the accused. Your Majesty is too equitable to permit during his reign the introduction of an innovation prejudicial to the rights of humanity.[79]

This was fairly strong language, but Louis replied to it by stating summarily that the nullification of the ruling at Toulouse had been proper and the evocation of the case to the Requêtes de l'Hôtel equally so. No principle of judicial procedure had been violated, he concluded, and that was that.

The Parlement, however, refused to accept this response as the final word on the subject and voted to remonstrate formally against the government's handling of the Marseillan affair and its use of decrees of cassation. Remonstrances were never actually made, as the court had to turn to other matters. Nevertheless, the judges, in speaking out on the Marseillan affair in 1779, revealed the same sense of legalism that had moved them the preceding year to protest the incarceration of an obscure artisan and distinguish painstakingly between the lawful suppression of mendicity and the unlawful pursuit of private vengeance. Admittedly, the parlementaires were conditioned by their perpetual sparring with the crown over fiscal and other public issues to object every time the government saw fit to intervene in the proceedings of the lawcourts.[80] Moreover, the judges were to a limited extent "politicians" in the sense that they were aware of a public attuned to parlementary pronouncements on all sorts of contemporary issues. Nevertheless, the government's evocations, cassations, and "private orders" (including the dreaded lettres de cachet) could affect any Frenchman at any time. In a regime commingling the roles of justice and public administration, the government could just as easily be accused as were the privileged parlementaires of exceeding a proper role.

The magistrates' concern for *justiciables* of all social ranks also appeared in their commentary upon disputes among inferior jurisdictions. An excellent case in point was the quarrel during 1779 between the royal and archiepiscopal bailliages at Rheims. Chapter 3 will fully examine the points at issue in this controversy. What is significant in this context is the fact that the officers of the Paris Parlement, in proffering their support for a compromise between the conflicting jurisdictional pretensions of the two courts at Rheims, underscored the popular inconvenience and hardship resulting from the dispute:

If anyone went into this affair in detail, he would be truly alarmed at the misfortunes resulting from the jealousy and greed of the inferior officers of these two tribunals. Every day one could witness parties being sacrificed by disputes that ordinarily result in ruin on both sides. There are administrative affairs taken under false colors to the royal bailliage where they do not belong, and other affairs initiated in this bailliage that certain underlings try to remove by all judicial tricks imaginable. A day does not pass without the competition between the two tribunals occasioning . . . duplicate legal investigations that are the ruin of the citizen.[81]

The officers of the Paris Parlement fully endorsed a proposal to readjust the jurisdictions of the rival bailliages at Rheims. The proposal, if implemented, would prove a boon to the people of Rheims, "establishing a better order of things and rescuing the subjects of the King from the cruel necessity of undertaking litigation merely to find out which court has the right to judge them."[82] Not at all surprisingly, this reference to the subject's welfare was immediately followed by recognition of the proposal's utility for the maintenance of law and order at Rheims. Concern for private convenience and concern for public order coexisted closely in the minds of magistrates who, as jurists and administrators, knew how intimately private convenience and public order were allied. For the parlementaires (as indeed for most authorities in most societies), humanitarianism was in part an expediential consideration.

Moreover, there were times when the humanitarianism deriving from the Parlement's judicial role was relegated to second place—or stifled altogether. Sometimes it was the magistrates' obsession about law and order that deafened them to the cries of individuals or groups. For example, at the court's plenary session of 19 August 1776, a member of the third chamber of Enquêtes denounced to his associates the kind of despotic act most frequently denounced in the Parlement: an imprisonment resulting from *ordres particuliers* from the government. In this case, two reputed physiocrats, the abbé Baudeau and the abbé Roubeau, had been reportedly arrested at the behest of certain entrepreneurs at Paris, apparently for crying up the virtues of free trade and attacking the privileges of the entrepreneurs. The speaker from the Enquêtes asserted that one of the defendants had been detained in the prison of the Châtelet and that he had not been allowed to defend himself against his accusers in court. Apparently sensing the lack of sympathy in his company for any partisans of the physiocratic cause, the speaker from the Enquêtes hastened to remind his colleagues that "it is not the persons and the works of the abbés Baudeau and Roubeau that merit the favor of the company." What really mattered, he insisted, was "the fact of ordres particuliers, which are always contrary to the laws and even more so when they tend to interfere with the order of justice."[83] This was precisely the issue that was to spark parlementary protests to the king in 1778 and 1779 and help raise the Parlement in defiance and the whole country in revolution in the late 1780s. On this occasion, however, the judges, fresh from their confrontation with Turgot over his physiocratic reforms, decided to let the matter rest.

They might lodge a protest at Versailles over the alleged mistreatment of harmless commoners in the king's courts and prisons; they were less eager to take up the cudgels on behalf of physiocratic agitators whose cherished economic freedom augured nothing but soaring prices for bread, popular discontent, and popular violence.[84]

The same stern advocacy of public order manifested itself among the parlementaires in September 1782. At that time, most of the magistrates were vacationing on their estates, but a number remained in the capital administering justice in the Chambre des Vacations under Presidents Lamoignon and de Gourgues. The Chambre des Vacations received a royal declaration of 21 September, which, in celebration of the birth of the dauphin, freed various prisoners from the Parisian jails.[85] Although the magistrates registered this declaration on 28 September, they simultaneously instructed President Lamoignon to seek assurances from the king that his act of goodwill "could not in any way prejudice the public security and tranquillity that is a special responsibility of the Parlement." After all, warned the judges, "the Public could be justly alarmed to see some subjects who had been juridically excluded from society now reenter that same society."[86] The jurists complained that those benefiting from such acts of pardon were liable to abuse the king's generosity by falling back upon their old, criminal ways. They furthermore recommended that the royal pardon embrace only those criminals guilty of the most minor offenses and that even those individuals, once set at large by the grace of the king, should be permanently barred from residing in Paris or in areas frequented by the royal family.

In fulfillment of the charge from his associates, Lamoignon corresponded with representatives of the government and was assured by Miromesnil himself on 1 October that all of the Parlement's concerns would be met.[87] Exactly what Lamoignon thought about the question cannot be determined from his papers. There can be no doubt, however, that the Parlement's fourth president remained wedded to the idea of a stern justice in France despite his genuine desire for reform. In 1788 Lamoignon might as keeper of the seals abolish one of the last vestiges of judicial torture in the kingdom; but in early 1781 his papers show him eager to prescribe ferocious punishments (including branding, the galleys, and banishment for life) for bankers and other moneyed individuals abetting gambling in the capital. His associate, Avocat-Général Séguier, felt almost as strongly about the matter as did Lamoignon, and his lengthy and heated indictment of the gaming activities of various *banquiers* in scandal-ridden dens within Paris spurred both the Parlement and the crown to take action against these activities in February and March 1781.[88] For the most part, the men of the Parlement, whether reformist or nonreformist, whether "zélantis" or "épiciers," believed in a rigorous justice.

But the judges' solicitude for the litigants within their company's jurisdiction could also be blunted by meaner considerations. It was all very
well to show compassion for Frenchmen victimized by the rival claims of
competing tribunals at Rheims or by despotic agents of the government.
It was quite another thing to be compassionate when the prerogatives or
conduct of the Parlement itself were in question. Thus, Séguier had objected in 1774 to an augmentation of presidial competence that had been
designed in part for the benefit of litigants; thus, he and his allies of the
Grand' Chambre had clung doggedly to their épices and vacations in
1783–84. Nor was the Parlement's reaction any more humanitarian in
1786 when an outsider, an officer of another parlement, had the temerity
to criticize the professional conduct of the Parisian magistrates in a trial
of the preceding year. In October 1785, the Paris Parlement's Chambre des
Vacations had condemned three men to be imprisoned and racked for
their crimes.[89] In the course of 1786, Dupaty, a président à mortier in the
Parlement of Bordeaux, had become outspokenly critical of the Parisian
judges' conduct in this case, charging that the trial procedure in the
Chambre des Vacations had been marred by irregularities and that the
final ruling itself had been unjustified and cruel. The affair became something of a cause célèbre, as Dupaty elaborated his critique in a *Mémoire
justicatif pour trois hommes condamnés à la roue*, while the magistrates
in the capital denounced President Dupaty for having meddled in their
affairs and for having fostered a spirit of revolt against the criminal ordinances and against the good old ways of doing things in French justice.
On 11 August 1786, the Parlement, adopting the recommendations of
Séguier who had spoken for the gens du roi, condemned Dupaty's *Mémoire justicatif* to be burned by the public executioner in the Palais de
Justice and announced further measures to be taken against the author,
printer, and distributor of the work.[90] The affair, however, terminated
to the discredit of the parlementaires during 1787: the three men who
had been found guilty by the Chambre des Vacations were set free by another tribunal, which, upon orders of the crown, reviewed the entire
proceeding.[91]

The Dupaty affair as well as other incidents of these years exposed the
ultimate failing of the parlementaires: their hostility to root-and-branch
reform of the laws and legal procedure. They could not or would not see
the forest for the trees. Their officers were expert at closing up loopholes
in existing regulations (when such action did not threaten their own interests); but their reaction to essays at more structural reform was invariably negative. Two incidents involving Guillaume François Louis Joly de
Fleury, the procureur-général, illustrate this problem.

In the first case, Joly de Fleury had remained unsatisfied with the legislation of December 1780 extending the competence of the Grand' Chambre. As a working jurist, he wished to revise the legislation in the interest

of various parties. For one thing, he immediately recommended that steps be taken to insure that defendants in cases involving commercial contracts could not delay disposition of such cases by alleging usury in the contracts under question (as the legislation permitted) unless they could prove that "usurious negotiations" had invalidated the contracts from the start. On the other hand, on behalf of all parties in all lawsuits covered by the December 1780 legislation, he advocated strict measures against unscrupulous proctors who might attempt to overtax their clients.[92] The Parlement incorporated these and other reforms in an arrêt of 21 February 1781.[93] But the court did not stop there. Less than a month later, again under the prodding of Joly de Fleury, it moved more decisively against the malfeasance of proctors in the court. The decree of 9 March 1781 assessed fines against procureurs who, acting for unwilling parties to a case, delayed the consideration by the parties' barrister of evidence germane to the litigation and delayed returning the evidence to the court.[94] The dilatory proctors would in fact have to pay two fines: one to the litigant or litigants inconvenienced by such tactics, and the other to the fund for dispensation of bread to prisoners in the Conciergerie. The jurists often acted in this manner to tighten up legislation from the government.

But the procureur-général and most of his colleagues would not challenge the mechanistic course of judicial procedure in France that occasionally invoked anachronistic and cruel practices to supplement inadequate evidence. A notorious case in point was the *question préparatoire*: torture that was still employed from time to time to extract a confession from an individual suspected of having committed a capital crime. In November 1779, Miromesnil sent the procureur-général a draft edict abrogating this practice. Joly de Fleury and some of his associates in the Grand' Chambre studied the document and debated the matter with the judges in the other chambers. Joly de Fleury later confided to a friend that he had been disturbed by some of the language in the preamble to the edict. "The style," he complained, "was a bit philosophical. . . . the author expounded on the ordinances concerning criminal procedure and argued about torture, etc." Indeed, the author had "left the door open for polemical writers to inundate the public with systems and new practices." Joly de Fleury continued, even more revealingly: "The matter was debated in court, and although the Parlement of Paris very rarely avails itself of the liberty of ordering the question préparatoire, it seemed that it could perhaps be rather inconvenient to deprive justice of that resource, which has upon some occasions been so very useful in uncovering the trace of great crimes and in procuring information important for public tranquillity."[95] Joly de Fleury's account suggests that there was some support in the Parlement for such a measure, and this is perhaps one reason why during 1780 he grudgingly cooperated with the keeper of the seals in abrogating the question préparatoire. He and his colleagues exacted their price, however: the "philosophical" language of the draft edict was watered down in the final version of the legislation so as to soothe sensibilities and allay anxieties at the Palais de Justice.[96]

This was the kind of mentality ascendant in the king's most powerful tribunal. And nothing changed in the ensuing decade as the ancien régime stumbled on toward its demise. When, at the height of the Parlement's quarrel with President Dupaty in 1786, a few voices in the court were reportedly raised in favor of reviewing the wisdom of criminal ordinances that could prescribe torture, Avocat-Général Séguier had his reply ready: "In these times of unrest a general cry has gone up against the criminal law, which some envisage as nothing but a vestige of bygone barbarism: the writings of the most famous jurisconsults, the monuments of the most ancient jurisprudence, and the decisions of the wisest legislators have all been proscribed. The most thoughtless individuals have applauded the intrepidity of a vindicator presumptuous enough to attempt to tear away the heavy veil which, he claims, obscures the law." The injuries and wrongs of slander, Séguier loftily assured his company, were merely "the homage that the philosophy of the century renders to the Magistracy."[97] Small wonder that Félix Faulcon should have written despairingly to a friend the following October that the parlementaires were "too gangrened" to reform themselves.[98] The "rights of humanity" that d'Aligre had preached in the royal presence in 1779 seemed far away. It would be simplistic to say that Joly de Fleury, Séguier, and like-minded magistrates were cruel men, but they certainly were hidebound conservatives unwilling or unable to transcend the attitudes of their profession. For this reason, and for other reasons discussed in other chapters of this book, the benison of parlementary justice was inadequate indeed.

No inventory of parlementary faults and foibles in the last years of the ancien régime would be fair in itself, for it would not tell the whole story. It would ignore or slight the fact that the parlementaires (and their counterparts in the other courts of the realm) dispensed nearly all the justice that was to be had in the eighteenth century. As later sections of this study will indicate, there were many times when Frenchmen, regardless of their social rank, were happy to receive the justice of the magistrates at Paris. Undeniably, that justice was flawed by the Parlement's corporate pride, by the precedence and privilege of its leaders, and by the majority of judges' stubborn adherence to the traditional ways of their profession. Yet these were failings common to all institutions in the ancien régime. In theory the crown, had it wished to, could have done something about the situation. In fact it had tried to, under Maupeou, and would try again, however briefly, under Lamoignon. But as this chapter has suggested, the crown was in a sense as dependent upon the Parlement's parti ministériel as was the latter upon the crown. If Lefebvre d'Amécourt and his allies clung to their powers and perquisites, the government clung with equal determination to its sources of revenue. If, more fundamentally, the parlementaires could not imagine justice other than it was, the government had always shown itself equally incapable of imagining absolutism and the social hierarchy other than *they* were. All of these issues, judicial and financial, constitutional and social, were ultimately interrelated. That the king and his magistrates seemed at times to be aware of this will appear more fully below. The tragedy for both Louis XVI and his parlementaires was the fact that they were ineluctably linked together in common defense of a regime for which the sands of time were rapidly running out.

CHAPTER THREE

The Magistrates and the
Monarchy, 1774–1786

The behavior of the Parisian parlementaires during the judicial controversies of the 1770s and early 1780s revealed how ambivalent their relationship with the crown could be. In the days and weeks following their professional reinstatement in 1774, the judges wasted no time in denying the monarch's right to compel registration of edicts after initial remonstrances, muzzle defiant members of the Enquêtes and Requêtes, and punish striking magistrates with forfeiture of their offices. Yet, just a few years later, the court's leaders used their ties with the government for all they were worth in beating back the reformist campaign of Lamoignon, Duval d'Eprémesnil, and their confederates. Thus, the politics of parlementary justice engaged a variety of interests at the Palais de Justice and elicited a variety of magisterial responses to Louis XVI and his ministers. But if this was true for the politics of parlementary justice, it was equally true for politics involving the government's judicial activities and finances. Yet, at the same time, the words and actions of the parlementaires show that in governmental as well as other matters they never forgot how their functions (and the immense prestige accruing from those functions) depended wholly upon monarchy in France. It was only with this reality in mind that the men of the Parlement proceeded to criticize the king and his government on judicial and financial issues.

This chapter will explore parlementary attitudes toward the crown in the twilight of the ancien régime. It will explain first of all how constitutional questions such as Gallicanism and the role of Necker's provincial assemblies spurred the judges to underscore the centrality of monarchy in France and associate their own authority with that of the crown. The discussion will then venture into more difficult waters. It will explore the ambivalence with which the parlementaires viewed the king: the king conceived as Supreme Magistrate, whose judicial preeminence was simultaneously sanctioned and delimited by law, and the king conceived as Governor, whose powers in political and administrative spheres were similarly limited. These considerations should further suggest that the magistrates' refusal during the 1774–86 period to concede the crown unlimited authority in judicial and financial matters directly anticipated the crisis in crown-Parlement relations that was to erupt in 1787 and help unleash the Revolution.

The Necessity of Monarchy in France

Service in the Paris Parlement tended to engender an awareness of a unique proximity to and association with the crown. True, the Parlement might summon the dukes and peers to the Cour des Pairs in December 1774 to fashion a defiant response to the government's legislation curbing magisterial politics; or then again, it might invoke the Estates General and chant the old litany of church and aristocratic privilege in its diatribes against royal taxation. Nevertheless, the justices ever seemed to be saying: let these same dukes and peers and all Estates General delegates and all clerics and nobles recognize and honor the unique bond between the sovereign and his oldest "sovereign court"! Such was the attitude prevailing at the Palais de Justice during the reign of Louis XVI.

For instance, sometime in the spring of 1785 President Joly de Fleury approvingly forwarded to an unidentified friend an essay treating the position of the dukes and peers in the French state. In closing, the essay was as concerned with the corporate supremacy of the Paris Parlement as it was with the *ducs et pairs*. The Parlement, so the essay asserted, "is the first of all the Corporations of the State . . . is never preceded by anyone . . . is even superior to the Estates General when they are in session and . . . can never be separated from the King by anyone or any institution whatsoever as is evidenced at general processions, at royal funerals, and at other great occasions. . . . The Parlement . . . is immediately attached to Royalty, without which it is neither a corporation nor a community." The dukes and peers and other *grands* of the kingdom might derive their prestige from "birth" and "hereditary dignities"; but the parlementaires enjoyed preeminence "as Officers of the King wielding royal authority." The essay underscored this bond between magistracy and monarchy with an exhortation to the king: "Finally, there is no one who should be more concerned to preserve that preeminence of the Parlement over all the rest of the State than the King himself . . . since the Parlement is nothing without Royalty and since it draws all of its authority from representing the King and wielding his authority. . . . the King, in preserving the Parlement's prerogatives, also preserves his own."[1] Joly de Fleury's correspondent returned this memoir in May, observing nostalgically that "the mold for such Memoirs has been lost."[2] There can be no doubt that Joly de Fleury agreed with him. His predecessors on the Grand Banc in the early decades of the century had gone to ridiculous lengths during the so-called "affair of the *bonnet*" to assert the supremacy of the Parlement over the peerage, a supremacy that derived from royal service rather than from pedigree.[3]

If the parlementaires stood, or felt that they should stand, between the king and his peerage, they claimed a similar precedence over the French Catholic church. Gallicanism had long been for the Parlement a way of defending the prerogatives of the crown (sometimes beyond the monarch's own wishes) and vaunting its own corporate supremacy. Although Gallicanism was not a major issue under Louis XVI, magisterial attitudes toward the Ultramontane philosophy associated with Rome remained unchanged.

In a series of essays on Gallicanism, Lefebvre d'Amécourt retold the story of church-state relations in France and once again forged the link between his company and the crown.[4] D'Amécourt spoke of how the Merovingian and Carolingian monarchs had combated the pretensions of the early medieval church: kings such as Pepin the Short and Charlemagne had continually convoked "assemblies called Parlements or Councils" that had aided them in matters concerning "ecclesiastical discipline" and "the principal affairs of State."[5] In this version of history, the Paris Parlement was foreshadowed long before its institution as a sedentary court at the capital. In discussing a later era, d'Amécourt portrayed the parlementaires as agents of a monarchical authority reasserting itself against the forces of feudalism, including the Ultramontane church, which had overwhelmed the last Carolingian rulers and long bedeviled their Capetian successors. The reestablishment of monarchical authority in France had been a long and painful process, and the Valois and Bourbons had found their magistrates to be indispensable auxiliaries. For example, in the midsixteenth century, Henri II had permitted the pope to commission several cardinals of the Gallican church to delegate to subordinates the power to root out Protestant heresies. But the cardinals had been granted this role by the king only "on condition that those whom they would delegate should take an oath to the sovereign, and that for the judgment of appeals in cities where Parlements existed, they would be obligated to choose up to ten persons, of whom at least six would be Counselors of the Sovereign Courts, and that those condemned would be given into the custody of the King's officers for execution of their sentences." Henri IV, according to Lefebvre d'Amécourt, had utilized his parlementaires in joining battle with the pope himself: "Henri IV having ordered his parlements to proceed against the Nuncio who had entered France without royal permission to censure those loyal to the king: The Parlements declared the Bulls abusive, prohibited their publication as a crime of lèse majesté, declared the so-called Pope Gregory XIV to be an enemy of peace and of the unity of the Church, of the King, and of his State . . . [and] ordered the seizure and trial of the Nuncio."[6]

This was of course the stuff of which many great Gallican controversies were made in the ancien régime. To recount such events was to document the parlements' growing importance as much as to celebrate the ascendancy of crown over church. Indeed, these two themes were necessarily complementary: the magistrates could not champion the restoration of royal authority in France without simultaneously reaffirming the influence they had come to wield in the kings' affairs.

That Lefebvre d'Amécourt's associates continued to share his Gallican sentiments under Louis XVI appeared in 1777, when the Jesuit controversy briefly flared up again. The parlements of the kingdom had furiously assaulted the Society of Jesus in the early 1760s. The government of Louis XV, powerless to stem the attack of the parlementaires against this emanation of the power of Rome, had, with its edict of November 1764, acquiesced in the destruction of the society in France.[7] However, the relentless Parisian and provincial judges had maintained their assault after 1764 with supplementary decrees circumscribing the movement and activities of the "ex-Jesuits," and the exile of the Maupeou years did little to quench their hatred of the proscribed society. On 11 April 1777, the Paris Parlement condemned a treatise advocating the reinstitution of the society in France and, upon the initiative of its présidents à mortier, launched a full-scale discussion of rumored "novel enterprises of the society within the kingdom."[8] The *Gazette de Leyde* reported that the presidents and "several of the oldest members of the company" argued strongly for renewal of the court's earlier strictures against the ex-Jesuits' activities, and the upshot was a decision to "name *commissaires* who would suggest the most proper means for heading off what would surely result from the present actions of the ex-Jesuits if they were not repressed."[9] A report by Séguier at the session of 11 April, which threw considerable doubt upon the veracity of the rumors concerning the defunct society, could not dissuade the majority of magistrates from resuming their campaign against a hated foe.

These denunciations in the Parlement stirred the government to intervene in the affair with "an Edict, which, granting to these former *Religieux* all the advantages they could claim as Citizens, attempted at the same time through appropriate restrictions to prevent the liberty granted them from endangering the tranquillity of the Kingdom."[10] The "appropriate restrictions" involved such matters as where the ex-Jesuits could live, what types of spiritual charges they could hold under the careful supervision of the ordinary clergy, and what kinds of pensions and other incomes they could enjoy. The edict, promulgated at Versailles during May 1777, was registered by the Parlement on the thirteenth of the month, but the judges insisted upon adding several conditions to the legislation.[11] They wished, for instance, to confine ex-Jesuits not possessing benefices to the dioceses of their birth and to ban them from exercising any public function of the ministry in the cities of the realm. Most significantly, the parlementaires ordered all ex-Jesuits holding benefices of any kind or acting as curates to acknowledge formally the destruction of their former society in November 1764, to accept all provisions of the present edict, and to swear "to maintain and profess the liberties of the Gallican Church, and especially the Four Articles of the clergy's declaration of 1682." The king was reportedly highly displeased at the Parlement's action, in part because former Jesuits nominated to preach before him at Versailles feared prosecution by the judges.[12] Louis no doubt signified his displeasure to his justices, and the following month brought a compromise between crown and Parlement that somewhat alleviated the ex-Jesuits' situation in France.[13]

To the end of their professional days, however, the parlementaires doggedly clung to their Gallican principles and thus to their exalted vision of monarchical—and magisterial—authority. The judges had occasion to remind Louis of this in the summer of 1783. For several years the bishop of Noyon had been disputing certain points of ecclesiastical discipline with his chapter of canons at Noyon. Litigation ensued between bishop and chapter, and the latter, charging the former with ecclesiastical abuse, was received as appellant *comme d'abus* in the Parlement's Grand' Chambre in May 1783. However, the bishop obtained a royal decree of 18 July withdrawing the case from parlementary cognizance and referring it to the King's Council. On 26 August someone from the first chamber of Enquêtes denounced this decree to his fellows in a plenary session of the Parlement. The bishop, he charged, "was depriving the Grand' Chambre of the exercise of its jurisdiction in ecclesiastical affairs and was in effect mocking its zeal for the preservation . . . of our liberties." After Séguier addressed the matter three days later, the Parlement sent First President d'Aligre to Versailles to complain about the evocation of the case from the Parlement to the royal Council. Of all kinds of litigation attributed to the parlements by the kings' ordinances, contended d'Aligre in the royal presence, the *appels comme d'abus*, involving as they did allegations of ecclesiastical abuse and conflicts between "the two powers" of church and state, were least susceptible of evocation. It was absolutely necessary, intoned d'Aligre, "that the ecclesiastical power, which often rivals your own and which is not exempt from prejudices contrary to the rights of your crown, be solemnly judged by the tribunal that joins to the greatest amount of experience the greatest degree of insight."[14]

Louis, unimpressed by this invocation of his regal prerogatives, failed to give the parlementaires any satisfaction on the matter. His Council was considering the contestation at Noyon, he said, and that was the end of the business as far as his good parlementaires were concerned. However, d'Aligre and his associates refused to let the matter drop. Their reiterated protests, delivered to the king the following February, drove the same points home once again and thus dramatized the continuity of magisterial attitudes on an age-old question.[15]

To be sure, the Parlement was all too capable of playing upon its special

relationship with the crown for petty purposes. During the judicial reform episode of 1783–84, the desire to preserve their unneeded fees had
in part motivated the senior jurists to warn Louis XVI darkly of the "fermentation," insubordination, and anarchy that must result if polemics
such as those of Lamoignon and his cohorts went unpunished. The king,
they had solemnly asserted, must beware lest disrespect for his principal
judges undermine crown as well as Parlement. For the most part, however, the parlementaires advanced such arguments in connection with issues of more substance than their vacations and épices. The classic example during the 1774–86 period would have to have been the controversy
over Necker's provincial assemblies. Starting in 1778, this affair provided
a battleground upon which the judges defended a wide variety of interests, and, not surprisingly, the survival of the parlements and of the monarchical "constitution" that justified their existence was one of the most
keenly felt of those interests.

Turgot had broached the idea of a system of provincial assemblies several years before. During his abbreviated ministry, his physiocratic confidant, Du Pont de Nemours, had drawn up a *Mémoire sur les municipalités* explaining Turgot's conception of a hierarchy of village and
municipal assemblies, intermediate bodies in the *élections* or *cantons*,
and assemblies at the provincial level.[16] Such assemblies, elected by and
composed of local landowners, would have assisted the Intendants and
their subordinates in assessing taxation among the élections and parishes, determining assessments for and supervising public works, and administering poor relief. Unlike provincial and general Estates, these assemblies would have ignored the traditional distinctions of three separate
"orders" or "estates" in society.

Turgot fell from power in 1776 and never submitted his plan to Louis
XVI, but Necker revived the idea in a different form two years later.
Necker's intention, emerging in the *arrêt du Conseil* of July 1778 provisionally establishing an assembly in the province of Berry, was to dispense with hierarchies of assemblies within each province and to fashion
instead a network of such bodies throughout France at the provincial
level alone.[17] These assemblies, with a more numerous personnel than
Turgot had envisaged, would furthermore be divided into contingents
from the three orders: the third estate would be doubled, and voting
would be by head rather than by order so as to please reformist interests.
Although the king would select the first sixteen members of the Berry
assembly at Bourges, those sixteen, under the direction of the archbishop
of Bourges, would designate the other thirty-two members from the
clergy, nobility, and third estate. Moreover, though the July 1778 decree
provided vaguely for the cooperation of intendant and assembly in such
matters as assessment of taxation in the parishes, public works, and poor

relief, it failed to mark out the intendant's and the assembly's spheres of authority in these areas.[18] This plan was adopted with modifications for assemblies in the Haute-Guyenne, Bourbonnais, and Dauphiné as well, though the latter two never actually materialized.

Necker's experiment was to stir apprehensions among the Parisian parlementaires even before they got wind of his criticisms of the intendants and parlements in the confidential memorandum on the provincial assemblies he submitted to Louis in 1778.[19] Nor were the judges alone in their concern about the possible constitutional implications of Necker's innovation. Indeed, some of their habitual foes shared their concern. Turgot himself greeted Necker's assemblies with a mixture of scorn and apprehension. "This present innovation," he warned, "if it is followed up, might end by changing the monarchical constitution." The former minister envisioned thirty provincial assemblies coming to an understanding "in times of trouble, feebleness, and minority." They could then form a "congress" like the one emerging at that very moment in America and claim the support of the whole nation. "If the military forces then turn against the monarchy, there would be a legitimate civil war," stated Turgot, "and republican principles would take the place of the monarchical constitution."[20] Whether or not the former controller-general was himself something other than a monarchist over the long run, he clearly saw Necker's scheme as capable of generating sudden and radical change in France.[21] His concern was echoed by a number of contemporaries—including one memorialist whose habitual criticism of parlementary pretensions did not prevent him from sounding, on this issue, much as the Parisian parlementaires themselves sounded.[22]

What, then, was the reaction to this innovation from the Palais de Justice? Commentary on the provincial assemblies, dating from as early as 1778 and 1779, appears in the papers of many of the leading parlementaires, including Lefebvre d'Amécourt, Abbé d'Espagnac, the Joly de Fleury brothers, and President Lamoignon.[23] The predominant fear of all of these jurists seems to have been that the new institutions would simultaneously endanger parlementary and monarchical prerogatives. Take, for instance, this apologia for the sovereign lawcourts in d'Amécourt's neat hand: "The sovereign courts in France exercise precisely those functions that the monarchical government can permit without inconvenience to itself. . . . they are never in a position to checkmate the authority of the sovereign power, they have none of the public revenues at their disposition, but they do have sufficient authority to present at the foot of the throne the needs and plaints of subjects without stirring up any ferment in the provinces."[24]

Obviously, many partisans of the crown would have accused this author of underestimating the parlements' capacity for obstructing the government when their own interests came into play. Just as obviously, however, the magistrates' own interests forced them to think in terms of the maintenance of royal absolutism in France. As Lefebvre d'Amécourt's papers put it: "To what perils . . . would the Monarch not be exposed if the representations that he receives . . . by means of his courts, were debated in the provincial assemblies . . . by persons representing the different orders who, united among themselves, would at the same time be the masters of all means needed to force the prince to assemble the Estates General?" [25] The similarity between this statement and Turgot's observations is evident. Turgot was primarily concerned for the monarch's prerogative, while the parlementaire here was probably worrying more immediately about a threat to his own professional and political activities; the keystone of reality for both perspectives, nevertheless, remained the institution of monarchy in France.

For the nub of the matter was that Necker's administrative experiment might overturn the good old ways of administering the kingdom. The system developed under the Bourbons had increasingly invested the intendant, a Bourbon creation, with the power to execute the royal will in the province or *généralité* to which he was assigned. In a parallel development, the parlements, acting more and more as self-styled tribunes for the classes and masses, had come to articulate popular grievances and denounce abuses allegedly arising from this regime, though customarily they directed their heaviest fire at the intendant's subordinates rather than at the intendant himself. It is not surprising that Lefebvre d'Amécourt's papers yield an elaborate defense of the intendant's administrative role.[26] D'Amécourt and his colleagues may very well have suspected, even before learning of Necker's confidential memoir to the king, that the director-general of finances would use a critique of the intendants to justify an administrative innovation potentially subversive of the complementary roles of intendants and parlementaires.[27] Naturally, however, the crucial point for the judges remained the status, present and projected, of the sovereign courts. The following observation, again from the d'Amécourt papers, went to the heart of the matter by linking constitutional change with the role of the king's tribunals: "One cannot avoid realizing that it will be impossible for the courts to preserve the importance they enjoy if the provincial assemblies take root. They [i.e., the courts] will be reduced one by one to purely judicial functions. The parlements will become as the judges of England, while the provincial assemblies through a joint effort will acquire the strength and the stability of the House of Commons." [28] The author here saw all too clearly that a constitutional monarchy, similar to that across the Channel, would separate legislative (and hence political) functions from judicial functions, stripping the high magistracy of that political role it had learned to relish over the years.

At about the time d'Amécourt recorded these observations, he and his fellow magistrates were learning of Necker's surreptitious critique of the intendants and parlements. Though the Parisian parlementaires had recently confronted the director-general over the *vingtièmes* and *corvée royale*, they bided their time on the question of the provincial assemblies.[29] But when, in early 1781, the government requested the court's registration of letters patent confirming the establishment of an assembly in the Bourbonnais, the grand' chambriers drafted a memorandum explaining to Louis that as custodians of royal authority they could not in good conscience promote his legislation. The Parlement's seniors claimed that they had failed to protest the institution of the first assembly in Berry two years before only because they had then regarded it as a mere experiment subject to termination at any time. With an oblique reference to Necker the grand' chambriers sought to justify themselves in the king's eyes: "We are not unaware that people have tried to attribute this delay to private motives; it is possible that a few persons have tried to profit from the occasion by involving their special interests, but we feel quite certain that the older magistrates have been occupied only with preserving royal authority, which the Parlements have always defended and indeed have so much interest to defend."[30]

This was no rhetorical flourish intended for public consumption but a disarmingly frank statement of magisterial dependence upon monarchy, destined for royal eyes alone. When the parlementaires proceeded, in their justificative memoir, to outline procedures that would maximize royal influence in the Bourbonnais assembly, they were responding as champions of a royal tradition that had always justified their own professional tradition, as advocates of a monarchical "constitution" that still maximized their own political and judicial significance.[31] The cooperation between the senior judges and the government that produced (after Necker's dismissal in May 1781) a compromise on the form and functions of the Bourbonnais assembly underscored the continuing interdependence of crown and Parlement on constitutional as well as other issues.[32]

Admittedly, the parlementaires had not mistrusted Necker's experiment for constitutional reasons alone. They were great landowners and tribunes of all taxpayers as well as servants of the crown, and in these roles they feared the provincial bodies as potential instruments of heavier taxation. The fact remains that the magistrates' reaction against the provincial assemblies, like their reactions against the *ducs et pairs* and the church, portrayed them as willing champions of monarchical authority in France. That the parlementaires did not view this authority as arbitrary and unlimited, however, emerged with equal clarity in connection with specific judicial and political questions of the period.

The King as Magistrate:
The Roots of Legitimacy

The magistrates recognized, indeed insisted upon, the magisterial quality of kingship. They paid homage to the king as Supreme Magistrate whenever he reenacted his ancient role in a lit de justice, however doggedly they might challenge the objectives of such sessions. Simultaneously, however, the jurists asserted that the king, as magistrate, must subject himself to the laws. In other words, legitimacy derived in the final analysis from the knowledge of when to apply self-restraint in the uses of power. As Avocat-Général Séguier had reminded the newly crowned Louis XVI in November 1774, the sovereign "must aspire to reign in concert with all the laws."[33] Obviously, that kind of legalistic attitude had implications for Louis in his political as well as his judicial role, and the parlementaires could never establish any hard and fast distinction between the two roles. Still, there were occasions upon which the jurists isolated the king in his judicial capacity and attempted to subordinate him in that character to the standard of law.

The controversy over cassation was an example in point. As indicated earlier, this term signified the royal nullification of a decree or judgment of one of the tribunals that the king considered illegal or self-contradictory. The right of cassation (like the associated prerogative of *évocation*) was a chronic bone of contention between the sovereign courts and the government during the eighteenth century. During the 1760s, the Paris Parlement inveighed with particular fury against the alleged abuse of cassation and evocation by "despots" wielding the king's authority in the government.[34] The Parlement's denunciations culminated in the tremendously long remonstrances of 5 June 1767.[35] Louis XV had his Conseil des Dépêches examine these protests and instructed two of its most distinguished members, Jean François II Joly de Fleury and Pierre VI Gilbert de Voisins, to tender him their reflections on the nature and legality of cassations.

The immediate political effect of the resultant treatise by Gilbert de Voisins is not pertinent in this context. What is pertinent is the fact that Gilbert de Voisins had formerly been a member of the Paris Parlement and continued to enjoy a unique stature in parlementary eyes long after his shift from a magisterial to a government career. At the height of the debate over judicial reform in 1784, President Joly de Fleury lionized him as one of the past giants of the judicial profession.[36] More to the point, Lefebvre d'Amécourt transcribed Gilbert de Voisin's excursus on cassations in its entirety and left it among his papers.[37] The treatise merits closer consideration, for it was a classic articulation of the magisterial view of kingship and left a permanent impression upon the parlementaires of the 1770s and 1780s.

On the one hand, Gilbert de Voisins unequivocally placed the king at the apex of justice in his kingdom: "In France, sovereign jurisdiction, as well as sovereign legislation, belongs to the King, as principle and as center of all public power, and the various degrees of jurisdiction established under his authority in the Kingdom return in the last resort to this principle and this center." On the other hand, this supreme judicial authority had always been "exercised with an order and under forms inhering naturally in the sacred character of this authority"—and the championship of this "order" and of these "forms" had largely been the function of the monarch's watchful courts, chief among them being the Paris Parlement. "In accordance with the ancient order of the Kingdom, the King's sovereign justice has been meted out, at least for the most part, in his parlement, whether by him personally or, in his absence, by his representatives. It has been the King's court, the court of peers, because the King has sometimes been attended by the peers on solemn occasions. The Parlement of Paris continues to embody these ancient traditions today."[38]

At the same time, insisted Gilbert de Voisins, this proud and ancient Parlement of Paris, and indeed all of the lawcourts that exercised an "eminent jurisdiction" for the sovereign, were "subject to rules," which the sovereign was ultimately responsible for maintaining. Most crucially, "the judges in the courts are dispensers and not masters of that authority which is entrusted to them." The monarch could thus intervene in his tribunals, indeed was obliged to at times, and this was the foundation of his right of cassation. Yet the monarch himself must always remember that "the power of judging is not arbitrary. The King himself in the order of his *puissance* does not wield this power arbitrarily, but according to the *esprit de règle et de conseil* that forms the proper character of his royal authority."[39] Gilbert de Voisins was treading the delicate and difficult line between magisterial constitutionalism and monarchical absolutism.

Gilbert de Voisins nicely balanced the opposing theses of crown and magistracy throughout his essay. He listed the circumstances that justified recourse to cassation of court decrees but more often than not hastened to qualify the royal prerogative he had just defined. For instance, the monarch had to intervene against a tribunal that presumed to *interpret* as well as publish and enforce royal ordinances; yet the distinction between *enforcement* of the ordinances (which was "entirely entrusted to the courts") and their *interpretation* was often so fine that recourse to cassation in all such instances "would not only cast these tribunals down to the level of the most inferior judges, but also unduly restrict their operations, against the ends of justice itself."[40] By minimizing the difference between court enforcement and court interpretation of royal ordinances, Gilbert de Voisins was in effect urging restraint upon the government in an area where it was especially prone to cross swords with the high magistracy. It was precisely tribunals such as the Paris Parlement that "interpreted" aspects of royal legislation (or "interpreted" what they took to be the king's will) by issuing administrative decrees of their own—thereby risking upon occasion the royal displeasure.

Again, even though Gilbert de Voisins viewed customary and Roman law in France as being "under the protection of the King's sovereignty" and hence justified cassation of judicial acts violating such local law, he saw the crown's prerogative as even more limited in this area than in the field of royal ordinances. The parlements had always enjoyed "a very ample power over customary laws, not only to interpret them but even to correct them if need be." As for Roman law, "its interpretation is as little subject to preconceived rules as is the interpretation of *coutumes*."[41] Thus, in this area as well, the crown must be circumspect in its use of cassation.

Gilbert de Voisins summed up his conception of cassation succinctly by concluding that "the more it must be accounted a proper means of authority reserved to the King for the maintenance of order and of observation of the laws in his kingdom, the less arbitrary its application must be and the less it must be employed beyond the dictates of necessity."[42] Predictably, the parlementaires of the following generation who so admired this minister and ex-magistrate placed greater emphasis upon his strictures against the abuse of cassation than they did upon his defense of its occasional use. Here, for instance, was Lefebvre d'Amécourt commenting upon the matter: "When our Kings reserved to themselves the useful right of examining in the wisdom of their Council, if the Sovereign Courts to which they had entrusted the laws, had respected or violated this sacred trust, it was not at all to favor caprice, intrigue, or oppression . . . nor to deprive justice of the confidence and respect which are its due, nor to permit anyone to trifle with its oracular pronouncements."[43] Needless to say, the Parlement in its recurrent dueling with the government over cassations and évocations stressed the "caprice," "intrigue," and "oppression" of those ministers whom it accused of interfering in the natural course of justice.

In this context, the magistrates' protest of 1779 against the cassation of a judgment rendered by the Toulouse Parlement and against the evocation of the case to the Requêtes de l'Hôtel at Paris appears in a new light. The judges' protest was an automatic response to a classic question of royal authority, as well as solicitude for the welfare of several humble Frenchmen.[44] When Louis, responding tartly to the judges' complaints, insisted that the affair was being handled legally in his Council and was no business of the Parlement, there was a swift reaction at the Palais de Justice. The judges voted for several of their number to look further into the particulars of the case; more significantly, they soon thereafter initiated conferences to reexamine the whole question of cassation.[45] It looked very much as though the judges were about to renew their furious antigovernment campaign of the 1760s. Ironically, the issue was eventually swallowed up by the debate over the vacations and épices, a debate that reminded the senior grand' chambriers of certain common interests with the crown. Still, the jurists' animus against cassations and evocations was an important aspect of their general indictment of "ministerial despotism," and it remained unaltered to the end of their professional days.

The Parlement had other opportunities to assert the limitations upon judicial kingship during those years. They did so in one case involving an obscure *roturier* named Jean-Baptiste Favriot. This case was cited earlier (in chapter 2) in a slightly different context as illuminating one area of the judges' professional mentality. It will be recalled that when the Parlement learned in July 1778 of Favriot's questionable arrest and incarceration, it immediately ordered a review of the matter. On 25 August the company sent First President d'Aligre to Versailles with information it had obtained concerning this artisan's arrest at Montgeron. But the first president did not go to Versailles merely to contend that one of the king's humbler subjects had been wronged; he was just as much concerned to make an abstract statement on the limitations of Louis's kingship. An excerpt from that statement seems worth quoting once again: "your parlement feels itself obligated to implore Your Majesty to contain within the limits of indispensable necessity or of obvious usefulness the dispensing of orders emanating from the supreme power. Be so good, Sire, as to insist with the most precise orders that there be no infringement of the liberty of your own subjects, against your intentions."[46]

The Parlement could take the affair no further, but it had once again reminded the king that he and his agents must endeavor to rule "in concert with all the laws"—which in this case meant utilization of the arm of justice to guarantee the liberties of Frenchmen regardless of social rank. Because the magistrates were willing on occasion to champion the rights of obscure commoners before the king, it was entirely logical that during the prerevolutionary tumult of 1787–88 they should apply the same legalistic argument in defense of the duc d'Orléans and several of their own number. Circumstances might at any given time determine the intensity of parlementary opposition to judicial "despotism," but the mentality behind that opposition remained constant.

Not that the senior parlementaires were necessarily loath to cooperate with the crown on specific judicial matters. Indeed, there were times (as during the 1783–84 reform episode) when the "ministerial" grand' chambriers positively drew the crown into a clandestine partnership for their own unenlightened purposes. But this relationship worked both ways. There is good evidence to suggest, for instance, that several of the tribunal's leaders were sympathetic toward the outraged Louis and Marie

Antoinette during the Diamond Necklace affair of 1785–86 and accordingly may have been biased against the cardinal de Rohan during his celebrated trial in the Parlement. The abbé Georgel insisted in his memoirs that First President d'Aligre, the Joly de Fleury brothers, Lefebvre d'Amécourt, and the two rapporteurs in the litigation "believed that the honor and dignity of the queen demanded that the cardinal be punished, if not as author of and party to the outrage . . . at least as having in effect contributed to it through liaisons unbecoming a man of his rank, name, and estate."[47] Georgel, as the cardinal's *vicaire-général* in the 1780s, was hardly unbiased in his account of the affair, but another observer commented that when the time came to pronounce judgment in the Grand' Chambre at the end of May 1786, Procureur-Général Joly de Fleury's conclusions were less than flattering toward de Rohan. Although he concluded that the cardinal had been duped by others in the unsavory incident of the necklace, Joly de Fleury reportedly suggested that de Rohan should ask the pardon of the royal couple "in the presence of the Court" for his indiscretion in regard to Marie Antoinette and should resign his offices and absent himself in future from Versailles.[48] According to Georgel, the two rapporteurs and a number of jurists "swayed by the discourse of the counselor d'Amécourt" seconded this opinion, but the decision of the majority was to acquit the cardinal, not only of all charges but also of all suspicion of indiscreet conduct.[49] Rumors that Avocat-Général Séguier had publicly accused his superior the procureur-général of having sacrificed the strict demands of justice to his sympathy for the queen, and some strained correspondence between Joly de Fleury and Duval d'Eprémesnil relative to another defendant in the trial, suggest further that some of the judges had been moved by other than professional considerations in this case.[50]

For the most part, however, the judges in the parti ministériel led their colleagues in the traditional policy of qualifying magisterial kingship, either by criticizing the government's administration of the sovereign's justice or by circumscribing the reach of royal jurisdiction in the country. The Parlement's reaction to the jurisdictional dispute at Rheims in 1779 exemplified the latter tendency.[51] At issue in this controversy was whether the archibishop of Rheims, acting upon the suggestion of the lieutenant-general of the royal bailliage of that city, should terminate a long-standing rivalry between his ancient archiepiscopal and seigneurial bailliage and its expanding royal counterpart by ceding most of his court's administration of civil and criminal justice to the royal court at Rheims. The Paris Parlement, under whose appellate jurisdiction this royal bailliage functioned, had taken an early interest in the affair in 1779, and one of the parlementaires—apparently either the current rapporteur d'Espagnac or Lefebvre d'Amécourt—drafted a memorandum expressing his company's position.[52]

As was noted briefly in an earlier context, this memorandum deplored the hardships imposed upon the populace at Rheims by the rivalry between the royal and ecclesiastical tribunals. It commented favorably upon the compromise proposed by the lieutenant-general of the former court. In return for the cession to the royal bailliage of most of the authority of his ecclesiastical-seigneurial bailliage, the archbishop would retain administrative rights over the archiepiscopal palace and its immediately dependent territories. In addition, he would obtain from the king the right to nominate one-third of the officers of the enlarged royal bailliage. The parlementary reaction was favorable, not only because the resolution of this dispute would simplify things for litigants at Rheims but also because both royal and ecclesiastical-seigneurial justice would gain something from the compromise. As the judges' memorandum put it: "The execution of this project will be useful to all parties. It will be useful to the King, and consequently to the royal bailliage whose jurisdiction and dignity will be augmented. It will be equally so to the Archbishop of Rheims, by stabilizing his authority, assuring the condition . . . of his justice, and according him new prerogatives."[53]

Naturally, the Parlement was aware that augmenting the competence of the royal court at Rheims would at least indirectly buttress its own position as well, insofar as litigation formerly bottled up in an ecclesiastical jurisdiction would henceforth be more directly appealable to Paris. Corporate spirit probably figured as always in attitudes at the Palais de Justice. Equally meaningful, however, was the judges' acknowledgment that seigneurial rights (in this case archiepiscopal rights at Rheims) could still exist alongside the authority of the monarch, thus qualifying to some degree the prerogatives of the latter.

The magistrates pursued their attempt to reconcile monarchical and seigneurial interests at Rheims in a second memorandum, written (again by either d'Espagnac or d'Amécourt) to clarify several legal points raised by Procureur-Général Joly de Fleury.[54] As a royal officer, Joly de Fleury had apparently questioned whether *any* circumstances could confer upon a seigneur such as the archbishop of Rheims the right to nominate subjects to positions in a royal court. To this, Joly de Fleury's confrere or confreres responded emphatically: "It is the King who gains here. If a seigneur purely and simply cedes his justice to the King, in return for being able to nominate subjects of the King to serve in the King's court, would not the Royal Domain be deemed as augmented? This is what the Archbishop of Rheims is doing here."[55] The memorandum reiterated that the compromise was "favorable to the public weal" and of considerable profit to the justice and authority of the king; simultaneously, it lauded the generous motives of the archbishop of Rheims, who was freely giving to the king's justice "a portion of the rights that belonged to him." Even though the magistrates as royal servants recognized the monarch as the ultimate font of French justice and watched over the rights of his domain, they continued to see the mandate of justice and its associated administrative functions as shared between the crown and the vestigial agents of feudalism. Thus, the parlementaires testified in their own distinctive way to the survival of certain ambiguities of judicial authority in the old regime. The compromise proposed for the rival jurisdictions at Rheims never came about. Although the archbishop was certainly reconciled to the diminution of his judicial authority, the officers of his court were not, and they managed to scuttle the proposal.[56] Still, this incident, along with others of the period, pointed up the judges' view that the monarch's supreme judicial power derived its fullest legitimacy from its responsiveness to French legal traditions—traditions that often argued against the arbitrary use and unlimited reach of that power. This conception of magisterial kingship was assuredly one of the basic prerequisites for revolution in France, for it inspired the parlementaires—and after them, representatives of all corporations and estates—to indict the absolutism of the Bourbons. But the magistrates' ambivalent conception of fiscal and administrative kingship struck even more closely at the continuation of Bourbon rule in France.

The King as Governor:
Raison d'état versus Property

The men of the Parlement were for the most part substantial landowners as well as royal servants, and from this simple fact flowed much of the ambivalence in their posture toward the operations and finances of the king's government. Admittedly, constitutional issues such as Gallicanism and the role of Necker's provincial assemblies compelled the judges, in part for self-serving reasons, to defend the centrality of monarchy in France. Moreover, when it came to government finances, the Parlement never seriously challenged the host of indirect taxes in the kingdom or (within certain limits) the immemorial levy of the *taille*.[57] But the eighteenth century did witness recurrent parlementary protests against impositions such as the *vingtièmes*, which lay upon the lands of parlementaires as well as peasants. The last fifteen years of the ancien régime brought the grand climacteric of such protest, thus underscoring the tenuous nature of the judges' support for the administrative and fiscal aspects of kingship.

In this connection, the reaction of the senior parlementaires to Necker's provincial assemblies is again illuminating. If, on the one hand, the magistrates, like Turgot and others, could see worrisome constitutional implications in a network of such bodies in the provinces, on the other hand, they could sense in this innovation a device by which unscrupulous "ministerial despots" would sidestep the registration and remonstrances of the courts to levy arbitrary taxes upon the defenseless population. Here is one of the parlementaires recording the misgivings with which the proprietors of Berry viewed their assembly:

> The taxpayers have sensed in the leaders of that administration nothing but views detrimental to the tranquillity of landowners [such as] . . .
>
> The desire to find out the true value of their property, so as to have then a pretext for increasing the vingtièmes.
>
> This is what the proprietors of Berry have discerned . . .
>
> And the fact is incontrovertible.
>
> . . . in vain have the members of the administration announced everywhere that their intention was not to determine the true value of the lands. . . .
>
> The proprietors of Berry have not heard these consoling voices at all.[58]

This observer clearly saw the Berry assembly as a passive instrument of Necker's current policy directed at "verifying" the values of all lands subject to the vingtièmes. And it is a fact that the government viewed such land valuations as portending in many cases an increased assessment of that imposition.[59]

Inevitably, the parlementary papers castigated the government for endeavoring on this issue to evade the natural defenders of all Frenchmen, the parlements:

> Is it not to be feared . . . that [the government] will use specious arguments to avoid the necessity of registration of taxes, thus destroying the ancient national maxim dictating such a procedure?
>
> The Minister, accustomed to dealing with these assemblies and demanding imposts which they will have to levy, will necessarily be tempted to throw over the constraints of registration in the courts and continue to deal solely with the assemblies on new taxation.[60]

The magistrates' apprehension was not unfounded. Necker's memorandum on the provincial assemblies, written solely for royal consideration, pointed toward just such an administrative arrangement, and the parlementaires must have found their worst fears confirmed when the director-general's sentiments became known.

The overall ambivalence of parlementary attitudes toward the provincial assemblies viewed as vehicles of taxation was summed up nicely in that statement of early 1781 justifying the court's refusal to register the edict confirming the establishment of a new assembly in the Bourbonnais. Would the members of the new body, queried this document apprehensively, be considered "representatives of their region" or "commis-

sioners of the King"?[61] As "representatives of their region," the members
of the Bourbonnais assembly would presumably have a chance to look
after the interests of local taxpayers, but as "commissioners of the King"
they would be mere tools of the ministry as it imposed heavier and heavier taxation.

As this commentary on the provincial assemblies suggests, the Parlement was raising the taxation issue on an associated front during
Necker's ministry. In November 1777 the director-general of finances
promulgated a decree regulating anew the assessment of the vingtièmes.[62] Among its provisions were the following. All lands subject to
the vingtièmes that had not been assessed for taxation since 1771 would
now be so evaluated by the intendants and their assistants. Lands assessed since that time would be taxed at their present rate for the next
twenty years. Each of the parishes would choose three "notable proprietors" to assist in all verifications of land values: these *propriétaires notables*, along with the *syndics* and *collecteurs des tailles* from the parishes,
would presumably safeguard their constituents against arbitrary assessments and thus against arbitrary taxation. In the future, however, all taxable lands must be reassessed periodically, that is, every twenty years.
Such a procedure would satisfy the general principle that taxation—implicitly, permanent taxation—should not be fixed at a given level but
should rather be proportional to the value of land, thereby following, "at
least at a certain distance, the increase in value of land."[63]

Even before the appearance of this measure, the Parlement had been receiving complaints about arbitrary verifications of lands by royal agents
within its jurisdiction. As a result, the court in August 1777 had instructed the procureur-général and his substitutes in the lower tribunals
of the jurisdiction to investigate the matter.[64] This inquiry can best be
treated later on for what it reveals about the magistrates' social attitudes.[65] For the moment, we must see how the judges, in private observations as well as in formal remonstrances to Louis XVI, reacted against the
principles of taxation enunciated by Necker.

In the first place, the parlementaires realized that the director-general
of finances, however willing he might be temporarily to forgo higher taxation of those lands assessed during the preceding six years, nonetheless
envisioned heavier taxation of *all* lands over the long run. But this meant
that the initiation of his policy was itself legally questionable in parlementary eyes. For the *arrêt du Conseil* of November 1777, like all such
"decrees of the Council," did not require the formal *enregistrement* that
all "declarations," "ordinances," and "letters patent" required; but the
judges insisted that any measure leading to increased taxation, even if
such taxation merely reflected rising values of land, must bear the
imprimatur of parlementary registration. As one parlementaire put it,
"the verifications proposed by the decree of 2 November can only be exe-

cuted according to registered laws: the form must be legal and uniform throughout the Kingdom." Otherwise, warned this magistrate, "any individual member of the Council who signs a decree will be more powerful than the King, because the will of a Minister will be able to restrain or extend the most sacred and immutable laws."[66] The Parlement and, by extension, all the sovereign courts were once more being cast in the role of bulwarks against ministerial despotism, mediators between the king (betrayed by his ministers) and his subjects.

Yet, looming behind this immediate constitutional question was the timeless confrontation between the state's fiscal needs and the rights—above all, the proprietary rights—of the subject. For the finance-minded government, this naturally had to be the cutting issue, because revenues were the sinews of ongoing royal policies. As for the Parlement, it could not for the moment obstruct a government bent upon increasing its revenues;[67] and yet the court's attitude was significant, not only because it revealed the jurists' woefully inadequate comprehension of the state's needs but also because it led these champions of proprietary rights to invoke the revolutionary principle of national representation.

The parlementary papers make it obvious that the judges did not accept the idea of permanent—and permanently increasing—taxation, at least as far as the vingtièmes were concerned. Here is one of the parlementaires reacting to a key provision in the decree of November 1777:

> *The revenues of the King must follow, at least at a certain distance, the growth of the value of lands. . . .*
>
> Here, the author of the decree betrays his thought and discloses his system for rendering taxes permanent.
>
> He calls them the *revenues of the King.*
>
> He wants them to increase with the land values on which they are levied.
>
> But taxes are, at the most, merely extraordinary revenues. They are momentary imposts.[68]

These "momentary imposts" were designed to meet the "needs of the State"—which this writer (or speaker) defined merely as the debts from the last war. Louis XV, he insisted, had affirmed the principle that such "momentary imposts" could not be increased. Yet here was Necker, in 1777, attempting to sing a very different tune. In effect, he was "announcing to the Nation that those money-saving measures so often promised are nothing but a mirage . . . that in time of peace, the debts of the State grow from day to day, and that the government aims to augment the proportion of the vingtièmes precisely *to meet these debts.*"[69]

The Parlement as a whole adopted these sentiments in the remonstrances it approved on 19 December and presented at Versailles on 26 January 1778. In decrying verifications of land values that would allow increased taxation, the judges resorted to hair-splitting interpretations of past legislation concerning the vingtièmes. For example, the government might claim that an edict of 1749 had expressly provided "that the vingtièmes would be proportional to the revenues of the taxpayers," and in the preamble of that edict Louis XV had admittedly stated that he preferred this mode of taxation because the vingtièmes were presumably to be levied on all ranks of society "in the proportion of their lands and their abilities to pay." But the parlementaires denied that the legislation of 1749 did anything but state (specifically, in its fourteenth article) that persons whose property had been assessed in 1741 were guaranteed *against* future increases in taxation. As far as the king's language in the edict's preamble was concerned, the magistrates respectfully observed that "one would have to ignore the evidence not to see that these last expressions established purely and simply a fact from which one could infer that, the declarations of 1741 having been sincere, the vingtièmes in 1749 were proportional to revenues; and not a principle from which one must conclude that the essence of the vingtièmes is to grow along with revenues."[70]

Necker was fully justified in riposting twelve days later (through the keeper of the seals, Miromesnil) by charging the judges with nit-picking on an issue of basic importance to the state. He might furthermore have mentioned his current efforts and future intentions to save state revenues by overhauling the government's administration of finances. This desperately needed reform, along with the actual fiscal exigencies of the American war, may at least have forestalled some parlementary criticism of his borrowing policies.[71] Still, some major revelation was needed to give the judges an adequate appreciation of burgeoning state expenses in the eighteenth century and to incline them toward accepting the notion that the monarch's revenues should increase with those of his landholding subjects.

For it is only fair to remark that the Parlement's attitude stemmed in part from the government's failure to enlighten the magistrates (and everyone else) about the true state of its finances. Not that this failure is surprising: before Calonne precipitated the issue in 1786 and early 1787, there were few or none in the government aware of the magnitude of the problem.[72] (Certainly, the king was among the uninitiated.) By the time of Calonne's ministry, the parlementaires would be incessantly (and justifiably) challenging the government to put its finances in order before seeking their approval of new loans. This tactic would culminate in the court's demand to examine the government's fiscal accounts in 1787. But the whole question of the regime's accountability in finances pointed in turn to an underlying constitutional issue, and it is crucial to note that the Parlement was beginning to define that issue as early as 1778 in its philippics against Necker's policies on the vingtièmes. These imposts, declared the January 1778 remonstrances, had never been anything more than *dons gratuits* patriotically (and temporarily) volunteered to the king by his loyal subjects. They were "extraordinary" gifts, not "ordinary" revenues. The remonstrances then spelled out the subversive implications of such an interpretation: "From the monuments of our history, from the principles of the French Monarchy, and from all well-ordered States, Sire, is derived that truth all too much forgotten but incontestable, that the sole means of legitimizing taxation is to consult the Nation; that, failing consultation of the Nation, the only means of rendering taxes supportable is to consult each individual."[73]

Probably the magistrates, like many literate Frenchmen, were at this time following the consequences in America of the British colonists' refusal to accept further taxation without explicit guarantees of representative government. Contemporary events must have made the parlementaires aware that the issue of national consultation, if raised in France, could be utilized on behalf of all Frenchmen and not just aristocratic landowners like themselves. True, the Parlement did not mention the taille or indirect impositions in these protests of January 1778. Nevertheless, the court was in this same period condemning various abuses of the corvée royale, which imposed heavier taxation upon commoners, and Necker would soon be promulgating legislation guaranteeing that the taille could not be increased without all the courts' consent.[74] Actually, "consultation of the Nation" was probably the last thing that most of the parlementaires, as pretentious royal administrators, desired. Still, it is significant that in sparring with the crown over royal finances these great landowners and self-styled tribunes of proprietary interests came to invoke the principle of national representation—the great revolutionary notion of the century.

The Parlement was unable to take its opposition to Necker's tax policies beyond reiterated remonstrances in March 1778,[75] but the deepening fiscal crisis of the following decade, complicated after 1783 by the antagonism between the senior parlementaires and Calonne, was to ignite new fires at the Palais de Justice and lead to the convening of the Assembly of Notables in 1787.

The resourceful and ambitious Lefebvre d'Amécourt was to play an increasingly prominent role in this last phase of the long duel between Parlement and crown. To be sure, nothing ever came of the incessant rumors earmarking d'Amécourt for a post in the government.[76] Still, he was able to score something of a coup within the Parlement's Grand' Chambre when, in July 1781, he succeeded the deceased abbé d'Espagnac as king's rapporteur. Contemporaries noted that this appointment, arranged directly or indirectly by the government, stirred resentment among the clerical grand' chambriers, from whose number the king's rapporteur traditionally came.[77] Though the precise role of the king's ministers in d'Amécourt's advancement is obscure, it is possible that Maurepas's long association with this parlementaire—and the government's recognition of his influence among his fellow magistrates—secured for him this position as the monarch's political spokesman in the court. In any case, as rapporteur, Lefebvre d'Amécourt (like the officers of the parquet) found his loyalties being pulled in opposite directions during the disputes between Parlement and crown.

Actually, the first chapter of this story, comprising the 1781–83 Ministry of Finance of Jean François Joly de Fleury, was generally peaceful. That the brother of the procureur-général and of the ninth president of the Paris Parlement was holding the portfolio for finances must have helped.[78] Yet more than kinsmanship was involved, since the new minister of finances had long been on close terms with the ubiquitous rapporteur Lefebvre d'Amécourt.[79] Moreover, the French had gotten themselves into another war, and the war had somehow to be financed. Thus Jean François Joly de Fleury found the key grand' chambriers in a cooperative mood when, in July 1782, he solicited their support for registration of a third vingtième to help defray government expenses.[80] Before registration of the new impost was secured, however, the Parlement's leaders, and indeed the court as a whole, voiced traditional misgivings in a manner boding ill for future crown-Parlement relations.

To begin with, there are anxious suggestions for reform in Lefebvre d'Amécourt's papers showing just how earnestly the judges wished to avoid new taxation.[81] Were there no alternatives to a third vingtième? Could not the government "brutally" abolish "all useless expenses"? Could it not reduce all pensions and reduce them drastically? Could it not manage the royal domain in a more efficient fashion? The judges were even to claim, nostalgically, that in bygone times the amount of revenue diverted to pensioners of the crown had been strictly tied to (and limited to) *les économies de la couronne*; today, however, royal pensions knew no limits and were paid out of the state's burgeoning tax revenues.[82] In what appears to have been a preliminary draft of protests to the king over the new impost, one or several of the parlementaires continued to hammer away at the idea that the sovereign should squeeze as much revenue as possible out of the crown domain and restrain his generosity with regard to pensions.[83]

But the exigencies of the moment clearly outweighed whatever traditional considerations might occur to the jurists. Such at least was the message that Lefebvre d'Amécourt, First President d'Aligre, and their closest associates conveyed back to the Parlement after a strategy session with members of the government late in June.[84] Accordingly, after the king's men of the parquet had formally submitted the proposal for a third vingtième to the court, rapporteur Lefebvre d'Amécourt spoke in favor of registration. However, the precise terms in which d'Amécourt appealed to his fellow magistrates are significant for what they disclose about the parlementary cast of mind.

In addressing his company on 9 July, Lefebvre d'Amécourt appealed for one more surge of patriotism to see the crown through one more crisis on the battlefield. He freely acknowledged the past exactions of the government but then espoused its cause:

> Without attempting to fathom the causes of our military reverses, we know that we have sustained them, and at the very moment when peace seemed imminent, when our enemies desired peace.
>
> The King's greatest desire is to enable his subjects to profit from just such a peace.
>
> But he cannot procure peace, he cannot render it permanent and advantageous, unless he can impose peace upon our adversaries by showing them the immensity and the inexhaustibility of our resources.

In one sense this was standard ministerial exhortation. The new impost was essential for its psychological effect upon the enemy; furthermore, it would help defray wartime expenses and serve as security for the loans the government would have to open to liquidate debts after the war. When viewed from the perspective of the Palais de Justice, however, the approach adopted by the king's rapporteur was something else as well: it was the only way to extract approval of new taxation from magistrates who still tended to conceive government finances as a disjointed series of responses to temporary crises, meaning, in most cases, war. Significantly, Lefebvre d'Amécourt at another point in his address referred to the third vingtième as being "added to the ordinary revenues" and underscored the need to levy this additional impost to help defray "the extraordinary expenses."[85] Not that the judges, or any others in the ancien régime, made hard and fast distinctions between "ordinary" and "extraordinary" finances.[86] What d'Amécourt was trying to do by associating the "extraordinary expenses" with the war effort was to portray the third vingtième as merely a temporary gesture of patriotism requested from the judges, a subsidy that would not long survive the event that had necessitated it.[87]

Moreover, d'Amécourt enthused over a provision in Joly de Fleury's edict that stated that the tax rolls already existing for the assessment of the first two vingtièmes would be utilized for the third as well and would remain otherwise unaltered. The king's advocate saw this article as assuring the taxpayers that they would "never again in the future be pestered by new verifications or by demands for declarations" of property values.[88] The pending edict did not actually make such a perpetual guarantee, but it is possible that the grand' chambriers received assurances on this score during their conversations with Finance Minister Joly de Fleury.[89] Phrases such as "new verifications" and "demands for declarations" harkened back to the controversy over the vingtièmes in 1777–78; the idea here perhaps was to reassure the parlementaires that taxes could not increase after the war. The king's advocate was accommodating his colleagues' traditional views on taxation in the very act of soliciting their support for the crown.

Rapporteur Lefebvre d'Amécourt accommodated his colleagues' views even further. In terminating his remarks he proposed that registration of the edict be accompanied by an *arrêté* stating that the parlementaires were all too aware of the "heavy weight" and "long duration" of taxation in France and lecturing the king once again on the need to establish a better order in his finances as the surest means of avoiding future taxes and loans.[90] D'Amécourt had thus fulfilled the charge of king's rapporteur in the Parlement, endeavoring (at least during the emergency of wartime) to mediate between and reconcile the stated needs of the government and the concerns of economy-minded, landowning jurists. Yet all the qualifications he had attached to ratification of the edict of July 1782 suggest that he would have been less amenable to an additional tax had there not been a war to finance and win. As it turned out, even the relatively moderate stance advocated by d'Amécourt and by d'Aligre and others failed of a majority in the court, which decreed instead that protests be made immediately to Louis.[91] The end result was the same, for the Parlement, after hearing on 12 July that the king had replied to these protests by demanding registration of the edict, obeyed this command. But it renewed its protests later in July, thus reiterating its misgivings about the king's finances and clouding the prospects for continuing cooperation between the monarch and his magistrates.[92]

Calonne became the controller-general of finances in November 1783, and his policy of borrowing to keep the government's finances afloat was to drive Lefebvre d'Amécourt and his confidants back into the arms of their colleagues' opposition. Admittedly, the judges had additional, more personal reasons for opposing the new controller-general. They had not forgotten his role in the government's prosecution of La Chalotais, the defiant procureur-général of the Parlement of Rennes.[93] Then again, there were unsavory stories about Calonne's involvement in the disgrace of his immediate predecessor as controller-general, Henri François de Paule Lefevre d'Ormesson, who boasted relatives and friends in the Paris Parlement.[94] The parlementaires themselves no doubt viewed Calonne's numerous ties with members of the financial community as having facilitated his intrigues rather than as likely to facilitate a sound stewardship of the state's finances.[95] Furthermore, rumor had it that Calonne had won out over Lefebvre d'Amécourt, among others, for the portfolio of finances, thus assuring himself and his policies something less than full support from the court's influential rapporteur.[96]

Yet it was those policies themselves that were most crucial. Necker's loans had been secured upon administrative and fiscal reforms and proposed in time of war; for these reasons, in part, they had encountered little parlementary resistance. But the tribunal, in protesting on 17 December 1783 against Calonne's pending loan of 100 million livres constituted in life annuities, reminded Louis XVI that it was now peacetime and implored him to secure fiscal reform:

> Your parlement, considering only its zeal for the success of Your Majesty's arms, thought that it should during the war register all the edicts submitted to it. . . .
>
> It anticipated that the advent of peace would bring the realization of promises, made so often and so solemnly, concerning a diminution in the public expenses.
>
> Your parlement, Sire, can only see with great sadness how the hopes of the people have vanished and how the condition of the finances still necessitates loans.[97]

The Parlement's disappointment over the failure of peace in 1783 to cancel the necessity for new financial expedients anticipated the more defiant reaction against the loan of December 1785, not to mention the Assembly of Notables' rebellion in 1787. It is obvious, however, that well before those events both Calonne and the parlementaires were engaged in a perilous game of self-delusion: he, by gambling that the state could maintain and even fortify its solvency and credit through a series of loans; and they, by seemingly expecting that the question of war and peace alone should determine whether the government needed more than "economy" and existing taxation to keep itself afloat. It was almost as if rapporteur d'Amécourt (who assisted in drafting these protests) was saying to the controller-general: "completely disregarding other legitimate interests, we leaders of the Grand' Chambre rallied to the king during the war; but the war is over, and there is nothing further you can legitimately expect of us. It should be enough that we do not decry every tax that lies upon the land in France."

The Parlement's stance was not without validity. Eighteenth-century taxation, crushing upon many *taillables*, may have also pressed many less-than-wealthy nobles who paid the vingtièmes but no tailles.[98] Could the king continue to exact such tributes from his subjects, commoners and nobles alike, without accounting for the policies and practices of his government? As Calonne continued to force his loans through the Parlement, the justices came close to posing this revolutionary question.

Thus, in the protests of 29 December 1784 the royal accounts themselves fell under their scrutiny:

> The delay in the liquidation of the war debts can only derive from the lack of order, of exactitude, and of regularity in the drawing up of the accounts. . . .
>
> There is a means worthy of Your Majesty's wisdom, the sole means that can prevent the total dilapidation of your finances, and it is to remedy the abuses that obscurity and confusion in the State's expenses always produce.
>
> That obscurity and confusion will soon disappear if Your Majesty will deign to order a detailed account of the amount and utility of expenditures proper for each department, order that funds be assigned to them only in proportion to necessary and useful expenses, make sure that these funds have been used as originally intended, and verify that each agent has observed the most exact order and economy in his disposition of such funds.[99]

In responding to these timely suggestions for development of modern bureaucratic procedures, Louis XVI might protest his exact knowledge of the state of finances in each "department" of government. The reality was otherwise; and the day was fast approaching when the king would have to account to the nation for his finances, and for much else besides.

Calonne proposed a third major loan at the end of 1785. This was more than the magistrates could take, and the resulting confrontation between the government and the court signaled the start of the finale of the agonizing quarrel between the two sides over the financial issue.

By December 1785, the controller-general of finances had to find some way to pay off the remaining third of the naval debts stemming from the 1778–83 war, as well as unexpected expenses in the administration of the colonies and the continuing and projected armaments expenses for 1785 and 1786. Calonne concocted a proposal that would in effect establish a loan and graft a second loan onto it.[100] The original loan, of 80 million livres, was to be financed through the sale of shares that would be reimbursed no later than ten years in the future at a median interest of 5 percent. The precise date of reimbursement for each investor would be determined by priority as established in a lottery. However, individuals participating in the original loan could use their reimbursed capital and interest to constitute life annuities that would be settled on one head at 9 percent and on two heads at 8 percent. The government, of course, would pay dearly in future reimbursements to its *rentiers* for its extended use of their funds.

According to one report, Calonne immediately got off on the wrong foot with the parlementaires by suggesting the revenue from the vingtièmes as security for the loan.[101] Certainly, the judges would have balked at such a proposal, which might have implicitly contravened the government's promise that the second and third vingtièmes would expire in 1790 and 1786, respectively. Eventually, Calonne had the *aides* and *gabelles*, indirect and unchallenged imposts, constituted as security for the loan. This detail and others were worked out at a meeting held in the presence of Miromesnil between the controller-general and several magistrates (d'Aligre, d'Amécourt, and the Joly de Fleury brothers) on 8 December.[102] At this session or shortly thereafter, Calonne entrusted to rapporteur d'Amécourt a memorandum justifying the new loan and invoking the magistrates' patriotism in its support.[103] Calonne doubtless saw his memorandum as conceding substantially to the Parlement's curiosity about the government's fiscal operations, and certainly the document discussed those operations at length. Unfortunately, it also resounded with optimism about the future, optimism scarcely justified in parlementary eyes.

If the controller-general was counting upon Lefebvre d'Amécourt to recommend registration of the loan to his colleagues, he was speedily disillusioned. Private remarks from d'Amécourt to President Joly de Fleury show that he was predisposed against registration, and the bookseller Hardy reported that the rapporteur was one of the first to speak against the proposed loan on 13 December when the procureur-général and his assistants presented it to the plenary session of the tribunal.[104] Criticisms of Calonne's edict came thick and fast, and before long the first president had delegated d'Amécourt and a number of his associates to prepare protests to the king.[105]

D'Aligre, accompanied by two other présidents à mortier, delivered the court's remonstrances to Louis XVI five days later. They presented nothing new, combining a severe critique of the proposed loan with a shrill demand that the king reduce pensions and other superfluous expenses and establish a better order in his finances.[106] Louis had heard all this before, and he ordered d'Aligre to return the next day with news of the registration of the edict. But the Parlement insisted upon renewing its complaints to the king. Louis, though growing more and more exasperated by the magistrates' stubborn opposition, authorized d'Aligre to bring him the court's reiterated protests the following day, 20 December.

When, however, the repeated denunciations of Calonne's policy failed to dissuade the king from insisting upon immediate registration, the Parlement took an even more defiant step. It registered the loan on the twenty-first, but only *du très exprès commandement du roi*, and it added a tremendously long arrêté which, by repeating the complaints and denunciations voiced the previous day at Versailles, wrote the Parlement's disapproval into the final, legalized form of the edict.[107] Two days later, the entire company was ordered to Versailles by lettre de cachet, and they watched as the king struck the offending arrêté out of the edict with his own hand. After completing this decisive act, Louis, in an aside to First President d'Aligre, signified his displeasure with Lefebvre d'Amécourt and ordered that he be replaced as rapporteur by another parlementaire. Looking back upon this contretemps, the cashiered d'Amécourt himself recorded, with evident satisfaction, that the court "remained for a long time without a rapporteur," and in fact some time passed before another grand' chambrier would brave the scorn of his colleagues by accepting d'Amécourt's position.[108] The rift between the monarch and his magistrates had widened ominously.

Procureur-Général Joly de Fleury must have been distressed by this turn of events, for he vainly endeavored to reconcile the two sides in the days following the dramatic scene of 23 December at Versailles. After an exchange of letters with Miromesnil and an interview with Calonne, he informed his brother the president that he had discerned at Versailles "no ill will . . . against anyone" in the Parlement and added that those in authority only wished that the king's former rapporteur "had been personally less opposed to the loan." Shortly thereafter, he remarked to his brother that everyone still believed Lefebvre d'Amécourt had "coveted . . . the place of M. de Calonne."[109] Although the ex-rapporteur heatedly denied this in a letter to President Joly de Fleury and attempted to blame the recent confrontation on "the intrigue of the opposing camp," his protestations were not altogether convincing.[110] His political ambitions had long occasioned Parisian gossip, and some lively comments in his personal journal, recounting Calonne's ministerial intrigues during 1783 and denouncing virtually every aspect of his subsequent ministry, spoke volumes about his hostility toward the controller-general.[111]

More important, the Parlement as a whole seemed predisposed against the reconciliation with the government that the procureur-général desired. Animosity toward Calonne no doubt played its part. Shortly after the events of December 1785, the first president, already on bad terms with the government over his personal finances, reportedly informed Calonne that he could discuss no business in his presence without the prior knowledge of his associates in the Parlement. Rumor also had it that the leading members of the tribunal had deliberately snubbed the controller-general by refusing to pay him the traditional courtesy call during their visit to Versailles on Sainte-Geneviève's feast day. But the tribunal's fundamental complaint concerned royal finances, and it restated its disillusionment with governmental fiscal policies in March 1786 when it remonstrated at length over Calonne's reform of the currency.[112]

The rising tide of parlementary opposition was certainly one of the factors Calonne had to take into account in the summer of 1786 when he gave Louis the bad news about his government's finances and suggested the convocation of an Assembly of Notables. The events of the 1770s and

1780s had demonstrated anew that the Parlement's traditional conception of the fiscal needs of the state, a conception reinforced by corporate and individual interests, could undermine the magistrates' support of administrative and fiscal kingship.

Parlementary attitudes toward the monarchy in the twilight of the ancien régime were complex. Sheer self-interest, the desire to perpetuate their uniquely influential role in France, motivated the jurists at all times to accept and indeed champion the centrality of monarchy. That they could proceed, within the framework of this royalist orientation, to view the exercise of magisterial and political kingship with ambivalence reflected to a certain degree their interests as great landowners and (in several cases) as men on the make who were always ready to condemn in others the same ambitions they themselves harbored. Nevertheless, their attitudes toward kingship just as surely reflected certain elements of their professional training and certain constitutional issues, which transcended the immediate politics of their quarrels with the crown.

The judges may have sought to limit the judicial prerogatives of the king, but if this mirrored on occasion their own corporate spirit it also sprang from their awareness that justice by its very nature should temper itself or be restrained by explicit guarantees for the security of the *justiciables*. In decrying arbitrary judicial acts by the royal ministers, the Parlement was exercising a crucial role of surveillance that the Revolution would soon acknowledge and entrust to more progressive tribunals. Again, the magistrates' jeremiads against applications of fiscal and administrative kingship reflected their own privileged status and bespoke as well their outmoded conception of governmental needs. But the king and his ministers did next to nothing to correct the judges' naïveté in the matter of state finances and at times seemed equally naïve themselves. Certainly the king failed to appreciate the seriousness of his government's financial dilemma, and this failure, which his parlementaires inevitably shared, testified to a momentous historical fact. The kings of France had long abandoned those representative institutions that alone could have enabled them and their subjects to collaborate in determining their respective rights and needs and obligations both in times of crisis and in ordinary times. Such an abandonment of national consultation may have inhered quite naturally in the whole course of French history; yet, for all that, the long-term consequences would be no less momentous.

The imperative of state finances gave rise to exchanges between crown and Parlement that mercilessly exposed this constitutional flaw in the twilight of the eighteenth century. The Parlement, for its part, attempted to reconcile its advocacy of monarchy in France with protests that served the interests of the king's subjects and justified doing so, at least in part, as a response to this central defect in French monarchy, the alienation of the king from his people. Hence, while in one sense it was not strange that the Parlement's eventual fate was that of all privileged bodies in the ancien régime, it *was* ironic that the Parlement fell victim to an upheaval that strove to harmonize government and society and so resolve the very problem that the judges had done so much to expose.

CHAPTER FOUR

The Parlementaires and the
Aristocracy, 1774–1786

If a complex of public roles and personal interests motivated the Parisian parlementaires to view the monarch and his government ambivalently, it also explains the ambivalence with which the justices regarded the aristocracy to which most of them belonged. On the one hand, Lefebvre d'Amécourt and his colleagues during the 1770s and 1780s moved in an opulent and glittering society that, converging on the capital and Versailles and dabbling in everything from ministerial intrigue to patronage of the salon and *souper*, fashioned innumerable ties between the highest families of robe and sword.[1] Furthermore, the magistrates' landed wealth linked them even more closely with their aristocratic cousins of the sword: the prominent grand' chambriers and many of their juniors were great seigneurs in the countryside, and it was to the management and enjoyment of their estates that they returned during the Septembers and Octobers of their lives. In such seasons, *vivre noblement* was certainly their style. Still, during the other ten months of the year, the parlementaires were officers of the crown who celebrated and fulfilled the duties deriving from that professional role. Moreover, in a society avid for privilege, the men of the Parlement found their professional rank conferring favors upon them, fiscal and judicial as well as merely honorific, that most nobles of the sword did not enjoy.[2] Robe and sword were probably drawing closer to each other in a general socioeconomic sense during the eighteenth century, but to the very end of the ancien régime the judges of the Parlement owed their unique combination of political and social prestige to their professional role in the monarchy.

These realities suggest that the parlementaires, in their judicial and political-administrative capacities, found it expedient to distinguish between an aristocracy viewed in more or less "static" terms, as a juridically sanctioned order whose privileges must be safeguarded, and an aristocracy viewed in potentially "dynamic" terms, as a caste that might strive to aggrandize its influence in the state. The magistrates were quite naturally concerned with many institutions and social groups other than the second estate during these years, but their reactions to certain judicial questions and public controversies involving noblemen do confirm that they made the distinction postulated above—and suggest furthermore that they favored a quiescent aristocracy over an ambitious one. This chapter will show first of all how the controversies over Turgot's attempted reform of the corvée royale in 1776 and Necker's policy on the vingtièmes shortly thereafter engaged the Parlement in a defense of an aristocracy conceived in static, traditionalist terms. Then, however, it will argue that the judges, through their judicial activities and pronouncements upon several administrative-political issues, combated various aristocratic pretensions that they regarded as inimical to the monarchy, the law, and the preeminence of their own corporation.

The Static Conception of the Aristocracy: The Corvée Royale and the Vingtièmes

There were several occasions upon which the parlementaires were challenged to defend the traditional hierarchy of estates. Probably the most famous (or most notorious) case in point was the confrontation between Turgot and the magistrates over the Six Edicts that the controller-general of finances submitted to the Parlement in the early months of 1776. Among these measures was a proposal to replace the royal corvée, or *corvée des grands chemins*, with a tax upon all those landowners subject to the vingtièmes.[3] Such an impost would therefore have affected all landed proprietors within the second and third estates. Turgot's praiseworthy intention was to compel these proprietors to contribute toward the upkeep of the royal highways, whose commerce and exchange, after all, enhanced the value of the proprietors' estates; at the same time, suppressing compulsory labor upon the *grands chemins* would benefit the *corvéables* and, through their increased attention to agriculture, would further stimulate this most crucial sector of the French economy. Unfortunately, Turgot's Six Edicts stirred up a hornets' nest of protest from special interests, and the lack of sustained support from the king eventually insured defeat for the Turgotist reforms. The Parlement had been predisposed against Turgot's physiocratic philosophy from the start of his ministry, and a stormy encounter between First President d'Aligre and Turgot's ally Malesherbes early in March 1776 underscored the reality of magisterial opposition to the controller-general's policies.[4] The Parlement protested formally against those policies in March and reiterated its opposition in remonstrances delivered to Louis XVI two months later, shortly after Turgot's disgrace.

The magistrates' opposition to the abrogation of the corvée royale and associated defense of the aristocracy stemmed from a variety of concerns. For one thing, there was the automatic and inevitable invocation of the hierarchy of orders in society. As some early suggestions for remonstrances in the papers of Lefebvre d'Amécourt put it: "The Constitution of this great monarchy is infinitely simple; it is formed of three distinct and separate Estates. . . . The clergy serves its sovereign by addressing its prayers to Heaven, the nobleman pours out his blood for the king . . . the taille and the corvées are the responsibility of the last section of the Nation."[5] Thus, the antediluvian scheme of *oratores*, *bellatores*, and *laboratores* to which the jurists stubbornly clung until the end of their professional days.

Yet, this predictable invocation of the three estates assumes a fuller significance when related to the central parlementary role of maintaining law and order, for one of the means toward this end was to champion the principle of hierarchy in society. Hierarchy in society meant social organization and, hence, social control. The preliminary draft of remonstrances in the d'Amécourt papers rejected the contention, put out by some, that the debate over the corvées constituted "a combat of the rich against the poor." What was involved here was instead a "question of State, the most important that can be discussed in the king's Councils." The commentary continued: "Providence did not want all men to be equal, and placed them in different conditions, giving each of them a particular genius, a particular character; the great order of the Universe consists in that infinite variety: The order of all political States also depends upon such conditions. Your people languish under the weight of their taxation; relieve their misery, but beware of removing men from their proper stations."[6] Destroy the traditional order, intoned this parlementaire, and you wipe away the foundation of the state. At another point he characterized the distinctions among the social orders as "the precious chain that links the Sovereign with his subjects."[7] The *avocat-général*, Séguier, would employ this figure of speech in addressing Louis at the *lit de justice* held on 12 March to enforce registration of Turgot's Six Edicts.[8] To be sure, these statements constituted a defense of aristocratic privilege and were in part self-serving; but they also betrayed an obsession with social order perfectly natural for judicial administrators who every day policed individuals, corporations, and communities within their court's unwieldy jurisdiction.

There was an additional reason why the judges were, at least to some extent, sincere when they claimed that the question of the corvée did not amount to "a combat of the rich against the poor." When the parlementaires defended the nobility against an impost additional to the vingtièmes to subsidize salaried labor on the kingdom's highways, they obviously had their own estates in mind, but they also realized that nobles as well as commoners could be sorely pressed by new taxation. Hence, an "economic" defense of the nobility figured along with the standard juridical apologia. In the protests against the legislation on the corvée royale delivered to the king on 4 March, the judges made this defense through two associated points, one regarding the relationship between many rural seigneurs and their tenants and the other regarding the economic status of the seigneurs themselves.

On the first point, the judges argued that both the lord and his tenant farmer were affected by the latter's obligation (under the corvée royale) to provide carts or other vehicles for the transporting of materials used in work on the roads:

> That kind of corvée is discharged for the most part by the tenant farmers, but the proprietor is no less adversely affected by it, because every tenant farmer who becomes a leaseholder calculates the duties and expenses in his lease and deducts them before paying what he owes to his landlord.
>
> What is true for the taille is consequently also true for this kind of corvée; the one and the other must be taken care of by the tenant farmer, but at the expense of the proprietor.[9]

The Parlement concluded that the suppression of this specific obligation and the compensatory levying of a new tax upon the proprietor would be "without interest for the tenant farmer." Such a conclusion was doubtless exaggerated, and like other assertions in the court's remonstrances it reflected the jurists' championship of privilege. Still, there is evidence that many seigneurs did share the burdens of their dependent peasants, either by receiving rents from which their tenants had deducted their own charges in advance or by paying themselves the tailles and other imposts of sharecroppers who were all too often impoverished.[10]

The parlementaires also made much of an associated fact: that for a number of reasons, including the financial interdependence often obtaining between lord and peasant, many nobles in the provinces were themselves of modest or even mean income. Did the government now wish to humiliate these faithful men of ancient lineage by subjecting them, like so many commoners, to a tax subsidizing labor on the kingdom's highways?

> Thus, the descendants of those chevaliers of past times who placed or maintained the crown upon the heads of Your Majesty's ancestors, of those poor and virtuous aristocratic families who for so many centuries poured out their blood for the aggrandizement and defense of the Monarchy . . . those nobles of race whose revenue is limited to the modest fruits of the inheritance of their fathers, which they cultivate with their own hands, often without the help of any servant other than their own children; such gentlemen, in a word, could be exposed to the humiliation of seeing themselves dragged down to the level of the corvée.
>
> Could anyone even assure the nobles that, once having been

rendered *corvéables*, they would not afterward be rendered *taillables* as well?[11]

This was not the first time, nor was it to be the last, that the magistrates, secure in their own functions and wealth, alluded in their remonstrances to the financial difficulties of the rural noblesse and extolled the virtues of a passive and frugal life spent on a rural seigneurie. How many provincial aristocrats actually conformed to the stereotype of the proud and impecunious *hobereau* was (and remains) an open question. The judges naturally did not bother to mention in these remonstrances of 4 March 1776 the vestigial privileges still attached to noble status that, even in the leanest of times and in the poorest of provinces, rendered the economic situation of the small seigneur superior to that of many luckless corvéables and taillables who enjoyed no fiscal immunities whatsoever.[12] Though they may have been most immediately occupied with the juridical or "constitutional" implications of Turgot's projected reform, the jurists were also aware of the fiscal implications of the legislation. For, after all, a new tax seemed now to be looming ominously over the estates of affluent nobles like themselves as well as over the more modest patrimonies of the small rural noblesse of the sword. Admittedly, the tribunal's criticism of the administration of the corvée royale as reinstated after Turgot's disgrace was to show that the magistrates were concerned about oppressive taxation of commoners in France as well. Nonetheless, the judges did oppose Turgot's generous effort to abolish compulsory labor upon the roads in 1776, and one reason for this was their determination to defend the economic status of the social elite.

This championship of nobility came into play again the following year when the Parlement declaimed against arbitrary assessments of lands within its jurisdiction by agents of Necker's ministry. As was mentioned before, the judges launched an investigation of these practices during August 1777. They had, however, been receiving complaints relating to both the vingtièmes and the corvées for over a year. The French historian Georges Lardé carefully studied this controversy insofar as it related to the vingtièmes.[13] His examination of pertinent documents in the Archives nationales—such as complaints from nobles and peasants addressed to the Parisian parlementaires and reports sent to the procureur-général Joly de Fleury from his substitutes in the inferior courts of the jurisdiction—convinced him that the government's agents were indeed often abusive and arbitrary as they traveled about assessing lands subject to the vingtièmes.[14] Nobles and commoners alike appealed to the Parlement for justice in this matter. Yet Lardé also found that the Parlement in remonstrating to Louis XVI magnified its findings out of all proportion. In doing so, and in castigating the intendants' subordinates for their abusive practices, the court betrayed a predominating concern for the privileges of the nobility.

In light of their outspoken sympathy for the provincial noblesse during the controversy over Turgot's legislation on the corvée royale, the parlementaires were indeed likely to be impressed by noble correspondents railing against alleged insults to their class in connection with the government's vingtièmes. As early as May 1776, for example, the procureur-général received a plaintive communication from one chevalier de Toussac in Poitou. This nobleman, after saluting the Parisian magistrates as the born protectors of the people, announced that he had "the honor to be a man of rank with a large family" and went on to denounce the way the *contrôleurs des vingtièmes* were assessing land values in his region. These agents were going "from town to town, from village to village, and under the pretext of alleviating the peasants' condition, provided that they declare what lands their masters owned, were assessing arbitrary taxes and . . . were liable to reduce the proprietors to misery." Especially pitiable, claimed the chevalier, was the situation of "those who because of their social rank could not sustain themselves unless they embraced professions that they were not born to follow." Although the chevalier implored Joly de Fleury and his associates to hear "the cries of an entire people plunged in dismay," the priority of his concerns was obvious.[15] Here indeed were all the hallmarks of the pressed rural seigneur, rich in pride and exclusiveness of caste and yet apparently on the verge of a derogating penury. The inquiry into the administration of the vingtièmes mandated by the Parlement and coordinated by the officers of the parquet and the *procureurs du roi* in the subordinate bailliages and sénéchaussées turned up similar stories in the waning months of 1778. The complaints of the chevalier de Toussac and other provincial proprietors were cited in the remonstrances that Lefebvre d'Amécourt and fifteen other counselors drew up in January 1778.[16]

The Parlement's resolve to defend the status of the rural lord or "gentilhomme" was stiffened by the issuance of the decree of November 1778, which systematized the surveying and assessment of taxable lands and so augured a higher return from the vingtièmes. The court's remonstrances of January 1778 detailed the abusive practices of the tax assessors in the countryside and chanted the customary litany of aristocratic and seigneurial rights, which the justices had always tended to equate with each other. Most interestingly, the judges' biases engaged them in a debate with Necker over some language in his November decree. At issue was that provision guaranteeing that all verifications of land values in the parishes would have to be approved by "three notable proprietors who will have been chosen by the proprietors of the parish."[17] Necker had hoped that this practice would safeguard landowners against arbitrary and inequitable assessments by the government's agents. His stipulation, however, succeeded only in rousing the ire of the traditionalists at the Palais de Justice. The parlementaires in their remonstrances lamented the fate of the seigneurs who must be assessed for Necker's vingtièmes: "Separated from the assembly of notables [in the parishes] by the constitution of the Monarchy, will they find the estimation of the value of their lands to be just if done in their absence? Will it be binding upon them? Without them, what will be the rights, the influence, and perhaps the intelligence, of this incomplete procedure? Would anyone argue that justice is not due to the seigneurs? Is an attempt being made to deliver them to the mercy of their vassals and divers government officials?"[18] As far as the magistrates were concerned, "three notable proprietors" could only mean three prominent commoners of the parish community. In their everyday work, the judges commonly applied the term "notable" to wealthy commoners from parish communities who were parties to litigation in the court.[19] Accordingly, the remonstrances of January 1778 differentiated between "notables" and "seigneurs" and assumed that Necker's provision, far from safeguarding rural seigneurs, would only expose them to the vengeance of their peasants and the malpractices of colluding government officials.

But this was not at all what the director-general of finances had intended. In his response to the Parlement, read by Keeper of the Seals Miromesnil on 7 February, Necker accused the judges of having quoted selectively from his legislation in order to discredit his intentions and muddy the issues. The term "three notable proprietors" included, and had been intended to include, representatives of the seigneurs. Thus he rejected the judges' attempt to portray the November decree as depriving gentlemen in the provinces of all influence in the surveillance over the assessment of taxable lands.[20]

The magistrates, however, were not mollified and almost immediately returned to the attack in reiterated protests, which were presented at Versailles in March.[21] Once again the judges spoke of "notables" and "seigneurs," but this time they went straight to the heart of their misgivings:

> By an abuse of words, imagined for the first time, they [i.e., the seigneurs] are being classified under the denomination of notable proprietors. The infinite respect of your parlement for all the acts that bear your name . . . does not permit it, Sire, to allow so grave a question as one involving the vingtièmes and the prerogatives of the Nobility to degenerate into a kind of grammatical exercise. But it must represent to Your Majesty that the decree of 2 November runs counter to the most just notions of rank and fortune, [and] involves the two Estates in opposition to each other.[22]

As the magistrates commented, they were not interested in pursuing a grammatical exercise; but for them the distinction between "nobles," "seigneurs," or "gentlemen," on the one hand, and mere "notables" from the rural villages, on the other, was critical.

This traditional conception of the social hierarchy, however, posed a real dilemma for the parlementaires in this instance. If, in each parish community, the lord should be one of the "three notable proprietors" provided for in Necker's legislation to watch over the assessment of the vingtième, the sacrosanct distinction between nobles and commoners would be violated. Could the seigneur function alongside *propriétaires notables* who were mere *roturiers* without suffering an intolerable affront to his dignity as local lord? But if, on the other hand, the seigneur cooperated with his "common" neighbors and with the government's men in overseeing assessment of the vingtième, yet was not accorded full say over the fairness or unfairness of his own lands' valuation, what then? In that case, warned the Parlement, in reference to all the seigneurs: "envied because of their social rank, possessing a superior wealth, crushingly outnumbered, their presence at the [parish] assemblies will be useless or mortifying for them; they will prefer to withdraw from the proceedings, and in so doing will leave the field free for assaults against their legitimate but envied superiority."[23] In other words, in their absence their social inferiors among the population might very well collude with unscrupulous government agents to assess their lands unfairly. And in the midst of all this, would the lords of the manors continue to enjoy that esteem of "vassals" and tenants to which their pedigree so richly entitled them?

In describing the rural nobility as "possessing a superior wealth," the jurists were tacitly admitting that the seigneurs' economic lot for the most part was not, after all, as pitiable as that of many among the provincial peasantry. There were no allusions in these protests to the marginal livelihood of provincial aristocrats. But this is hardly surprising. For one thing, most of the judges were themselves substantial seigneurs and as such were as adamantly opposed as other landowners to seeing additional taxation upon their estates. Beyond this, however, the judges held strongly to an idealized and nostalgic vision of a nobility resident in the countryside, a nobility whose affluence might vary but whose rank was constant. The parlementaires were defending the status as well as the property of the noblesse, and their quarrel with Necker over the vingtièmes turned to some extent upon this traditional concern.

Louis XVI once again rejected the magistrates' protests, but the Parlement insisted upon having the last word. Upon the report of Lefebvre d'Amécourt, the abbé d'Espagnac, and the other authors of the remonstrances, the court on 12 May adopted an arrêté that declared, dramatically if ineffectually, that the current policy on the vingtièmes could not be implemented without "striking a direct and lasting blow at the property of all orders of citizens, without violating in particular the original exemption of lands of the Nobility from taxation, and without making the hierarchy of orders disappear."[24] During the preceding month Necker had issued a decree aimed at remedying some of the abuses resulting from the assessment and collection of the vingtièmes,[25] but this corrective legislation could not really come to grips with the central concerns of the traditionalists and proprietors of the Palais de Justice.

In summation, the Parlement's reactions to the fiscal reforms of Turgot and Necker produced an endorsement of noble status that was inspired by a variety of considerations. The parlementaires were jurists schooled in French legal traditions and accustomed to applying them to social as well as purely judicial questions, and so they defended the nobility as a juridical entity. They were also administrators aiding the government in the enforcement of law and order in the capital and throughout their court's huge jurisdiction, and so they defended the nobility as a crucial order in the hierarchy, or link in the chain, that held society together. As great landowners and nobles, the magistrates linked the status of nobility to the principle of inviolability of property. Finally, as self-styled intermediaries between the sovereign they claimed to serve and the subjects they claimed to represent, the men of the Parlement pointed out occasionally that the tributes demanded with increasing frequency by the state could exact a considerable toll from nobles as surely as from commoners.

But if the magistrates most certainly idealized the aristocracy, they were idealizing a status, and prerogatives accruing from it, that had existed for centuries. They were not endorsing any recent social development within aristocratic ranks, let alone any increment of aristocratic political power. The parlementaires' favorable conception of the aristocracy was in this sense a static, not a dynamic, conception. Of course it is perfectly obvious that the judges in championing the traditional privileges of the kingdom's nobles were simultaneously defending their own privileges. Self-interest was a vital spur to their attitudes. But this in turn reminds us that the parlementaires jealously exercised judicial and political functions that they denied to most of their cousins of the sword. Thus, they rejected a social elite viewed in activist or dynamic terms—viewed, that is, as challenging parlementary pride, parlementary interpretation of law, and parlementary functions.

The Dynamic Conception of the Aristocracy: Judicial Affairs

Acting in their primary capacity as jurists, the men of the Parlement combated the pretensions of aristocrats more than once during these years.

There were incidents that manifested an abiding tension between robe and sword in the Paris-Versailles milieu and elsewhere; yet more significant, if less publicized, were the occasions upon which the judges, in the quiet exercise of their profession, opposed the standard of law to actual or potential ambitions within society's upper ranks.

Creditable testimony to a continuing split between the magisterial and court nobility survives from the late eighteenth century. When, in March 1771, Louis XV summoned Malesherbes, then first president of the Paris Cour des Aides, to witness his annulment of the arrêt of Malesherbes's court protesting the judicial reforms of Maupeou, an observer was struck by the reception accorded the embattled magistrate and his associates. As President de Boisgibault later recalled:

> It was noted with astonishment that in entering and traversing the two apartments that led to the cabinet of the King, where a large number of Seigneurs, soldiers, and courtiers of all ranks had foregathered, the crowd arranged itself in two lines, on left and right, and saluted these Messieurs with an air of respect, of consideration, and of consternation, which was all the more striking because the men of the Robe are ordinarily regarded with an entirely different eye at the Court and sometimes have a hard time entering even when the King has requested their presence.[26]

De Boisgibault was apparently impressed more by the courtiers' sudden and uncharacteristic respect for the robe than he was by the substance of the occasion itself.

Another memorialist, Bésenval, noticed the same phenomenon at Versailles in the 1780s. In fact, in the course of his narration of the controversy over judicial reform during 1783–84, Bésenval paused twice to remark upon the disparity of perspective between Versailles and the world of the Parisian robe. He claimed that in 1783 he endeavored to arouse some interest in Lamoignon's campaign at Versailles, "but the barrier that separates the robe from the court is so strong that anything concerning the former seems totally foreign and irrelevant to the latter. I had difficulty even getting the court to comprehend what was at issue and found indifference and distraction reigning supreme."[27] At a later point in his relation of the reform episode, Bésenval returned to the indifference of the courtiers toward the magistracy and saw this attitude as in part to blame for the defeat of Lamoignon and his faction. "I have already said that Justice, or anything having to do with Justice, is so foreign to the courtiers that they never have the slightest interest in it and occupy themselves with it only in the case where some personal litigation, some major collision between the authority of the sovereign and the parlementary power, drags them out of their indifference on that subject."[28]

Arguably, leading parlementaires such as Jean Omer Joly de Fleury and

Lefebvre d'Amécourt, with their rumored political ambitions, could have bridged this chasm easily enough on their way to new, ministerial careers. (In 1787 their adversary Lamoignon would—briefly—succeed where they had failed.) That is one reason why the denunciations of intriguing courtiers in the papers of d'Amécourt ring rather false—all the more so in that they were penned soon after the author's confrontation with Calonne and consequent dismissal from the post of king's rapporteur in December 1785.[29] Again, the leaders in the Grand' Chambre pocketed pensions from the government just as surely as did the aristocratic hangers-on at Versailles. But, obviously, the parlementaires were in no sense dependent upon such largesse, and insofar as pensions in the Grand' Chambre symbolized anything, it was the crown that was dependent upon magisterial cooperation in important public affairs rather than the reverse. This state of affairs made it all the easier for the judges to round upon the government in the 1780s, admonishing it for doling out so many gratuities to aristocratic sycophants at court.[30] In addition, the Moreton-Chabrillant trial of 1782 gave the Parlement an excellent chance to defend a member of its own profession against a haughty young representative of the sword nobility at Versailles and to reassert the pride and prerogatives of the robe.

The case in question involved the youthful comte de Moreton-Chabrillant, captain of the guard of the comte de Provence, and a proctor in the Parlement named Pernot-Duplessis.[31] A scuffle between the two men had taken place at the Comédie-Française on its opening night, 9 April 1782. Pernot-Duplessis claimed that he had been deprived of the seat he had paid for that evening and had been insulted by Moreton-Chabrillant, after which he had been forced from the balcony on the order of the latter and temporarily detained. The parlementary proctor failed to receive satisfaction for his alleged outrage when his case was heard at the Châtelet early in the summer of 1782, and so he appealed the decision to the Parlement.

Significantly, the brief prepared under the supervision of Duplessis's procureur in the Parlement retold the story in terms likely to appeal to the magistrates (mostly grand' chambriers) who judged the case in the Tournelle. The brief characterized the appellant as "an honest man in all respects, and known by the mildness of his manners and the graciousness of his disposition," and stressed that he had been, on the evening in question, "dressed in the customary fashion of his estate, in black with long hair." His apparel was contrasted to that of the comte de Moreton-Chabrillant, who had appeared on the balcony of the Comédie-Française some time after Duplessis, "in rose-colored coat, with sword and plumed hat." The brief then explained in careful detail what had happened next:

This individual, absolutely unknown to M. Pernot, stared at him, and saw a black coat and long hair. . . .

"What are you doing there? [demanded the comte.] Withdraw immediately."

Monsieur, I am at my place.

"Withdraw, I say to you."

Monsieur, I have a right to be here, for my money, as any other person. I have paid for my place. I am not going to withdraw. I shall remain.

"A f—— *robin* dares to resist me!"

And he shoved M. Pernot with his hand to make him leave.

"You're a rascal, a scamp. I'll teach you to know with whom you're dealing. You'll go into detainment. I'll have you sleeping in prison."

That will not be, Monsieur, I assure you.

"I am *monsieur le comte de Chabrillant,* captain of the guard of Monsieur, the King's brother. I have the right of command here. I command here. It is by order of the King. Into prison, scamp, into prison; and now follow me. . . .

Monsieur, no matter who you are, a man like you cannot make a man like me spend the night in prison without cause.

The upshot was that the guard was summoned and Pernot-Duplessis, despite his protests, was conducted downstairs, at one point being allegedly yanked by the hair without provocation; then at Chabrillant's orders he was shut up for over four and a half hours and not released until long after the conclusion of the evening's performance. The brief arguing Duplessis's case cited a number of witnesses to substantiate this version of the affair and emphasized the concurrence of two of them that the comte had spoken of the appellant as a "f—— *robin*" and had used other unflattering terms such as "thief," "fraud," and "swindler."[32]

Chabrillant evidently feared that his opponent's case, argued in such terms, would win the sympathy of the parlementaires, for at his initial hearing he implored the judges to note "that, far from believing that he was speaking to an officer of justice, he necessarily thought, given the *rude conduct* of M. Pernot, that he did not belong to the robe despite his dress. The UNSUITABLE *denomination* of 'robin,' assuming it had truly escaped his lips, could therefore only be taken in this sense. . . . Certainly he was far from being *unaware of the respect that is due to the body of the magistracy!*"[33] The argument prepared for Chabrillant stated rather lamely that the defendant had simply been trying to gain his seat in the balcony at the Comédie-Française but had been blocked by Pernot-Duplessis; that in calling the guard the comte had not meant to accuse his antagonist of being a thief; and that the appellant had only been grabbed by the hair when trying to slip away into the crowd at the theater.[34] It was to be hoped that the magistrates would look upon Chabrillant as no more than an impetuous "*jeune militaire* in whom the principles or prejudices of his estate have not inculcated a habit of moderation." The brief also claimed that several parlementaires had offered their services as mediators between the two parties but that Duplessis, bent upon revenge for the insult or supposed insult to him and his profession, hoped to find a similarly vindictive attitude in the Tournelle of the Parlement. He evidently expected the tribunal to view his cause "as the cause of the entire Robe, of the entire Public."

If these were in fact the appellant's expectations, they were rewarded. The attentive journalist S.-P. Hardy reported that the case came up in the Tournelle on 31 July "in the presence of a prodigious multitude of spectators of all ranks." So obvious was it that most of the magistrates and observers wished to see the appellant victorious over his insolent opponent, said Hardy, that only with difficulty was an attorney of the court, Martineau, found to undertake Chabrillant's defense. Hardy reported after the second session a week later that Duplessis's attorney Blondel had "stressed the general interest of the Public, in defending an individual whose simple status as citizen should have warded off any kind of insult, in a place where money alone put nobility and commoners on the same footing, according them an equal right." Even those *militaires* attending this second hearing of the case were swayed by Blondel's reasoning, according to Hardy. Finally, on 19 August, before a "prodigious assemblage of interested spectators," the attorney Martineau, "shamed and embarrassed by his own espousal of the cause . . . of the comte de Moreton-Chabrillant," entrusted his client's fate to the judgment of the court.[35]

The second avocat-général of the Parlement (yet another Joly de Fleury) announced the Tournelle's decision.[36] Not surprisingly, the judges found in the appellant's favor. They ordered Chabrillant to pay his opponent 6,000 livres in damages and to avow in open court that the man he had insulted was "a man of honor and of probity." It would be hard to believe that the social terms in which Blondel had so cleverly cast his client's argument did not have their effect upon the magistrates of the Tournelle. To be sure, the "cause of the entire Robe" had also become the cause "of the entire Public" along the way. Still, Moreton-Chabrillant's insistence at his interrogation that he was "far from being unaware of the respect that is due to the body of the magistracy" had been pointedly underlined by the attorney of Pernot-Duplessis in the document submitted to the judges' consideration and may be taken as a further, if indirect, reflection of magisterial pride on the eve of revolution in France.

If an affront to one of its inferior officers spurred the Parlement to punish a contumelious young aristocrat, issues of a more systemic nature could provoke a more basic parlementary critique of the aristocracy. A graphic example of the tribunal's tendency to combat aristocratic usurpation in the field of justice was its reaction in 1784 to the affair of the vicomte de Noé.[37] To simplify a complex case, Noé, who was both a nobleman and the mayor of Bordeaux, had twice imprisoned a guard, who, upon the orders of the military governor of the province, had refused entrance at Bordeaux's theater to Noé and the other members of the municipal corporation. The military governor in question was one of the marshals of France, the maréchal de Richelieu. The marshals, led by Richelieu, had persuaded the king to order the liberation of the guard after his first incarceration. After repetition of the episode, however, they had tried the mayor of Bordeaux before their own tribunal as a *militaire* who, through his alleged disrespect for the maréchal de Richelieu, had affronted all the marshals of France. The vicomte de Noé had attempted to appeal his case to the Paris Parlement during May 1784, but Louis XVI (apparently influenced by the marshals or by their spokesmen at court) had evoked the case to his own Council. Soon after, however, the case was thrown back into the lap of the marshals' tribunal, which in June upheld its earlier judgment against Noé.

On 6 July a magistrate of the Enquêtes, almost certainly Duval d'Eprémesnil, rose to denounce these proceedings in the Parlement.[38] He warned his colleagues that "a purely military tribunal is arising in the Kingdom, which arbitrarily disposes of our compatriots' liberty, encroaches upon local municipal administration, and usurps royal justice. ... This tribunal, Monsieur, is the Assembly of the Marshals of France." The speaker related what he knew of the affair to the other magistrates and concluded with an impassioned plea for parlementary intervention. "The Throne is surrounded by the Marshals of France. A quarrel, trivial in appearance, could have the most serious consequences, clearing the way for exorbitant pretensions sustained by armed Judges in all provinces."[39] The Parlement immediately ordered the parquet to investigate the matter; the king's men provided further details in their report to the company on 3 August; and the court decided on that day to draw up remonstrances protesting the treatment of the vicomte de Noé by the marshals.

Duval d'Eprémesnil was one of the judges named to the commission charged with preparing the remonstrances and submitted to that commission an excursus on the history of the marshals of France.[40] In that work, entitled *Du Connetable, des Maréchaux de France, de leurs fonctions, et de leur pouvoir*, Duval d'Eprémesnil belittled the marshals' historical role, lumped them together with other elements of the aristocracy that had usurped royal power in medieval times, and reasserted, in true parlementary fashion, the priority of the king's chief magistrates over all great nobles of the sword. Even at coronations and lits de justice, declared the d'Eprémesnil essay, the chancellor's proximity to the sovereign signified that, however much the nobility's swords might protect the sovereign, justice remained "his true force and his true dignity." Therefore, the essay affirmed, as long as the kings deigned "to listen to the counsel of their Parlements, which have no interest and no authority other than the interest and authority of the Throne . . . the ambition of the Marshals of France" would remain but "an idle fancy." Duval d'Eprémesnil was in 1784 what he would be to the end of his days: an active and articulate man of basically royalist orientation.

These sentiments found many an echo in the remonstrances that d'Eprémesnil, Lefebvre d'Amécourt, and some other magistrates drew up during August 1784.[41] The Parlement, in adopting these protests on 31 August and presenting them to Louis XVI five days later, showed unmistakably how its judicial training and philosophy precluded approval of any increase in aristocratic judicial power. The judges made three essential points: they subordinated the military tribunals of the land to the "ordinary" courts headed by the Paris Parlement, they distinguished painstakingly between "gentlemen" and "officers of the robe," and they gave to the corporative rights in question at Bordeaux a priority over caste pretensions.

On the first of these themes, the judges grimly warned Louis: "States survive only through the laws, and they perish with them as well; the establishment of a military power is the most certain presage of their common subversion. Sooner or later, one sees the armed forces failing to respect the authority that counts upon their support. . . . the kings who preceded Your Majesty . . . elevated Justice above force."[42] The ensuing argument revealed the judges' concern about the activities of courts staffed by the high military aristocracy. The marshals of France were, admittedly, still empowered to judge "military misdemeanors or contracts, committed or concluded by men of war, without distinction of birth," and when assembled with their dean they could decide upon "points of honor" between "gentlemen and those of your subjects who follow the profession of arms."[43] Nevertheless, the marshals must recognize that, even in these circumscribed areas of dispute, their decisions were subject to appeal by the "offended" party to the ordinary royal courts: after all, the marshals were not "the chiefs of the Nobility; only Your Majesty fills that role."[44] In particular, no citizen, whether a man of the sword or not, could lose his "honor" definitively in the marshals' tribunal, and "as far as the person of a gentleman is concerned, it can only be judged by your bailliage personnel in first instance and by your parlement, the Grand' Chambre assembled, on appeal. Those are, Sire, the French maxims."[45] The jurists also condemned dueling as an irrational manifestation of aristocratic pride and cited the attempted abolition of this practice under Louis XIII as a specific example of the curbing of unruly behavior among the nobility. Thus, the magistrates, vaunting their corporate spirit and association with the judicial prerogatives of the crown, seized the occasion to reassert their supremacy over one of the highest aristocratic courts in the land.

Second, the judges continued to whittle down the authority of the marshals' tribunal by stressing the distinction between robe and sword and denying the marshals cognizance of litigation involving *any* officer of the robe, even in matters supposedly concerning "points of honor." Seventeenth-century legislation had not differentiated satisfactorily between sword and ultraprivileged robe: "It remained necessary to do away with exceptions to the essential rights of officers of the robe which could result from this situation: this is what the edict of 1704 did, in stipulating that the judges of their persons would also be the judges of their offenses. At that point, the work of our laws on the point of honor was complete."[46] In other words, "men of war" or "gentlemen who were not officers of the robe" would "in points of honor" remain subject, at least in first instance, to the marshals' jurisdiction, while that special *privilégié*, the man of the robe, would be judged in *all* cases by the civil courts.

All of these points were immediately pertinent to the case under examination because of the king's failure to allow the vicomte de Noé, regardless of his social and professional status, to appeal his earlier conviction to the Parlement at Paris. But it is even more intriguing to see how the remonstrances, in coming to grips with the specific incidents at Bordeaux, defended the integrity of the municipal *corporation* there against the provincial governor's attempt to divide it along lines of *caste*:

> The facts in this affair are common knowledge, the controlling principles equally acknowledged. . . . by virtue of a first order that the governor gave the guard . . . the entrance to the theater was forbidden to the municipal corporation; the order was rescinded insofar as it affected the mayor, the undermayor, and the gentlemen of the corporation, but it was renewed for the barristers and merchants of the corporation. This was an improper and humiliating distinction. . . . In effect, the policing of the theater belongs to the entire *corps de ville*; the gentlemen members are only deputies there. . . . By such an order . . . an indivisible body was divided.[47]

Thus, if, on the one hand, the parlementaires championed the right of Noé (whether as militaire or as officer at Bordeaux) to appeal his case to them, on the other hand, they insisted that the provincial governor, the maréchal de Richelieu, had had no right to favor Noé and the other gentlemen administrators over the barristers and merchants at Bordeaux. The magistrates probably viewed all the members of the corps de ville at Bordeaux as being of privileged society in a general sense, but in a controversy pitting professional and legal principles against social pretensions the judges' instinct (indeed, as they saw it, their duty) was to advocate the former rather than the latter.[48]

Bookseller and memoirist S.-P. Hardy noted on 24 July, well before the preparation of these remonstrances, that the original denunciation of the Noé affair in the Parlement had been clandestinely published and that the Parlement, though suppressing this work on 20 July, had failed to pursue the matter with its wonted rigor.[49] Hardy's fear that the publicity given to the affair might "greatly inflame the Marshals of France against the Parlement" and leave the tribunal powerless against "the sword blows of the Militaires" was exaggerated, although Louis XVI did reject the judges' remonstrances out of hand, stating that the marshals' affairs were subject to his judgment alone.[50] The magistrates could take the controversy no further, but their lack of enthusiasm in suppressing a published version of their remonstrances in September 1784 further underscored the message in those protests.

Despite occasional protests to the king on controversial decisions of other courts, however, the Parlement tempered aristocratic claims more effectively through the unsensational but steady application of law to litigation, which was, after all, its primary function. The problem of the corvées illustrates this fact. If the magistrates insisted that the corvée royale rested squarely upon the shoulders of laboring commoners, they were less positive about the validity of every seigneurial corvée claimed as a vestige of past glories by the provincial nobility. This uncertainty appears from time to time in those papers of Lefebvre d'Amécourt devoted to definitions and explanations of eighteenth-century laws, customs, and obligations.[51] Here is the working jurist, endeavoring to discuss seigneurial corvées in a way that would take into account the bewildering hodgepodge of customs and usages in France: "The *special corvées* are those which are due to some Seigneurs, in virtue of the law of the locality or of some particular title. . . . Most of the special corvées have been acquired, as it has often been said, by usurpation: but since the customary laws have been written down, there has been an attempt not to permit any of these servitudes, if they do not seem founded upon a legitimate cause or title." D'Amécourt's commentary went on to state that in regions of written codes these corvées were "reputed to be seigneurial rights" but that in regions of customary law "people do not at all consider them to be ordinary rights of Seigneuries and Justice, but rather to be *an exorbitant and not very favorable right, which cannot be extended, and must be kept within its just limits.*"[52] At other points this parlementaire went into the matter of seigneurial corvées in meticulous detail.[53] Such commentaries reflected the difficulties encountered by the royal jurists of the eighteenth century in the settlement of litigation between lay or ecclesiastical lords and the commoners from whom they exacted, or expected, corvées and myriad other seigneurial duties.

Precious insight into this matter can be gained from consultation of the series of official conclusions by the procureurs-généraux of the Paris Parlement in litigation, a series preserved at the Archives nationales in Paris.[54] Even a cursory look through these written conclusions, which resulted from the intervention of the procureur-général in parlementary lawsuits and stood as the court's final judgment, suggests that the magistrates' decisions depended upon how they interpreted the laws locally in force rather than upon the social status of the parties involved.

There was, for example, the dispute in 1782 between the "Sieur Dumay and other summoned individuals" and "the inhabitants of Mouilleron."[55] Several members of this community, led by one M. Dethalomesse, sought parlementary review of a lower-court decision awarding several rights of corvée to the lords at Mouilleron. The appellants claimed that the obligations imposed upon them by the disputed judgment were invalid. After examining the evidence on both sides, Procureur-Général Joly de Fleury agreed with them, concluding among other things that the inhabitants of Mouilleron were to be "discharged from the condemnations pronounced against them" by the lower tribunal and that Dumay and his correspondents were to reimburse the appellants for the monetary equivalent of the rights of corvée wrongly exacted from them. Furthermore, Dumay and the other involved parties enjoying seigneurial rights were in the future to refrain from demanding the disqualified services from M. Dethalomesse and his fellow parishioners at Mouilleron. At the same time, Joly de Fleury, speaking for the king and for his parlementary colleagues, refused to accord the victorious parties a total dispensation from the obligation of the corvées. He stipulated that the Parlement's ruling did not affect those rights of corvée at Mouilleron established by legitimate records and contracts, and he provided for future parlementary intervention, should that be necessary to adjudicate conflicts between the seigneurs and the community over the obligations of the latter. Nevertheless, the main thrust of the ruling was to whittle down the claims of the seigneurs upon their inferiors, and the court was willing to deputize a judge to insure that future arrangements honored this ruling.

There were times when rights asserted by commoners, rather than by their lords, were at issue, and in these situations likewise the court could rule in favor of the *roturiers* while simultaneously qualifying the concessions granted. A dispute broke out between the Seminary at Rheims and the inhabitants of nearby Neuf-maison during the years 1782–83: at issue were certain rights of woodcutting in the forest of Fahazard claimed by the residents of Neuf-maison.[56] The court, Joly de Fleury speaking, ruled in the commoners' favor. They had, and would continue to have, the right to go to the forest to cut dry, dead wood and even some "green" wood from living trees and would store that wood in areas "that will be indicated to that effect each year by the officers wielding administrative control over the said forest." All opposition raised to these claims by the Seminary at Rheims was and would remain null and void, although typically the procureur-général went on to specify that the victorious parties would be fined and punished in other appropriate ways should they attempt to cut wood outside those areas indicated by the aforementioned officers. The king's servant in Parlement was not taking away with one hand what he had conferred with the other but only qualifying judiciously the concession he had just granted the commoners at Neuf-maison.

It is just as easy, admittedly, to find the court rejecting the suits of commoners in other litigation, and the distinctions drawn in the Mouilleron ruling between the temporary *abuse* of a seigneurial prerogative and the lawful nature of the right itself show how firmly committed the magistrates were to a status quo in France that still permitted vestiges of feudalism. Nevertheless, a random sampling of approximately two thousand conclusions pronounced by Guillaume François Louis Joly de Fleury in Parlement from 1 July 1782 to 30 July 1783 reveals that, although very few of the lawsuits in this period pitted identifiable seigneurs against identifiable commoners, those that did were almost as likely to terminate in victory for the commoners as to go in the opposite direction.[57] If in their professional capacity the jurists never betrayed the slightest desire to war against established vestiges of the feudal past, they were equally disinclined to favor litigants of a specific social rank at the expense of the standards of French law.

The jurists' ingrained conservatism also motivated them at times to circumscribe seigneurial prerogatives in the exercise of justice itself. The outstanding case in point during this period was the Parlement's unsuccessful attempt to mediate between the officers of the archiepiscopal bailliage at Rheims and the personnel of the city's royal bailliage. As the previous chapter showed, several of the senior grand' chambriers at Paris asserted over and over in two successive memorandums of 1779 that the compromise suggested by the archbishop of Rheims, and enthusiastically endorsed by the Parlement, would substantially increase the powers of the royal court and so serve the royal and (what was the same thing) the public interest. Moreover, in distinguishing between *seigneurs apanagistes* and *tous autres seigneurs de fief* in connection with jurisdictional issues arising at Rheims, the parlementaires threw an additional obstacle in the way of possible seigneurial usurpation of royalism in France.[58] The ordinary *seigneurs de fief* could freely choose officers for their own courts from among the king's citizenry and could, in circumstances such as those of the archbishop of Rheims, nominate some of the personnel of a royal tribunal. The *seigneur apanagiste*, who was a lord temporarily enjoying without owning a portion of the crown domain, could under no circumstances whatsoever exercise such a right, said the jurists. As in so many other connections, the Parlement in responding to the jurisdictional issues at Rheims defended the crown domain and its associated rights of justice, laying down a precise boundary between monarchical and seigneurial prerogatives. Not that any seigneur apanagiste had anything to do with the contestation at Rheims; indeed, there were only a few of these special lords in France.[59] But in emphasizing these lords' *total* inability to influence royal and public justice, after having so narrowly defined the rights of ordinary seigneurs such as the archibishop of Rheims to influence public justice, the magistrates of the Parlement were reconfirming their conservative professionalism.

The justice meted out by the Paris Parlement and the other lawcourts of the ancien régime was marred by the social inequality of litigants, as it was by the survival in court of anachronistic procedures, laws, and attitudes. But the jurists' conservatism could and did cut both ways: against sorely needed reform, on the one hand, but equally against the use of justice for "social" purposes, on the other. The judges clung to the old ways of doing things, and they also clung to the contradictory corpus of French law they had inherited from their predecessors. The question that remains is whether the parlementaires showed themselves equally conservative in dealing with aristocratic involvement in matters having political implications.

The Dynamic Conception of the Aristocracy: Political Affairs

The political aspect of the relationship between the judges and the aristocracy turned primarily upon the Parlement's right to examine and register (or protest) important royal legislation and its more general role of articulating the interests of corporations and individuals within its jurisdiction. The issue of the "plenary court" in 1774–75 spurred the parlementaires to defend the integrity of their company's functions and to belittle certain elements in the aristocracy perceived as menacing those functions through their projected membership in such a plenary court. The controversy over the provincial assemblies several years later stimulated a more explicit parlementary critique of administrative and political ambitions within the first and second estates.

This study has already had occasion to note the jealousy with which the Parisian judges defended the preeminence of their company within the judicial hierarchy and their insistence upon justifying that preeminence by associating themselves with the king. The treatise that Jean Omer Joly de Fleury sent to a friend in 1785 celebrated the Parlement as

"the first of all the bodies within the State" and reasserted the insepara-
bility of Parlement from king.[60] Of greater relevance at this point is the
distinction in this treatise between the Parlement and the great aristocracy of the realm, a distinction that flowed naturally from the association
of the former with the crown. "The situation is not the same for the
Dukes and Peers and other great men of the kingdom, who although ever
dependent upon the King . . . claim to derive their establishment and
their social rank from their birth and hereditary dignities, and not from
their capacity as officers of the King exercising royal authority."[61] The
parlementaires intended in all cases to make such a distinction between
themselves and the nonjudicial aristocracy.

Something of this determination surfaced when the court in its protests of 8 January 1775 condemned the plenary court that the government
had threatened to employ in future trials of refractory magistrates. Predictably, the Parlement trumpeted its status as the first court of the realm.
The Parlement was the "Court of France," the "first court of the Realm,"
and therefore any tribunal created by the government with a "right of
judgment and consequently superiority over the Parlement" would "de-
grade" and "pervert" it and do irreparable harm "to the judicial order."[62]
The Parlement of course recognized the right of certain great aristocrats—
the princes of the blood, the dukes and peers—to attend the solemn convocation of the Court of Peers. But this was as far as its generosity would
extend, and its characterization of other *grands* who might usurp its corporative prerogatives was not very kind. Thus, it scornfully likened the
envisioned plenary court to "the assemblies to which the King might
have called some great vassals, some officers of his palace, and the people
who held the personal court of the King in the palace" in past centuries.
Such people "were not and have never since been . . . members of what
the government sees as an eventual plenary court." Furthermore, the Parlement continued, this so-called plenary court would embrace "officers
other than those whom the ancient usages have introduced into the
Court of Peers" as well as "other great and notable personages . . . who,
however, have merely a right of honorary attendance [at the Court of
Peers] even in the case of lits de justice."[63]

Doubtless, the Parlement would defend the privileges of the king's
"great vassals," the "officers of his palace," and "other great and notable
personages." But let these glittering figures in the aristocracy not forget
their place: let them not aspire to usurp the Parlement, to sit in judgment
upon the king's true magistrates. Idealization of the seigneur who con-
tentedly cultivated his lands and his rustic virtues in the countryside,
idealization of aristocratic privilege in general—that was one thing. Approval of even a hypothetical role for "great and notable personages" in a
plenary court—that was quite another.

The parallel between the magistrates' conflicting fears on this question and those aroused by the controversy over Necker's provincial assemblies shows even more forcefully how ultraconservative the judges were when it came to the apportionment of judicial and political authority. The Parlement vacillated between apprehension that the provincial assemblies might become independent of and thus dangerous to the monarchy and contrary fears that they might become tools of "ministerial despotism" and arbitrary taxation. It vacillated between similarly contradictory fears in its 1775 protests over the plenary court. On the one hand, such a tribunal could very possibly become a sounding board for all kinds of selfish interests and intrigues and thereby prejudice the reputations, the very lives, "of the most important persons in the State and of all citizens exposed to the play of great passions and powerful hatreds." On the other hand, the judges, with an ever-wary eye to their old adversary the government, could simultaneously see such a tribunal as a "mere commission controlled in advance, ready to be summoned and used as a tool for all the purposes determined by powerful ministers."[64]

The plenary court suggested by the legislation of November 1774 would not have actually assumed the judicial and political functions of the Parlement in the event of that tribunal's suspension of activities. The 1774 legislation reserved that role to the rival Grand Conseil, which consequently drew a bitter parlementary attack in the protests of January 1775.[65] But, in deriding the personnel of the envisaged plenary court, the magistrates obviously had political issues in mind. Once established, susceptible of becoming a "tool for all the purposes determined by powerful ministers," what powers might it not assume at the behest of despotic government? And, in fact, Lamoignon, as keeper of the seals, was to revive the idea of the *cour plénière* in 1788, establish its personnel, and endow it with both the Parlement's role of *enregistrement* and a curtailed power of remonstration. Although the Parlement never had the chance to protest formally against an innovation that was to be as short-lived as its author's ministry, the renewed menace of a plenary court provoked some unflattering reflections on the history of the French aristocracy, which will be cited later on in connection with the prerevolutionary crisis of 1787–88.

But the Parlement's disqualification of various "great and notable personages" for high magisterial office in January 1775 hardly anticipated the vehemence of the attacks against the ambitions of the aristocracy that appeared in parlementary papers several years later. The reaction of some of the leading parlementaires to the political and administrative questions posed by Necker's provincial assemblies illuminates the judges' conception of the aristocracy quite as much as it does their posture toward the monarchy.

We have already seen that some of the magistrates feared (justifiably, as it turned out) that Necker wanted eventually to dispense with the intendants altogether, confine the parlements and other "sovereign courts" to a strictly judicial role, and invest the provincial assemblies with the primary role of administration in the provinces. With increasing certainty, the magistrates saw these bodies as appropriating their own cherished role of intermediary between sovereign and subjects, and their suspicions were confirmed in 1781 when they got hold of Necker's confidential memorandum to Louis XVI.

The parlementary critique of the provincial assemblies becomes of special relevance to the question of social attitudes in focusing upon the personnel of Necker's institutions. Just as the material cited earlier from the papers of Lefebvre d'Amécourt, the abbé d'Espagnac, Lamoignon, and the Joly de Fleury brothers pointed to the disruption of current administrative practices as being the potential villainy of the piece, so it indicated the representatives of the first two estates as the primary villains. To be sure, there are references in these papers to ambitious men within the third estate, warnings against pitting commoners against clerics and nobles. But this was to be expected from custodians of hierarchy and order and does not change the fact that the first two orders bore the brunt of the critique.

Take the clergy, first of all. In establishing an assembly in the province of Berry, Necker in his *arrêt du Conseil* of July 1778 had conferred the presidency of the new body upon the archbishop of Bourges. According to the commentary in the papers of Lefebvre d'Amécourt, such an arrangement could establish a perilous precedent. "By instituting provincial assemblies, they have reduced the power of the Intendants to a nullity; but Bishops are put in their place: are there not many reflections to make on this change? Could not the consequences be dangerous?" D'Amécourt seemingly answered his own question at another point in his papers: "The clergy seems to have acquired great advantages, and its authority would even seem to have been augmented frighteningly, if it should want to abuse it: in effect a Bishop will always be the president of each assembly. . . . one cannot avoid concluding that the internal administration of these assemblies will truly be in the hands of the clergy."[66] That is to say, the clerical members of the assemblies, habituated to obeying their bishops in all matters, would be putty in the hands of the presiding ecclesiastic, fit tools for the establishment of clerical domination. Moreover, the service of provincial clerics in these assemblies would jeopardize the unique prestige of the first estate, which derived from its spiritual role. The bishops would acquire "too much civil authority" and in becoming "assessors and distributors of taxation" would acquire in peoples' minds "the kind of ill repute associated necessarily with that function." If they would only confine themselves "to exposing the needs of the people of their dioceses, they would remain their protectors and their fathers."[67] As for the *curés* in the parishes, they might similarly find participation in the activities of the assemblies to be a mistake. If their parishioners were burdened with a heavier taille, these taxpayers might suspect the hand of their priests in it. After all, why not suspect the curés, who "by their rank and by the nature of their revenues almost never support the least portion" of such taxation?[68] Again, if the practice of voting by head rather than by order should be extended from the Berry assembly to all other assemblies, then "the Third Estate, more numerous, will reject the burden of taxes and throw it back into the lap of the Nobility" with the result that "the Clergy, tranquil because of its fiscal immunity, will leave the Nobility at daggers' points with the Bourgeois."[69]

Several parlementary concerns were at work behind this critique of the first estate. D'Amécourt and his colleagues may to some extent have genuinely feared for the spiritual mission of the clergy in those provinces represented by the new assemblies. Perhaps something of the old Jansenist moralism found an echo here; there is precious little evidence to prove so, but observers did note the survival of a strong Gallican animus against the Jesuits, especially in the Grand' Chambre, after the reinstatement of the old magistracy in 1774.[70] However, the comments cited above exposed two very substantial motives for parlementary distrust of clerical participation in the new assemblies: the magistrates as noble proprietors resented the immunities from taxation enjoyed by the clergy, and above all they viewed the clerical assemblymen as part of that unprecedented personnel that might seize power in the provinces or conspire with the government to rob the intendants and judges of their administrative-political functions.

Far more interesting is the critique of the secular aristocracy, which appears at different points in the papers of all the aforementioned grand' chambriers. President Lamoignon, for instance, penned some comments that typified fairly well the concerns of all these parlementaires. In the long run, he evidently felt, the practice of voting by head in the provincial assemblies might enable the third estate to tip the constitutional balance against the clerics and nobles and subvert their privileges. For the time being, however, the "superiority of the power and influence of the principal Gentlemen, who already have a keen sense of their strength, will leave them all manner of ways to escape the burden of taxation and throw the entire burden back upon the people."[71] But if the provincial nobility should endeavor in this way to take advantage of Necker's innovation, this might have drastic consequences. In medieval times the French monarchs had taken concerted measures "to whittle away at the political authority of the principal gentlemen in the provinces and give the people, by degrees, the civil and free existence they had not had previously." Now, however, the nobility, by seizing control of the assemblies' deliberations on taxation, might very well force the government in self-defense to engineer a greater coup de force, destroying the nobles' resistance to taxation and other government programs but also destroying the privileged status of the first two orders into the bargain.[72] The Lamoignon commentary, by tying the past assertion of monarchical power over the unruly feudal aristocracy to the projected perils of aristocratic activities in Necker's assemblies, graphically underscored the conservatism of the parlementary outlook. Aristocratic privilege was countenanced only within a static constitutional framework, a framework that could no more tolerate the concession of new administrative powers to nobles and clergy than it could concede new powers to the third estate.

Some observations in the papers of Lefebvre d'Amécourt depicted in unflattering colors the actions of individual seigneurs likely to follow from their participation in the new assemblies. Some of these gentlemen delegates would betray the interests of their seigneurial constituents by manipulating the assessment of taxation so as to shift the burden of the taille and perhaps even the vingtièmes upon those other lords and their peasants. This would inevitably lead to internecine jealousies and rivalries within the ranks of the nobility, to "specific quarrels, hatreds, and animosities . . . between gentlemen who will reproach each other because of their higher taxes. That cause is the source of eternal divisions reigning in the parishes among the taillables; how much more intense must such divisions be among the great proprietors agitated by commensurately greater interests."[73] One of two consequences must follow: either some of the more "turbulent" and ambitious aristocrats would oppress those around them, seizing the opportunity offered by their new administrative role to become intolerably powerful; or the government would step in at the first sign of trouble and restore its own absolute prerogative by destroying the first two orders, privileges and all. In either case (and here the second was seen as following almost inevitably from the first), to entrust new powers to members of the clergy and nobility would be foolhardy.

The remarks in the papers of these parlementaires suggest an ambivalent view of the third estate. One author feared that their membership in the provincial assemblies might give the delegates of the third the means "in future times to destroy the privileges of the Clergy and the Nobility."[74] Another author assailed the division of third estate representatives in the Bourbonnais assembly into two contingents, the *bourgeois des villes* and the *propriétaires des campagnes*. To permit such a novelty was to sanction "a fourth order in the monarchy, or at least . . . the present form means that it will be possible to upset the balance established in ancient times between the clergy, nobility, and Third Estate."[75] Yet this same author could at another point view the third estate as likely to be dominated, even oppressed, by the other two estates in the new assemblies:

The Third, that is to say, its permanent representatives, dependent upon the nobility and clergy, will have neither the ability nor the desire to defend themselves. . . . In actuality, reputation, the power to protect, territorial riches are all in the hands of the clergy and nobility at present. The slightest knowledge of the provinces forces one to admit that it will be impossible for the bourgeois of a town, the resident in the country to oppose the Bishop or the Seigneur of a great estate who will want his opinion on some issue to be accepted.[76]

Such a prediction might lack credibility in postrevolutionary eyes, but it would ring very true in the context of the ancien régime: after all, even when the kingdom was stumbling into revolution during 1787 and 1788 those in authority envisioned as much of a threat from society's upper ranks as from the crown's traditional allies in the third estate. To portray Necker's assemblies in the late 1770s as being potential vehicles of aristocratic influence over the less prestigious elements of provincial society was a perfectly natural reaction for contemporaries who would tend to view the present through the lens of the past.

And, after all, what would the past bring to mind if not the usurpations of the royal writ by the aristocracy in its feudal heyday? Hence, it is not surprising that one of the Joly de Fleury brothers in the Parlement should have painstakingly transcribed several essays containing vociferous attacks against the aristocracy and should have recommended these "reflections, so very wise, upon all that is dangerous and new in the administration of the Monarchy."[77] The main thrust in these essays emerges in the following remarks:

In summoning the Nobility and Clergy to the intermediary government of affairs of State, you turn their thought toward politics, you make them savor the pleasure of domination and the allurement of taking the helm of the State. . . . soon therefore one will necessarily see some hotheads in the Nobility passing from the heart of idleness to the arena of political affairs, and the feudal spirit attempting to take back its former rights to the detriment of the people, and aspiring to rule in the provinces to the cost of absolutism.[78]

What would follow would be the evolution of an "intermediate aristocracy" among the provincial assemblies: not the stabilizing element of quiescent seigneurs idealized in many a parlementary protest but rather a turbulent class of men whose ambitions and activities would sap the foundations of royal authority and jeopardize the security of the people: "The result must be . . . on the one hand a weakening of [royal] power, on the other a reduction of liberty: the Kings in little time are sure to lose an increase in authority, which only centuries of skillful policy have purchased, and the people are going to fall back into the state of bondage of medieval times."[79] Not a very complimentary vision of aristocratic activism in the twilight of the old regime, but a vision, nevertheless, meet for parlementary purposes.

The papers of Lefebvre d'Amécourt had stated frankly that the government should look to magistrates "accustomed to discussing and handling public affairs in the courts" and to the intendants rather than to "proprietors taken at hazard in the provinces" for cautious and capable administration,[80] and in 1781 the Parlement's leaders relayed similar advice to Louis XVI. We have already had occasion to note that the senior parlementaires sent two memorandums to the king at about the time of Necker's disgrace, justifying their company's refusal to register an edict finalizing the form of the Bourbonnais assembly. Most significant in connection with the magistrates' social attitudes is the fact that the second of these two apologias came down hard upon elements within the rural aristocracy: "The taste for administration has become a fad that it is important to terminate; the most secret departments of the domestic government have been exposed to public scrutiny, it is becoming urgently necessary to stop all kinds of speculation; each provincial gentleman has deemed himself capable of governing the State and we must try to emulate those times when people speculated less on operations [of state] that can be directed only by those who have made of them a lifetime's study."[81] Here was the clearest possible rejection of an aristocracy viewed in dynamic terms. The magistrates would ardently defend *chaque gentilhomme de province* when it came to his seigneurial rights and his overtaxed lands, and just as ardently oppose him should he deem himself "capable of governing the State."

It is only against the background of these parlementary attitudes that the full significance of the judges' suggestions for the assembly in the Bourbonnais emerges. As the preceding chapter noted, the judges in their two memorandums of 1781 advised the king to maintain the assemblies already functioning in the Berry at Bourges and in the Haute-Guyenne at Montauban in their original form for the time being. As for the assembly in the Bourbonnais, they proposed a new administrative scheme.[82] The delegates of the three estates should not deliberate in common but rather convene separately, the clergy during a short interval of the first year, the nobility during the second year, and the third estate delegates the year after. The opinions and complaints of each estate regarding local matters such as taxation, upkeep of roads, and poor relief would then be reported by a representative of each order, or *syndic*, to the intendant of that province. These syndics, and not the assembly itself, would cooperate directly with the intendant in the administration of the province. As a result, "all would be done in the King's name, but at the request of the syndics of the orders."[83] What this system would preserve would be the centrality of the intendants' role in provincial affairs—and, implicitly, the judges' cherished role of mediation between sovereign and subjects on issues not taken up, or adequately resolved, by the intendants. What it would exclude would be the possibility, anathema to the parlementaires, of the delegates of the three orders coming together and administering the provinces themselves in consultation with Versailles.

In offering this plan to the government, which the latter accepted, the men of the Paris Parlement reaffirmed their social conservatism.[84] In their first memorandum to Louis, they had declaimed against Necker's division of the third estate contingent in the Bourbonnais assembly into *députés des bonnes villes* and a novel *ordre des paysans*.[85] They might have declaimed far more strongly against this arrangement and against the third estate in general had they realized how much energy, ambition, and confidence was accumulating within the upper strata of that estate at this juncture in French history. As it was, the parlementaires, reacting to the past rather than prophesying the future, were more concerned to castigate provincial gentlemen than to belabor the bourgeoisie. Magisterial ambivalence toward the aristocracy, as toward all other institutions in Bourbon France, reflected the fact that the Parisian parlementaires were so situated as to enjoy very nearly the best of two worlds, social and political, and would brook no attempt from any quarter to deny their enjoyment of either.

Any assessment of parlementary attitudes toward the nonrobe aristocracy during the years from 1774 to 1786 must recognize that magisterial and aristocratic interests were seldom clearly antagonistic in that period. Indeed, if there was an aristocratic regrouping and resurgence in the late ancien régime, the judges had neither the time nor the inclination to seek to identify and then oppose most of the symptoms of such a development. For example, the Parlement never had anything to say against the aristocracy's monopolization of prestigious posts in the church, diplomatic corps, and armed forces during the closing years of the eighteenth century. Again, there is no evidence that the court, had it been able to, would have thwarted every seigneur's attempt to put the screws more tightly upon his tenants and sharecroppers. The laws governing such relationships on the land were varied and complicated, and furthermore no amount of judicial training and service could make the jurists oblivious to their own interests as privileged landowners, interests betrayed in many a defense of seigneurial prerogatives. If such tendencies be interpreted as signs of a caste reaction in late eighteenth-century France (though this is increasingly debatable), then the Parlement did not in these areas oppose a *réaction nobiliaire*.

But evidence does suggest that judicial and political issues forced the parlementaires at times to choose between aristocratic and opposing claims. Whether the opposing claims were those of the crown, individual commoners, or privileged corporations such as the Parlement itself, the judges were quite capable of upholding them against the aristocracy and often did so in a manner underscoring their pride of profession. This was true in the judicial field, where the Parlement's rulings and diatribes against aristocrats attested to the continuing tension between robe and sword as well as to the jurists' respect for the standards of law. It was equally true in the political field, where the magistrates championed their roles of registration and remonstration against all aristocratic comers.

Thus, the parlementaires not only distinguished between a static and a potentially dynamic role for the aristocracy but condemned prospects for the latter role whenever they saw such prospects as capable of challenging their own company's prerogatives or its interpretations of the laws. It is in this sense that the judges would have adamantly opposed an aristocratic resurgence in late eighteenth-century France. Such a stance would have been only natural, for the parlementaires were inextricably involved in their country's judicial and administrative royalism. They were aware of this fact and prided themselves upon it, as well they might, for it fortified their self-esteem by maximizing their influence upon events in the old regime. Any resurgence of the aristocracy threatening to disrupt the monarchical system in France must simultaneously have called into question the parlementary influence that was an integral part of that system.

CHAPTER FIVE

Counselors, "Corporations," and
Commoners, 1774–1786

The Parisian parlementaires had a number of ways of viewing the middle and lower ranks of old regime society. They envisioned the third estate as a juridical entity, an order in the sacrosanct hierarchy of orders in France, and desired that it neither dominate nor be dominated by the first and second estates. They held a corporative vision of society and therefore committed themselves to defend the myriad *corps et communautés* that embraced so many commoners in the kingdom. The judges also found certain issues engaging them in an advocacy of the interests of the mass of unprivileged or underprivileged people within their company's jurisdiction. They defended these *roturiers* against overweening clerical and gentlemen seigneurs, against allegedly unscrupulous "men of business," and against despotic agents of the central government. The pages that follow will examine these parlementary attitudes and activities. They will show the magistrates championing various "corporations" and taking up the cudgels on behalf of commoners—commoners viewed as consumers in need of essentials such as bread and firewood, and commoners viewed as *corvéables* and *taillables* obliged to work on the roads and to pay taxes but entitled to humanitarian treatment. The discussion will also show that, in these areas as in all others, the parlementary role stemmed from a multiplicity of motives: concern for *privilège*, concern for social order, distrust of entrepreneurs and government agents, a desire to curry favor with the public, concern for the Parlement's prerogatives, and an unquantifiable pinch of humanitarianism.

The Counselors and the "Corporations"

When Turgot, actuated by his physiocratic faith in economic freedom, attempted in 1776 to abolish the maze of guilds and other privileged associations in the capital, he provoked a classic parlementary defense of corporative privilege. In one of his Six Edicts, the contrôleur-général attacked the *jurandes et communautés de commerce, arts, et métiers* as obstacles to commerce and industry, as depriving workers of their "natural right" of subsistence through a freely chosen profession, as prejudicial to state finances, and as corruptive of Parisian manners and morals.[1] Yet Turgot, as aware as anyone of the Parlement's objections to the doctrine and practice of economic freedom, attempted in his legislation to disarm what he anticipated would be the inevitable magisterial opposition. Regulations governing certain critically important professionals—pharmacists, goldsmiths, booksellers, and printers—were to continue unchanged for the time being. The status and activities of butchers, bakers, apothecaries, and other entrepreneurs were spelled out in the edict. Turgot also provided carefully for the policing of commercial and industrial activities, for the adjudication of all disputes arising between merchants and their artisans and workers, and for the payment of debts contracted by the defunct associations. Finally, he predicted that the new competition in the professions arising from his reform would decrease the price of commodities, enhance rather than reduce their quality, and insure their more equitable distribution.

In the early months of 1776, however, the Parlement was deluged with petitions from those whose privileges were threatened by the impending legislation: the wine merchants, the lemonade makers, the linen merchants, the hatters, the grocers, the soap makers, the dressmakers, and so on.[2] Although there were countless and colorful variations on the main theme, all of these *privilégiés* predictably assailed Turgot's impending reform, foretelling all kinds of economic and moral ills should it be implemented. The aggrieved merchants and guild masters elicited a sympathetic response from the judges at the Palais de Justice. Both in the remonstrances of 4 March and in Avocat-Général Séguier's response to the forced registration of the Six Edicts at the lit de justice of 12 March, the Parlement took up the case of these privilégiés and exposed the main elements of its own corporative philosophy. Four considerations outstanding in this apologia were: (1) a frank defense of venality of office and associated privileges, (2) a highly "qualitative" view of commerce in society, (3) a restatement of parlementary judicial prerogatives, and (4) an organic law-and-order conception of society.

Perhaps it would be as well to begin with the last of these themes, for the magistrates' obsession with law and order was a natural concomitant of their daily judicial-administrative function and undergirded their championship of all existing institutions in the kingdom. Séguier's famous exposition of this attitude at the lit de justice of 12 March 1776 has been cited by many authors and was mentioned briefly in this book in an earlier context, but insofar as it so beautifully capsulated the parlementaires' corporative vision of society, it must be quoted here at greater length:

> All your subjects, Sire, are divided into as many different bodies as there are different conditions and professions in the Kingdom: the

Clergy, the Nobility, the sovereign courts, the inferior tribunals, the universities, the academies, the companies of finance, the companies of commerce, indeed living bodies in all parts of the State, which one can regard as the links in a great chain, the first one of which is in the hands of Your Majesty, as chief and sovereign administrator of all that constitutes the body of the Nation.[3]

In this vision, even the clergy and nobility became as the guilds of Parisian "industry" and commerce: living bodies, links in the great chain of being of French society. Séguier went on to paint a dark picture of Parisian society without the established relationships between masters and artisans and workers, without the established regulations governing what could be produced and where and how much and by whom and at what price. "Independence," warned the senior avocat-général darkly, "is a vice in the political constitution, because man is ever tempted to abuse his liberty; the law is intended to prevent frauds of all kinds and remedy all abuses." Therefore, let the traditional system of *jurandes* and other bodies continue. It "watches equally over the interest of the one who sells and of the one who buys; it maintains a reciprocal confidence between the one and the other; it is, so to speak, upon the seal of the public faith that the tradesman displays his wares to the buyer and the buyer receives them from the tradesman's hands in confidence." Abolish the guilds, abolish their sage regulations, and you will "destroy all kinds of resources essential to the conservation of commerce; each manufacturer, each artist, each worker will consider himself an isolated being, dependent upon himself alone and free to indulge in all extravagant acts conjured up by an unsettled imagination; all subordination will be destroyed; there will be no uniform weights and measures; the thirst for gain will animate all workshops."[4] Séguier's words only reinforced the message delivered to Louis XVI eight days earlier in the Parlement's initial remonstrances. Those protests had presented the Parisian guilds, with their associated powers of police, as the sole means for keeping rough, uneducated, and potentially unruly apprentices and journeymen in their proper places and for insuring that the poor, "who can only gain from disruption," would never have that chance.[5] The message was an old one in parlementary counsel to the king: no stability of relationships, no public confidence; no public confidence, no flourishing of commerce and the arts. But above all the judges liked to pause upon that first stage of their argument, to conjure up the specter of anarchy and dwell upon its fearsome implications.

As the preceding has already suggested, the judges' obsession with the need to maintain a traditional system of economic and social control also implied an old-fashioned, "qualitative" view of commerce and manufacture. For the parlementaires, *privilège* was the keystone of the traditional system and was consequently the crucial determinant of the quality of society's goods. Here were the parlementaires, accounting in their remonstrances of 4 March for the supposed ascendancy of French merchandise in Europe:

> And how did our commerce rise so rapidly to this degree of splendor? By means of these privileges which this minister [Colbert] knew to be so necessary to the progress of manufacture. How have our glass manufactures, and those of porcelain, completely vanquished the manufactures of Venice and rivaled those of Japan and Saxony? By the privileges accorded to them.
>
> The inventor works without courage when he works for others; he has no incentive to perfect his work without the incentive of personal gain.
>
> Under the sway of privileges, he has two resources, either to profit from their special exemptions if his funds allow him to do his own work, or to choose a tradesman who appreciates his discoveries to pursue them for him. . . .
>
> Today, what interest will engage him to perfect his work if his inventions are immediately imitated by others? He will sell desperately to head off competition and will have no time to perfect his work and will be ruined.[6]

Abolition of the regime of privilege would inevitably mean a fatal deterioration in the quality of all French goods. Foreign purchasers would look elsewhere for their merchandise; French inventors, artisans, and merchants would be demoralized; and the king's revenues derived from foreign and domestic manufacture and trade would fall off drastically. The judges even warned of large-scale migrations of commoners from the countryside to the cities, as would-be artisans and inventors, seduced by the prospects of an unregulated field of endeavor, forsook their farms in search of quick and cheap commercial gain.[7] The truly skilled and dedicated craftsmen would be lost in the crush of inferior workers flocking to the cities and towns; quality would be sacrificed to quantity; and the ascendancy of French merchandise, insisted the parlementaires repeatedly, would become a thing of the past.

Turgot had heard all this before, and his reply to the court's initial remonstrances, given by Miromesnil at the lit de justice of 12 March, reasserted the physiocratic belief in the virtues of a free, or at least relatively free, commercial and manufacturing economy.[8] It was only too true, he agreed, that men were prone to abuse an absolute liberty, but he insisted that his legislation provided adequately for the policing and administration of the new regime. Yet the controller-general could have no satisfactory answer for two other magisterial concerns: the principle of property in the enjoyment of privilège, and the extent of the Parlement's own judicial prerogative. Both matters were inextricably part of the justices' corporative philosophy.

At the lit de justice, Séguier unabashedly broached the question of property and privilège: "To accord to all your subjects, without distinction, the right to run a store, to open a shop, is to violate the property of the masters who make up the associations. The mastership is indeed a genuine property for which they have paid and which they enjoy on the good faith of the ordinances; they are going to lose . . . that property, from the moment they share the same privilege with all those desiring to enter the same trade." To champion the *maîtrises* of the guildsmen was as natural for Séguier as to defend parlementary offices or seigneurial (or peasant communal) rights: the maîtrises were, like these other things, property, and defensible in court. Furthermore, said the avocat-général, the government itself should keep something else in mind, something involving its own finances: "the price of a great portion of these masterships . . . has been paid directly to the royal treasury, and if the other portion has been given to the societies, it has been used to reimburse the loans that those societies had to make to the State; that resource, which the government has perhaps availed itself of too frequently, but which has always been useful in urgent circumstances, will from now on be closed to Your Majesty, and the public revenues will themselves be quite considerably reduced."[9] Moreover, pursued Séguier, the government would now have to burden itself with the obligation of paying off the debts contracted by the various guilds and communities, and in addition it would have to indemnify those merchants losing their privileges by reducing or forfeiting altogether its levy of the *capitation* upon them. Actually, Turgot's legislation provided in a number of ways for the liquidation of these socities' debts and for other expenses incidental to the reform.[10] Séguier, however, glossed over such provisions in invoking a fiscal argument that might further dignify his case for property and privilege.

Finally, there was the matter of the Parlement's own powers. Turgot's edict said nothing about them explicitly, but it would affect litigation that was receiving or might ordinarily through appeal receive parlementary consideration. All cases involving allegations of inferior workmanship by members of the guilds or arising from contractual disputes between masters and men would, at least up to a certain money value, be judged summarily in last resort by the *lieutenant-général de police*; contestations involving more than 100 livres would continue to be judged "in the ordinary manner." Other types of litigation, concerning such matters as disputes over guild privileges and seizures of property and currently pending in lawcourts, were to be either thrown out of court immediately or attributed by the government to the "appropriate tribunals."[11] Avocat-Général Séguier, however, speaking for his fellows at the lit de justice of 12 March, saw nothing to commend in such arrangements, and the remonstrances presented at Versailles eight days earlier had spoken darkly of the mischief and abuse likely to result from them: "The overthrowing of judicial procedures, the arbitrariness of decisions, the contempt of superiors, caprice, harshness, oppression ... the abuses of all kinds practiced by underlings of an independent power, are frightful misfortunes for the people. . . . Could [Your Majesty] also take from them the advantage of being judged only by the courts that ought to judge them, and submit all ranks of citizens without distinction to a jurisdiction that ought to have immediate power only over the lower classes?"[12] This oblique assault upon the attribution of certain categories of litigation to the lieutenant-général de police, and the more general indictment of all judicial innovation, mirrored the pretensions of both the Parlement and the inferior tribunals within its jurisdiction. The Parisian guilds figured prominently among the multitudinous associations whose litigious affairs so often required parlementary or lower court justice.

The magistrates' response to the Turgotist legislation on the guilds was not entirely negative. Séguier, speaking at the lit de justice of 12 March, conceded the need for specific reforms here and there: the abolition of useless associations (the flower girls, the greengrocers), the merging of similar groups (the bakers and pastry cooks, the carpenters and cabinetmakers, the tailors and dealers in old clothes), the admission of women into the masterships of the embroiderers and hairdressers, and so on.[13] Further than this, however, he would not go. Séguier's colleagues reaffirmed their objections to Turgot's legislation in remonstrances of May 1776, but by that time the great controller-general of finances had already fallen from power.[14] Legislation of August 1776 and subsequent parlementary decrees restored much of the old system of regulation, and thus the magistrates' views in this area prevailed over physiocracy for the remainder of the ancien régime.[15]

Turgot's attempt to reform the guild system in 1776 produced the most revealing statement of the judges' corporative philosophy during the reign of Louis XVI. Nevertheless, the Parlement continually occupied itself with administrative matters involving the many constituted bodies within its jurisdiction and in doing so articulated a wide variety of concerns. A few examples follow.

Turgot's legislation on the guilds had envisioned no immediate changes in the regulations governing the book trade, but the government's decision in 1777 to modify the privileges of the Parisian booksellers and printers touched off an intermittent debate within the Parlement.[16] Duval d'Eprémesnil, petitioned by *libraires* and *imprimeurs* in the capital, denounced the 1777 legislation to his fellow magistrates: taking up the arguments of the aggrieved parties, he urged the Parlement to remonstrate formally over the matter.[17] He was able to induce his company to delegate a number of judges to look into the affair, but the sessions of the resultant commission dragged on inconclusively through much of 1778 and 1779. On 23 April 1779 d'Eprémesnil himself read out to the assembled company a long *Récit sur l'état de la librairie*, in which he ardently defended the privileges of the Parisian booksellers and printers and predicted that any reduction in those special rights must endanger society's control over the written word.[18] D'Eprémesnil's assault upon the 1777 legislation ultimately failed, for Avocat-Général Séguier in a later report argued that no intolerable wrong had been done to the libraires and imprimeurs and reiterated that the Parlement would continue to cooperate with the government in maintaining proper control over the book trade. The court followed the counsel of Séguier to avoid remonstrances over the matter. Still, the amount of time consumed in parlementary discussion of the book trade underscored the judges' espousal of privilège and concomitant "qualitative" view of culture, more specifically literary culture, in the ancien régime.

At about the same time, the Parlement was far more concerned to protest a royal declaration affecting the Collège at Auxerre, in the process underscoring its readiness to defend interests identified largely with the third estate. The declaration in question, promulgated during October 1776, removed effective control of the Collège at Auxerre from the municipality of that community and vested that control in the religious Congregation of Saint-Maur.[19] This collège was one of a number of educational institutions in France at which the king had recently established new military schools favoring the sons of the nobility. The declaration of October 1776 stressed the importance of the Collège at Auxerre in the campaign for improving the education of the noblesse. The declaration vested the "administration" and "enjoyment" (if not full ownership) of the lands, properties, and pensions of the collège in the Congregation of Saint-Maur, subordinated the collegiate bureau of administration (in which the Paris Parlement figured) to the congregation, and ordered the congregation to report directly to the secretary of state for war on all matters concerning the *école militaire* and its noble students.

The Parisian parlementaires were unhappy with this legislation, registering it only on 10 June 1777 at the *très exprès commandement du roi*. Before that ceremonious and grudging act of submission to the royal will, however, the magistrates had already voiced their dissatisfaction with the declaration in formal remonstrances.[20] Although the judges were no doubt annoyed by the government's attribution to a religious congregation of a corporate administration in which they participated, their protests, presented at Versailles in April 1777, concentrated upon two other points, namely, the Auxerre municipality's loss of control over its collège and the new emphasis at the collège upon the military education for the nobility. On the first point, the magistrates' reaction was a predictable one. What right had the Congregation of Saint-Maur, they asked, to administer the collège traditionally administered by the municipality of Auxerre and to manage those properties and draw those revenues traditionally reserved to Auxerre for its government of the collège? As in so many other situations, the parlementaires here defined rights of *propriété* and alleged a violation of those rights. On the second point, the judges' reaction was especially interesting. They looked askance at the new stress upon military studies for sons of the noblesse at the collège. "Indeed, Sire, it will be in vain that the students are separated for their lessons, for the students will yield, as young people are liable to yield, to the seductive allure of military instruction; the spirit of these kinds of courses will become general in the collège and the military kind of education will become dominant and soon exclusive." What course of action would then be available to those citizens of the commercial classes at Auxerre who had intended that their sons be grounded in nonmilitary subjects? To be sure, they could remove their sons from the collège, thus frustrating the original purpose of the institution, but even so the evil might not be contained. The *esprit militaire*, "good in itself, but out of place in a city of commerce and trade," would soon invest the very homes of the students, and as a result "the inhabitants of a city, already unjustifiably deprived of their property, would be reduced to the harsh necessity of excluding their children from being educated at their own collège, or even in their own city."[21] Louis XVI predictably rejected these protests out of hand, denying that Auxerre had been deprived of any rights and insisting that his legislation would strengthen the collège and so benefit all classes and all interests in the city. The magisterial advocates of property and of the commercial classes at Auxerre failed to be convinced by Louis's response and so signaled this attitude by registering his declaration "at the express command of the king."

The magistrates' reaction to the affair of the Collège at Auxerre illustrates how, upon occasion, they embraced the cause of a particular sector of French society. At the same time, their reaction reminds us of more constant concerns motivating the parlementaires' defense of corporative rights, such as the concern for private property and the concern for the court's own administrative role. Equally important, of course, and ever lurking beneath the surface of the court's acts and pronouncements, was the concern for public order. Yet the magistrates, to a degree not always appreciated, attempted to balance that indispensable public order against the rights of individual Frenchmen, and not just in fiery indictments of "ministerial despotism." During the summer of 1783, for example, the Parlement was investigating the various prisons and asylums within its jurisdiction. The tribunal from time to time ordered the lieutenant-général de police or his subordinates to appear before it with information about conditions within these establishments.[22] The court received a general report from the lieutenant-général and his men on 29 July. They assured the counselors on this occasion that "they had noted nothing in these establishments that could be prejudicial to law and order, to the public safety, or to the legitimate liberty of the King's subjects." Members of the two sexes were being kept separate as they should be; most of the pensioners in these establishments were there because of insanity or epilepsy, and all were treated with "gentleness and humanity"; the spiritual as well as physical needs of the inmates were receiving proper attention; and those unfortunates entrusted to these *maisons de sûreté et de santé* by their families were not detained any longer than was absolutely necessary. The Parlement expressed its appreciation for this accounting, exhorted the lieutenant-général and his agents to maintain their close surveillance over these institutions, and charged its own first president to watch over the situation through his correspondence with the municipal police.[23] Whether realities inside the prisons, asylums, and hospitals of the capital justified the assurances of the lieutenant-général de police and his men cannot be ascertained from these minutes of parlementary proceedings. But the judges' stated concern for the public safety and solicitude for individual rights ring very true indeed, for they faithfully echo the more militant and publicized sentiments of the court's recurrent polemics against governmental absolutism, economic freedom, and "subversive" social reform.

The mention of governmental absolutism serves to introduce one other concern articulated by the men of the Paris Parlement in dealing with privileged associations within their jurisdiction. The parlementaires helped to bring down the old regime by voicing their misgivings over the central government's finances, and at times they evinced precisely the same concern in criticizing lesser institutions within France. For instance, after consenting on 31 December 1782 to register letters patent prolonging the life of the *octrois* or tolls on foodstuffs and wines entering the capital, the Parlement voted to remonstrate to the king on the need for a reform of the municipal administration. Only such reform, the judges felt, could enable the city eventually to terminate the octrois and other charges that supposedly went toward the liquidation of the municipal debt.[24] Furthermore, in the decree accompanying the registration of the letters patent, the Parlement took it upon itself to prohibit the city from ordering new construction, opening new loans, or engaging in other fiscal maneuvers without the approval of Procureur-Général Joly de Fleury. The court also ordered the chief officers of the municipality to present in the Parlement within one month a complete statement of the city's revenues, expenditures, and fiscal operations.[25] The court's initiative provoked an immediate response from the government. First President d'Aligre was ordered to appear at Versailles on 26 January 1783, at which time Louis expressed his disapproval of the Parlement's action and stated that he himself would see to the "condition of the city of Paris."

D'Aligre nevertheless used the occasion to relay to Louis his colleagues' criticisms of the waste and inefficiency in the administration of the Parisian Hôtel de Ville, and in September of the same year he returned to Versailles with even sharper language about the need for fiscal and administrative streamlining in the city's bureaucracy.[26]

This was an ever-present concern, almost an obsession, in parlementary minds and was likely to surface whenever the jurists reviewed the operations of this or that body within their purview. In fact, just a matter of days before First President d'Aligre was reiterating his company's criticisms of the Parisian municipality, in September 1783, the Parlement was urging the king to adopt a new administrative statute for the hospitals at Lyons. "The new ordinance," said the judges, "in assuring relief and subsistence to the paupers of that city and to the other poor who flock there from all sides, must rigorously prohibit all operations not directed toward the public weal." Overzealous administrators must not be allowed to throw money away on nonessential construction, and the hospital administrators ought every year to publish their records of expenditure and revenue and make these records available to the citizens of Lyons. How better to insure efficient use of existing funds, and guard against future loans and taxes, than to expose the workings of the hospital bureaucracy to *la publicité*, to the light of day? Louis XVI was as unreceptive to this counsel as he was to the recommendations for better management of the Parisian municipality—all the more so in that the judges, in discussing the hospitals of Lyons, drew a pointed analogy between their government and the management of the kingdom.[27] For the parlementaires, however, surveillance over provincial hospitals and surveillance over the central government were equally natural—because equally necessary.

In setting forth its corporative view of society during the 1770s and 1780s, and in dealing with specific institutions under its sway, the Parlement exposed a complex variety of concerns. Certainly the championship of privilège, and of the kind of world privilège implied, was one of the most crucial of those concerns. But just as certainly, the magistrates had other reasons for acting as they did. The most convincing proof of this is the time and energy they devoted to problems involving those individuals, such as small urban consumers and rural *corvéables*, who profited relatively little from the regime of privilege.

The Counselors and the Consumers

During the last two decades before the Revolution, the Parisian parlementaires struck out repeatedly in defense of Parisians and others whose precarious existence (especially during the bitter winter months) depended largely upon bread and firewood.[28] The citizens referred to in the remonstrances, correspondence, and decrees of this period were certainly not all from the ranks of the *menu peuple*, but the reasoning of the parlementary arguments on behalf of consumers leaves no doubt that the judges sought a "popular" role and prided themselves upon it.

In part, this role reflected a long-standing magisterial suspicion of *gens d'affaires*, entrepreneurs who were in a position to dupe and exploit the public. In leafing through the folio volumes of the Lefebvre d'Amécourt collections, the researcher continually comes upon lawsuits documenting the fraud and chicanery of entrepreneurs into whose hands various individuals had unwisely committed their property and affairs. From such rascals one could expect nothing but "arrogance, hardheartedness, chicanery, and delay," and the Parlement's sentences in cases involving such individuals were invariably severe.[29]

Given such an attitude, it was perfectly natural that d'Amécourt and his fellows should seize every opportunity to attack those economic theorists advocating freedom for the commerce in grain and other essential commodities. The tirades of Avocat-Général Séguier against "physiocrats" and "economists" predated the exile of the Maupeou years and were legendary.[30] This same prejudice manifested itself in the late 1780s in Lefebvre d'Amécourt's manuscript notices upon the ministers of the old regime. This influential grand' chambrier spoke of the theorists who had "inveigled" Turgot into accepting and applying their notions on the grain commerce. These "philosophers who preach nothing but humanity and patriotism" had gotten their way, and for France the result had been hardship and famine. The principles of these pseudophilosophers had been answered by "the reproaches of all of starving France."[31] D'Amécourt's remarks, of course, indicated in retrospect one of the principal disappointments of the Turgot ministry; they also suggested that the parlementaires were willing to seize upon every incident of past economic troubles to justify their predisposition against the physiocratic doctrines.

Turgot obtained a preliminary *arrêt du Conseil* on 13 September 1774, authorizing anyone within the kingdom to participate in the transport, storing, and selling of grain. This decree was followed by letters patent on 2 November confirming and amplifying the provisions of the September decree.[32] The Parlement did not receive these letters patent until 12 December: its immediate reaction at that time was to name *commissaires* to examine them.[33] The magistrates' apprehension about the practical effect of the proposed legislation may have been quickened by a petition they received during this period from the officers of the grain measurers' association.[34] The grain measurers complained that the letters patent would rob them of their intermediary function between the merchants and the purchasers of grain at Paris. It was the grain measurers, so their petition claimed, who ascertained the amounts of grain being sold at the markets and insured that there was no spoiled grain that might harm or even endanger the lives of the citizens. Moreover, the grain measurers warned the magistrates that the new regime of economic freedom, by permitting the Parisian bakers to buy wheat and other cereals anywhere they were displayed rather than restricting them to certain designated areas, would open the door to monopolization of a precious foodstuff. And what might such a monopolization by the bakers not lead to in times of scarcity? These *officiers mesureurs de grains* also sought (predictably) to enlist the judges' sympathy by portraying their function as a legitimate and endangered patrimony, but in stressing the perils of economic deregulation they demonstrated their familiarity with the parlementaires' predisposition against the doctrine of Turgot and his partisans.

The court eventually registered the controller-general's legislation, but according to two contemporary journalists it did so only after prolonged debate and a vote that showed how deeply divided the judges were on the question.[35] S.-P. Hardy commented in his journal that the magistrates, always sensitive to public opinion on controversial issues, feared that their approval of the measure would lead the people to suspect them of complicity with the hated monopolizers of grain.[36] That the issue was very much on the judges' minds was evidenced by their decision to accompany their grudging ratification of the letters patent with a statement to the monarch spelling out their misgivings. The Parlement, "obligated by its position to articulate the needs" of the people, had been willing to register the legislation only because it was persuaded that the king's prudence "would suggest to him the most proper means to insure that the public markets were capable of providing" for the "daily subsistence" of his subjects.[37] This statement was probably compounded of several attitudes: fears of popular unrest in times of scarcity, a desire to signify to the lower classes, however indirectly, that the court was espousing their cause, and a genuine concern for their lot in hard times.

The parlementaires viewed the so-called *guerre des farines* that broke out in the following spring as a confirmation of their misgivings. Lefebvre d'Amécourt was later to characterize this unrest as "a revolt resulting from the exporting of too much grain" and to assert, somewhat hyperbolically, that, "from that moment forward, the Economists had no more influence in political affairs."[38] The parlementaires were all the more eager to return to their critique of Turgot's policies at this time in that the controller-general had authorized the summary provost courts to handle all prosecutions stemming from the grain riots. This policy was necessitated by the momentary emergency in the environs of the capital, but it was nevertheless resented by the Parlement as an infringement of its own functions. In an arrêt of 4 May the court ordered all inferior tribunals in its jurisdiction to refer cases arising from the riots directly to the judges in Paris and to proscribe illegal gatherings. Simultaneously, it invoked the popular cause, imploring the king to have measures taken "to make the price of grain and bread fall to a level commensurate with the needs of the people and thus deprive all ill-intentioned individuals of the opportunity ... to stir things up."[39] The next day the judges were forced at a lit de justice to register letters patent legitimizing the summary procedure in the provost courts, and Séguier again raised the subsistence issue by entreating Louis to "take a truly paternal interest" in the popular welfare.[40] The judges would not let the king forget what they considered to be the root cause of the disturbances in and around the capital: government policies that led to a scarcity of bread and resultant high prices.

Less than a year later, the Parlement was preparing remonstrances against a royal declaration that removed the few restraints still existing upon the selling, buying, and transport of wheat and other foodstuffs.[41] Duval d'Eprémesnil allegedly harangued his colleagues on the issue, denouncing the "insolent and dangerous sect" of economists, which included the controller-general himself.[42] The protests that were drafted, approved, and eventually presented to Louis developed two predominant themes: the advantageous position of the grain merchants vis-à-vis the purchasers of grain, and the close connection in times of scarcity between popular misery and popular revolt.

On the first theme, the magistrates reviewed the long series of measures implemented over the years to control the commerce in the most vital commodities. These measures, they asserted, "grew more necessary from day to day to the extent that commerce, catching up in its toils the population of the countryside, entrusted the lives of more and more citizens to the discretion of the traders in grain." The judges lauded the past efforts of the municipality to oversee, in the popular interest, the movement of grain into Paris and its sale in the marketplace. They bemoaned the fact that "this ever-vigilant police that was watching over the subsistence of so many unfortunates" was now going to disappear, "leaving the field to the selfish speculations of the trader, who always sells more dearly than he has bought and, thinking only of himself, subordinates to his own interest that of all others." And the parlementaires went on to explain how the imperative needs of the people worked in the favor of the seller:

> There is, Sire, a vice inherent in the commerce in grains, a vice that has not perhaps been sufficiently appreciated by the partisans of economic liberty: it is that, in this trade unlike all others, the seller dictates to the buyer, because here it is stark necessity that is buying, necessity that does not stop to think about prices when it is extreme. To clarify the argument, if any kinds of cloth became too expensive, all the less expensive cloths would have so much popularity that the manufacturer, fearing for his investment and trade, would be forced to lower the price of his product. However, in the

commerce in grain, everything would have the same value, because all grains, even those of poorest quality, are priceless when reckoned by need.[43]

As a result, there could be no true competition among the grain merchants, all of whom could speculate and sell their commodity at the dearest possible price.

The Parlement's remonstrances went into other aspects of the popular dilemma. They argued, for instance, that in an economic emergency the "indigent class of consumers" inevitably suffered from the discrepancy between wages and rising prices. Harsh experience, they claimed, demonstrated that wages never quite caught up to prices, and especially not in hard times, when prices exploded without warning and idle hands desperately sold themselves for meager wages. Had the partisans of the "system" of economic liberty taken such things into account? "Had they calculated . . . what a moment of distress could mean in terms of the discouragement and sorrow of that unfortunate class that had nothing going for it but its labor and the more immediate protection of the laws?"[44] The little man was at the mercy of the market forces both as a wage earner and as a consumer.

Not surprisingly, the parlementaires then probed more deeply into the popular mentality in hard times, linking popular despair with popular revolt:

> A popular movement becomes a popular riot, and then the instruments of suppression must come into play to restore law and order, a law and order that would always be best guaranteed by the constant and vigilant authority of the law.
>
> It was, Sire, because they had weighed these drawbacks that our fathers multiplied precautionary measures in the interior of the cities; they regarded need as the primary force moving all men: need moves the scoundrel toward crime, and excites paupers to unrest . . . it plunges the people into despair or holds them in a state of agitation; one does not reason at all about necessity, for it involves one's own existence.[45]

This analysis reflected the experience of the old regime, with its food riots, its *taxation populaire*, and its ruthless methods of suppressing such disturbances; at the same time, it anticipated to some extent the popular mood during the recurrent food crises of the Revolution. To be sure, the magistrates in discountenancing at one point the hoarding of food by upper-class Frenchmen spoke merely of "indiscreet precautions on the part of the rich," and such relatively mild language testified indirectly to the stake held by the parlementaires themselves in the status quo.[46] Nevertheless, their denunciations of the "selfish speculations" of the grain merchants, and general indictment of the free market, would find many an echo in the revolutionary politics of the 1790s. The judges' identification of need as "the primary force moving all men" was crucial, and they refused to let this insight become submerged in a sea of platitudinous calls for "law and order."

This same recognition of the public interest emerged strikingly in the associated remonstrances defending the Parisian guilds. If the primary thrust here was a defense of privileged producers and proprietors, the judges hypothesized just as frankly about the effects of the abolition of the guilds upon the consumer: "One is even more frightened, Sire, when one considers those professions that hold the lives and safety of men in their hands; the bakers, the wine merchants, all those in general who sell foodstuffs, who will inspect them? . . . The grocers ought to have been regulated more carefully [in Turgot's legislation] than the apothecaries; poisons pass from their boutiques into pharmacists' laboratories and into the hands of artists who use them; is it not more dangerous to multiply the merchants who distribute them?"[47] Such language dignified the defense of the *jurandes* and their monopolies, but the parlementaires were probably sincere in maintaining that past regulations, now to be overturned by the Turgotist legislation, had benefited the consumer as well as the privileged producer by setting standards for prime commodities and by subjecting violators of those standards to the police and to the hierarchy of courts headed by the Parlement.

Turgot had as little patience for these arguments against his economic reforms as for those against his abrogation of the corvée royale. Indeed, he had anticipated many of them in his legislation on the guilds and grain trade.[48] Yet, the provisioning of food to the capital was still an uncertain business, and the public remained susceptible to rumor and panic on a subject that concerned it so closely. In view of these realities, it is doubtful whether Turgot's somewhat doctrinaire economics of laissez-faire could have justified themselves in the immediate future. They might have worked over the long run, assuring that supply sought out demand and thus reduced prices and enhanced the purchasing power and living conditions of all; but the magistrates, in their daily role of social surveillance, could not wait.

It is important to stress this daily role in characterizing the Parlement's defense of the consumer. It did not require the provocative innovations of a Turgot or a deluge of petitions from privileged officers and masters of guilds to spur the Parlement to defend consumer interests. The court's archives abound with arrêtés attempting, in the public interest, to control the production, sale, and transport of articles of consumption vital to the public, and most often, if not always, the poorer public. The bookseller Hardy reported during February 1783 that the Parlement, hearing of a pending exportation of grain to England and fearing that this might lead to shortages of bread at home, passed a "rather severe decree" forbidding the exportation. According to this observer, the king immediately summoned d'Aligre to explain his company's action, and the first president responded "with respect, but at the same time with energy," by voicing his associates' apprehensions about a possible scarcity of bread.[49] On this occasion the court received royal assurances that the problem would be taken in hand by the government, but the magistrates charged their chief officer to continue to pressure the monarch and his ministers on the necessity to insure the townspeople an adequate supply of bread. Then, during the exceedingly dry summer of 1785, the Parlement issued a decree ordering all persons, "no matter of what rank and condition," to buy only as much hay, straw, or other fodder as was absolutely necessary for the maintenance of their livestock. The decree also stated that "those who might have fodder to sell would have to sell it to the proprietors, farmers, and cultivators of their parishes who might need it solely for their personal farming and consumption" and stressed that these "proprietors, farmers, and cultivators" should have priority in any purchases over strangers from outside their parishes.[50] The ever-observant Hardy, commenting upon this parlementary decree, asserted that it was designed primarily "to head off the deadly effects of drought and frustrate the enterprises of the greedy monopolists, [who are] always ready to swallow up, so to speak, the really essential commodities as soon as they have reason to hope that circumstances may allow them . . . to profit from higher prices."[51] In view of the Parlement's protests against physiocratic policies during 1774–76, Hardy's interpretation of this decree of 1785 was probably on the mark.

But the magistrates' orientation toward the consumer manifested itself most clearly in connection with their protests during 1784 and 1785 over the provisioning of firewood to the capital. This was another area in which the Parlement intervened continually on behalf of the Parisian population. The judges were interested in seeing that the correct kinds and amounts of wood were being sold at reasonable prices to the people who needed it in order to preserve some warmth against the bitter winters of the 1770s and 1780s, as well as to the bakers who needed it in order to fire their ovens. The municipal administration would often take the initiative in this area, adopting measures for controlling the supply of wood and sending its chief officer, the *prévôt des marchands*, to the Palais de Justice to secure parlementary approval of these measures. Often the Parlement, finding such provisions inadequate, would issue its own decrees supplementing the measures of the municipal administrators. Of course, the ministers at Versailles could also become involved in this sphere of administration and often did during these years.[52]

On 6 July 1784 the Parlement, after ratifying an ordinance presented by the prévôt des marchands to suppress various fraudulent practices in the commerce of firewood, issued a lengthy decree on the subject.[53] Among other things, this decree prescribed in minute detail the construction and dimensions of the wooden instrument (*membrure*) used to measure the size of the firewood stacked in timber yards near the river prior to being sold. The parlementaires hoped that this would assure equity to both seller and purchaser in such transactions. Three days later the judges received a royal declaration on the same subject.[54] The declaration prescribed the measuring, marking, and stacking of firewood and divided it into three categories: the *bois blanc*, which usually went to the poorer townspeople at a relatively low price, and the more expensive *bois neuf* and *bois flotté* habitually transported to the capital on the Marne and Seine.[55] Furthermore, the "rights of entry" upon wood entering Paris, traditionally lower for the bois blanc, were henceforth to be the same for all three types of wood, which meant that the total price to the consumer of the bois blanc, formerly between seventeen and eighteen livres per cartload, would now be over twenty-two livres per cartload. The higher price of the bois blanc presumably would serve as an incentive to merchants to supply this wood more regularly than in the past.

The Parlement immediately decided to remonstrate against this legislation, and d'Aligre delivered the resultant protests to Louis on 31 July. The judges, realizing that wood had a variety of uses in Paris, feared that the proprietors of forest lands and the wood merchants might attempt to profit from the higher prices accorded the cheap wood by concentrating upon marketing that type to the exclusion of those types needed for construction purposes. The magistrates also suspected that the merchants' partisans might have alleged an exhaustion of forests in the area to justify higher prices because of longer distances of transport of wood from other regions; but they claimed that the merchants had failed to demonstrate such a shortage of wood in the environs of the capital. In any case, the rise in the price of the bois blanc would not sufficiently compensate the merchants for their allegedly higher costs of transport, and thus the only lasting effect of the legislation would be to pass this higher rate on to those in Paris least able to support it— "the consumers." The parlementaires complained that the taxes on the wood entering the capital had risen from the original 16 sous per cartload in 1726 to the present level of 110 sous. This was bad enough for the rich, who consumed the superior grades of wood; but was it not even more unfair to expect the poor to pay the same high tax upon the only type of wood they were used to buying?

> Because of unforeseen events, such as falling water levels or an accumulation of ice in the rivers, the dearth of other types of wood could make the bois blanc, which in all probability would still abound in the timber yards, a very precious commodity for the poor.
> The poor make no advance plans.

The poor constitute the great majority.

Finally, the poor, in the case of essential commodities, must be the special, if not the only, object of the Sovereign's enlightened solicitude.

The "rich," in a pinch, could usually take care of themselves, said the magistrates, but the poor were not so fortunate. Would it not therefore be fairer to tax the cheapest grade of wood at a lower rate, thus giving the poor a margin of relief in hard times? Having made this point, the magistrates concluded by suggesting more humane and efficient means of assuring the city its wood: in emergencies, the authorization of "special fellings of trees" to provide wood in a hurry, and for the long run, the reduction of tolls, the improvement of canals used for the floating of wood, and more careful management of the forests supplying the wood.[56] In response to these pleas, the king promised to study the Parlement's suggestions, but he also insisted upon immediate registration of his declaration. The magistrates, after hearing the first president's report on 3 August, registered the legislation and let the matter rest for the time being.

However, their argument against the wood merchants took on a cutting edge the following summer, when the government issued a new declaration reducing the price of the bois blanc by two and a half livres per cartload but increasing the price of the bois neuf by three livres per load.[57] In remonstrances received by the king on 31 July 1785, the parlementaires asserted that the motive behind this legislation was to give the merchants a new incentive to supply wood rather than to benefit the people, because the reduction of two and a half livres applied only to 60,000 cartloads of cheap wood and the larger increase of three livres would affect nearly 250,000 cartloads of wood of higher quality. The parlementaires denied the efficacy of the incentive for the merchants and scornfully alluded to the preamble of the declaration, which justified these measures as a response to the very dry summer the Parisian area had been experiencing: "But when the municipal administration yielded to such an extraordinary request, could it have thought that if the low water levels retarded at this time the provisioning of Paris, the augmentation [of the price of the bois neuf] would facilitate navigation?" No, declared the judges, the moving force behind this legislation was the cupidity of the wood merchants, and not the dryness of the summer and the low waters in the rivers. Moreover, according to the Parlement's intelligence, the merchants were engaged in a conspiracy to bleed the public.

But, Sire, your parlement does not have to go so far to find the causes of the so-called dearth of wood. It can inform Your Majesty that, according to the records furnished by the City, there are today 500,000 cartloads on the quays of the Seine, of the Yonne, and of the Marne; that this momentary fear of lacking wood is only the result

of a fraudulent cooperation among the merchants; that they thought
they could use the appearance of a scarcity to frighten the Government and cozen it into granting a new price augmentation. . . . It can
finally inform Your Majesty that this fraudulent cooperation is now
accompanied by the maneuvers of several companies which, in acquiring some considerable bonus payments, have supposedly made
some major commitments; but if these commitments are sincere,
they must therefore know where the wood is and how to get it here.

But such companies, claimed the judges, always defaulted on their prom-
ises after having grabbed an advance portion of their payment, leaving the
essential work of provisioning the capital to the government. The sole
remedy for these ills, they insisted, was the execution of the "wise and
ancient regulations" and enforcement of engagements by which the merchants would be obligated "to supply, year after year, a certain quantity of
cartloads" of wood.[58]

Not unexpectedly, the king replied that his declaration was the best
way to facilitate the provisioning of Paris, "in assuring to the wood merchants a known and legitimate profit." Furthermore, he reminded the
court, the cheaper grade of wood would now be available to the people at a
reduced rate.[59] If this reminder was Louis's way of questioning the sin-
cerity of the Parlement's protestations on behalf of the *menu peuple*, the
magistrates could with justice reply that they had objected strenuously
the year before to the increased cost of the most popular grade of wood.
They could add with equal justice that the poor as well as the affluent
would pay dearly in the long run for the government's habitual accession
to the merchants' demands for higher prices. Indeed, when the judges at
the king's insistence registered his declaration on 9 August, they appended a long arrêté stating that the court reserved the right to renew and
enforce "the provisions of the established regulations to assure the provisioning of Paris and prevent maneuvers by the merchants that might
cause the said city to experience the crisis of a scarcity of wood, a concern
that could in the future serve as a cause or pretext for more requests for
higher prices."[60] Louis was also urged to find ways to expedite the current
provisioning of Paris so as to justify a rolling back of the prices established in the latest legislation.

The court did not relax its surveillance in this important area. On 14
October of the same year, a member of the Chambre des Vacations announced to his fellows that yet another variety of wood floated on the
Marne part of the way to Paris was now selling, like the aristocratic bois
neuf, at twenty-seven livres per cartload, though previously it had sold for
less. An investigation revealed that an *arrêt du Conseil* of 20 May of the
same year had granted this price increase to the merchants. In this case,
however, the court's intervention had at least a temporary effect, for the

president of the Chambre des Vacations was able to announce to his colleagues on 25 October that the King's Council had promulgated another
decree rolling back the price increase on this particular grade of wood.[61]
However, at this same session, yet another abuse was denounced. The
wood suppliers, claimed an indignant judge, were not only selling the
wood floated part of the way on the Marne at the same rate of twenty-
seven livres set for the bois neuf but were also, in direct violation of the
laws, mixing all types of wood together in many of the timber yards along
the Seine. Hence, they were charging the public twenty-seven livres per
cartload not only for the wood floated down the Marne but also for the
lower-quality bois blanc. "These troubling facts," the judge asserted, "derived from the lack of publicity given to that decree [of 20 May], which
had, in a manner of speaking, been kept secret, and from the lack of vigilance of the municipal commissioners and wood inspectors."[62] The Parlement charged its gens du roi to investigate these alleged transgressions
by the wood merchants and to report back to the full company after the
vacations. Before the jurists could take any definitive action, however, the
prévôt des marchands appeared before them to obtain their endorsement
of two new ordinances policing the sale of wood. In a long speech, the
prévôt des marchands, Le Pelletier de Mortefontaine, explained the two
measures, defended the efforts of his municipal administration to assure
a sufficient supply of wood for the capital, and lashed out at the greed
of the merchants.[63] Before the end of the year, the parlementaires had
approved the new regulations proposed by the municipality, casting them
in the form of one of the most comprehensive and ambitious decrees
ever issued by the court to control the machinations of the wood
entrepreneurs.[64]

This decree required all those contracting to supply the city with wood
to tell the municipality exactly how much they committed themselves to
provide and what profit they expected from their operations. The pledged
amount of wood had to be cut, transported, and sold in Paris and nowhere
else within two years, under penalty of confiscation of all wood left un-
sold in the timber yards at the end of that period. The merchants were
expressly forbidden to sell along the routes of transport, whether on water
or land: stiff penalties were to be meted out to those selling part of their
wood before reaching Paris. Finally, the court's decree stipulated that the
three primary grades of this commodity—the bois flotté, bois neuf, and
bois blanc—as well as all other varieties were to be stacked and marked
separately in the yards along the river. Any merchant attempting to mix
the various kinds and to charge the consumer the higher rates of the bois
neuf for all of his wood was liable to a fine of 500 livres. The efficacy of
this decree is questionable, but its promulgation was hailed by S.-P.
Hardy, who claimed that Parisians had "never been so vexed and so mo-
lested in a thousand ways" as they were, in the 1780s, by wood en-

trepreneurs who seemed to be "as thick as thieves" and possibly in league with "monopolists in high quarters."[65] A similar attitude motivated the judges until the end of the old regime.

The Parlement's defense of the consumer during these years admittedly was not simply an exercise in humanitarianism. The magistrates were dourly suspicious of entrepreneurs who seemed at all likely to escape the *police* of the ancien régime. They also knew very well that public misery could breed popular disturbance. But their very obsession with law and order sharpened their awareness that most men would prefer a decent minimum of comfort and security to the uncertain career of the agitator and thus reinforced their conviction that it was right as well as expedient to defend the people against those who could deny them subsistence. Perhaps the judges were also playing for a bit of popular acclaim, but the consistency with which they cast themselves in the role of "consumer advocate" regardless of the tug and pull of other interests suggests that most of them viewed this role as an obligation. Within limitations imposed by their conservative outlook and personal interest, the men of the Parlement also revealed "popular" sympathies in connection with the troublesome issue of the corvée royale.

The Counselors and the Corvéables

To discuss parlementary attitudes toward the corvée and the corvéables means first of all to recognize that the judges' opposition to Turgot's abolition of the corvée royale in 1776 was *not* simply a matter of defending the privileges of the nobility. One of the Parlement's most persistent critiques during the eighteenth century dealt with royal finances, and this critique was employed on behalf of commoners as well as nobles. It is useful to see how in 1776 one of the leading parlementaires treated Turgot's proposed tax replacing the corvée as just another example of sloppy government finance: "If these funds are employed for other purposes, that diversion of revenues will be part of the general problem: a new imposition would be neither just nor reasonable, it would be crushing for the people, who could not be sure that the new revenues were being properly applied, since to the contrary they have to bear continual witness to the fact that government expense has no principle other than the government's whim."[66] The government, warned this parlementaire, would sooner or later find excuses for diverting tax moneys originally earmarked for the upkeep of roads to other, supposedly more "urgent" needs and might then use the resultant deterioration of the kingdom's *grandes routes* as an excuse for restoration of the old forced labor. Turgot's plan might work, but only if the government adopted rigorous measures to separate these moneys from the other revenues and to insure that the special funds were employed for their original purpose: the construction and repair of the main highways in France. This *parlementaire* then proceeded to detail practical measures toward this end.[67] Turgot's edict suppressing the corvée prescribed similar measures, at least partly in anticipation of a parlementary financial critique.[68] The Parlement had additional reasons for opposing Turgot's reform, but the critique of government spending argued a humanitarian concern and was to reappear subsequently in the parlementary campaign against abuses in the corvée system.

Later in 1776 the magistrates proposed their own alternative to the aborted reform of Turgot: retain the old *corvée en nature* but exert every effort to ensure its implementation in the most humanitarian way possible. One of the judges—probably either Lefebvre d'Amécourt or the abbé d'Espagnac—presented what was in effect a blueprint for the administration of the reinstated corvée. An excerpt follows:

> Two principles, equally true, must lead to the restoration of the corvées.
>
> The first, which no one contests, is the necessity of having roads.
>
> The second, the impossibility of repairing and maintaining them by taxes rather than by simple labor.
>
> But in restoring the corvées, it is essential to demand from the people only a contribution that does not prejudice agriculture or their own subsistence.
>
> It is likewise essential that this duty be directed with reflection and discrimination and that it be executed only for things useful to society.[69]

Therefore, let no corvéables be ordered to labor on someone's road "as a private favor." Let no community be ordered to send its peasants more than two leagues to extract materials for roadwork or to perform the requisite work itself. Let no corvées be ordered in seasons when the corvéables must be in their fields. The number of days of labor must be "irrevocably fixed." The number of carts and other vehicles provided by the corvéables must be similarly fixed. The schedules of work must be posted in the villages so that every man would understand his obligation and no man could be overworked. The publicity given to these arrangements would be the best possible guarantee against abuse at the lower administrative level, although any corvéables who felt that they were being unfairly used could apply to their intendant for redress of grievances.

The consistency of parlementary attitudes, from issues of bread and firewood to the problem of the corvée, is striking. Whether railing against free trade, castigating greedy wood merchants, or proposing a blueprint for the reimplementation of the traditional corvée, the counselors of the Parlement wanted to circumscribe the activities of suspect gens d'affaires and lower-echelon government agents. Hence, their desire to see strict limits placed upon how far the corvéable could be expected to go to fulfill his task, how much and what kind of work could be exacted from him, how long he must labor, and what vehicles and implements, if any, he must provide.

Hence, as well, their dissatisfaction with the actual terms of the government's reimposition of personal roadwork after Turgot's disgrace. The declaration of August 1776 promulgated by Turgot's brief successor Clugny to set the corvée back on its old footing left much to be desired by parlementary standards, for beyond promising that the king would at some point devote "special attention" to alleviating the conditions of roadwork, it said nothing specific about the administration of this task.[70] The Parlement registered Clugny's legislation on 19 August but appended a request that Louis impose humanitarian guidelines upon the corvée and allow those individuals who did not wish to work on the roads to purchase their exemption from the intendant and his subordinates.[71]

There was widespread dissatisfaction with the reestablished corvée from the very start.[72] Not surprisingly, in some areas this stemmed from the very reinstatement of the old system: Turgot's reform had been humanitarian and had attracted much support. Yet it seems that many communities within the Parlement's jurisdiction were bothered more by the haphazard and occasionally vexatious manner of the corvée's reimposition than by the principle of the corvée itself.[73] In September 1776 Clugny sent instructions in the form of a circular letter to all the intendants, instructions granting the communities two options. Either they could execute their work personally, with individuals paying others to perform their tasks if they so wished, or the communities *as a whole* could turn over their assigned labor to entrepreneurs and *adjudicataires* hired by the intendants and their agents. These entrepreneurs would hire gangs of workers to perform these tasks, and the resultant expenses (workers' salaries, entrepreneurs' compensation, and so on) would be defrayed by a tax additional to the taille assessed on the commoners of the community. Another circular to the same effect was sent to the intendants by Clugny's titular successor Taboureau des Réaux the following April. Necker himself did not seem to care which method was implemented, just so the corvée was administered in each *généralité* "according to each Intendant's sense of local realities."[74] The result was that within a number of généralités, whole communities paid others (through additional taxation) to do their work for them. The standard procedure was for the intendant to secure a government order (*mandement*) entitling communities within his généralité to adopt this so-called *corvée par adjudication*. According to Chaumont de la Millière, intendant of the bridges and roads, the new system was modeled upon "the principles adopted previously in the généralités of Caen, Rouen, and Alençon" in Normandy.[75] At least one minister had misgivings about the corvée par adjudication: in his circular of April 1777, Taboureau des Réaux stated that, though he knew that some communities had switched voluntarily to the new corvée, he nevertheless feared all administrative innovations of this sort and reminded the intendants that they were to implement the new corvée only at the request of "the parishes themselves."[76] A majority of the intendants were sooner or later to establish the new system in their généralités.

The Parisian parlementaires had their doubts about the new system from the start. Some of them may have been indirectly affected by local commutations of the corvée to the extent that the substituted tax lay upon their own tenants and sharecroppers, although as privilégiés the magistrates obviously had no direct stake in the manner of implementation of the corvée. Nevertheless, as critics of the "administrative monarchy," the jurists suspected that the corvée par adjudication might lend itself to abuse. Their misgivings were confirmed during 1776 and 1777. A number of localities within the court's jurisdiction reported abusive practices on their roads and bridges: some of these complaints were directed against the traditional corvée, but others involved the fiscal corvée par adjudication. From Rheims came an undated letter detailing abuses in that area during 1776 and 1777. Another letter from the same region described the way the peasants were being overworked on the road from Châlons to Rheims. On 17 April 1777, one Fréton, an official at Achères in the généralité of Orléans, wrote to complain that the intendant in that region was forcing some peasants to labor at a distance of three leagues from their homes and had arbitrarily imprisoned others, reducing them to misery.[77] As advocates of law and order, the judges must have been especially distressed to receive a letter in December 1777 from the village of Cosne-sur-Loire in the Orléans généralité stating that the community's jailer at the local prison had been dragged away to labor on the roads, making honest folk fear for their safety from vagabonds and criminals on the loose![78] But undoubtedly the kind of complaint that most nettled the judges at Paris involved the imposition of a new tax upon the corvéables and taillables to finance the roadwork performed by gangs of men in the pay of various entrepreneurs. At the court's plenary session of 22 August 1777 the same magistrate who called his colleagues' attention to alleged abuses in the administration of the vingtièmes also asserted that in a number of généralités the king's agents "were levying 4, 5, or 6 sous per livre on the assessment of the taille for the construction or repair of the main highways."[79] The court immediately ordered an investigation of the situation, charging the procureur-général to obtain from his subordinates in the lower tribunals of the jurisdiction information as to the nature and extent of abuses in the administration of the corvées.

The investigation lagged seriously at the local level, for the circular letter sent by Joly de Fleury to the procureurs du roi of the bailliages on 4

September had to be reinforced by a more imperative order two months later requiring information immediately on the vingtièmes and corvées.[80] As late as 9 December, Avocat-Général Séguier, collaborating with the other members of the parquet on the investigation, informed Joly de Fleury that twenty-four bailliages had still not complied with the Parlement's orders. At least one local procureur du roi (a certain Filleau, at Poitiers) tried to atone for his tardiness by intimating in a letter that the results of his inquiries would be significant when fully documented: in his jurisdiction, he claimed, "as in all the provinces of the kingdom, everyone is complaining about taxes, and no one can explain satisfactorily how these types of imposts have been established."[81]

The Parlement's investigation also may have encouraged other communities in the jurisdiction to detail their grievances to the judges at Paris. At some point during this period, the procureur-général received an undated letter signed by representatives of a large number of communities in the généralité of Amiens. In this letter, which must have confirmed many a parlementary suspicion, the corvée par adjudication was denounced:

> The petitioners do not at all claim to be exempt from the obligation of contributing something to the upkeep of the main highways, but they would like to contribute their own labor and would especially like to obtain tasks that would be fixed and immutable. Henceforth, this is the only possible way to put an end to the brigandage and vexations of the supervisors and engineers of the roads and bridges, and of all the other subalterns who, under the reign of the best of Kings, are more interested in enriching themselves and in pillaging the countryside than in solidly repairing the highways.

The letter went on to describe the many ills visited upon the heads of the luckless corvéables of that region, but the gravamen of their complaint was that they were not allowed to do their work and were instead burdened with a tax "all the more terrible in that it will always be arbitrary, it will have no limit other than the very avidity of those who have established it and collect it."[82] Several other communications detailing similar hardships and imploring the protection of the magistrates arrived at the Palais de Justice during the Parlement's campaign to secure royal action curbing the abuses uncovered by its own investigation.[83]

It was not until the end of January 1778 that Séguier reported the findings of the investigation to the assembly of chambers. The labors of the parquet and subordinate tribunals yielded results in all seventeen généralités that lay wholly or partially within the Parlement's jurisdiction.[84] The results were mixed. In five of these généralités (Alençon, Dijon, Limoges, Nancy, and Orléans), there did not appear to be many problems, although it was reported that some communities had been coerced by lower-echelon government agents into accepting a tax additional to the taille and leaving their roadwork to various "entrepreneurs" and their road gangs. That few abuses were reported from Orléans was attributed to the efforts of the intendant there, Cypierre, to encourage the roturiers to perform their assigned tasks themselves and prevent the "drivers, supervisors, syndics, and foremen" from interfering in the people's work.[85] Even in the généralité of Alençon, Séguier claimed, there were all too many communities forced "by all kinds of methods" to subsidize the labor of others by paying additional taxation.[86] In the other twelve généralités covered wholly or in part by the parlementary inquiry, abuses were more varied and detailed. This was especially so for Paris itself and for Poitiers, La Rochelle, Soissons, and Tours. These were some of the findings in the Parisian area:

    1. At Châteaulaudon they collect different moneys, and [yet] they neither make repairs nor construct anything.

    2. The King has earmarked 20,000 livres to level out a mountain and the work has not been done at all.

    3. At Corbeil, those corvéables who have not provided the requisite vehicles are condemned to pay 30 livres per vehicle and 10 livres for each horse not provided.

    4. At Montereau, a considerable sum is included each year in the taille for the upkeep of the pont de Samois, and this bridge has not existed for more than two centuries.

    5. Orders have been obtained from the Intendant for the construction by corvée of a road of half a league leading to the gates of the chateau of M. de Bonnaire des Forges, Maître des Requêtes, a road that is totally useless. Those refusing to obey have been condemned to pay a fine . . . and then have been forced to do the work during the harvest.[87]

In the *généralité* of La Rochelle, widows and septuagenarians were being subjected to taxes for the corvée and punished arbitrarily if they could not afford to pay them. At the same time, younger men were being required to work leagues from home in seasons when there was not enough daylight to allow completion of assigned tasks.[88] Séguier denounced "a multitude of abuses" in the généralité of Tours: young men were being forced to work five or six leagues from home, some workers had to wheel handbarrows and carry their tools for inordinately long distances, others were left for several days at workshops without work, and so on.[89] Similar reports came from Poitiers and Soissons.

It is not easy to assess the significance of these dossiers in the parlementary archives. Probably some of the procureurs of the bailliages, motivated by their own distrust of government agents and gens d'affaires and eager to impress their superiors with their industry in tracking down abuses, painted as dark a picture as possible by embellishing incidents here and drawing unwarranted conclusions there. The Parlement's gens du roi, for their part, certainly did not go out of their way to draw their company's attention to those localities expressing general satisfaction with the way their corvée was being administered. They obviously wanted to seize upon every specific report of abuse as justification for their mistrust of gens d'affaires and government agents, a mistrust that was soon to loom large in their colleagues' remonstrances over the vingtièmes. Still, an impartial examination of the material turned up by the parlementary investigation necessitates the conclusion that there were extensive abuses in the administration of the corvée after its reestablishment in 1776. These abuses were indicated by unsolicited complaints to the Parlement as well as by the court's own inquiry, and they arose both from reversion to the old-style corvée en nature and from implementation of the fiscal corvée par adjudication.

In reporting for his colleagues of the parquet to the full membership on 30 January 1778, Séguier augured a parlementary protest to the king by lashing out at unscrupulous government agents and entrepreneurs battening off helpless corvéables. He voiced his confidence that Louis XVI would be "touched by the deplorable state to which those of his subjects most in need of relief have been reduced" and was sure that the king would want "to shield them from the vexations that lower-level administrators multiply to enrich themselves."[90] The Parlement responded by appointing a commission of judges to study the material deriving from the parquet's investigation, and on 17 February the company charged its first president to inform Louis of the abuses in the administration of the corvée and to request royal action on that score.

In his subsequent discussions with the king and his ministers, First President d'Aligre apparently utilized a fourteen-page Résumé des plaintes adressées au Procureur général du Roi, sur les corvées.[91] This document incorporated many of the findings of the Parlement's investigation and resounded with criticisms of despotic government subdélégués, unscrupulous "entrepreneurs," and their agents' inhumane treatment of corvéables upon the roads. Although it denounced abuses arising from the traditional as well as the newer type of corvée, its primary thrust was against the so-called corvée par adjudication. A portion of the summation follows: "All these deeds have the same object: (1) to force the corvéables by a thousand vexations to accept commutation of their corvées rather than to perform their work themselves; (2) to make that commutation as expensive as possible and turn it into an impost that equals and even surpasses sometimes that of the taille; (3) finally, to eternalize the projects that have given rise to the commutation, and thus to perpetuate the tax." The Résumé claimed that the king was now in a position to appreciate past parlementary counsel on the administration of the corvée. The king must realize now, as a result of his Parlement's inquiry, that the commutation of the roadwork of whole parishes, far from alleviating the people's situation, would only serve "to augment the burden of popular taxation and expose the people to multiple vexations." There was no substitute for the old corvée en nature: let the corvéable do his allotted work "under wise regulations," unburdened by any additional tax and undisturbed by greedy "entrepreneurs," and all would be well.[92]

This was the message d'Aligre bore to Versailles at least three times during the spring and summer of 1778. For a while the Parlement's chief officer could elicit from the government nothing beyond vague assurances that it would "busy itself with that matter and try in all conceivable ways to satisfy the company."[93] On 28 August, d'Aligre informed his associates more specifically that orders had been given to the intendants to conform to the royal declaration of 11 August 1776 and allow individual corvéables to perform their own work or pay to have it done by others, as they desired. Furthermore, the government through d'Aligre asserted that it was adopting the limitations upon the duration and severity of roadwork that the parlementaires had been demanding all along.[94] The magistrates might have been willing to see individual corvéables (as opposed to whole communities) paying to have others perform their work—and in fact, as the government reminded the Parlement through d'Aligre's announcement of 28 August, the parlementaires had endorsed this practice in registering the declaration of 11 August 1776. But as there was still no evidence that the government was going to issue strict guidelines for the administration of the corvée in all généralités, the impatient judges decided to take matters into their own hands. After hearing d'Aligre's report on 28 August, they issued a decree ordering the procureurs du roi in the bailliages of the jurisdiction to send "detailed memoirs" to the procureur-général at Paris describing any abuses incidental to the administration of the corvée in their areas. The parlementaires were particularly concerned to hear from the bailliages in cases where "the corvées might be indicated in seasons when they would interrupt necessary agricultural labors, where they would draw the corvéables more than three leagues from their homes, where the tasks would exceed the strength of the workers, where the number of days for the actual work, as well as the number of vehicles required from each proprietor or farmer, would not be fixed."[95] But the court's arrêté went even further. It attempted to strike at the heart of the corvée par adjudication by forbidding the imposition of any additional tax upon any community and by forbidding the assignment of tasks to road gangs hired by entrepreneurs under the authorization of the intendants.

Thus, in effect, the Parlement was attempting to outlaw administrative innovations that some of the intendants had already been authorized to introduce into their généralités. The government was bound to see the

Parlement's arrêté as an unwarranted intrusion into administrative affairs and, more specifically, as intolerably restricting the work of the intendants and their subordinates. It reacted immediately: after being informed of the Parlement's initiative by Procureur-Général Joly de Fleury, Keeper of the Seals Miromesnil wrote to him expressing the king's "surprise" and displeasure and ordering him, d'Aligre, and two other presidents to appear before Louis on 30 August.[96] Both the first president and the procureur-général immediately replied, protesting that their company had only intended to keep Louis abreast of possible abuses in the administration of the corvée.[97] At their audience with the king, the officers of the Parlement presumably were told that he had authorized some of his intendants to experiment in their généralités and would not brook the court's interference.

Nevertheless, the following day (31 August) the magistrates voted to prepare further protests on the corvée to be presented to Louis after the vacations. These protests were apparently never put into final form, but a rough draft still survives in Lefebvre d'Amécourt's papers. It posed questions testifying to unchanging magisterial concerns. Why not promulgate a "clear, precise law that will declare what is abuse and what is not abuse, that will provide guidance both for the administrator and for the corvéable? And, that law given, why not charge the Parlement with seeing to its execution, as it is charged to see to the execution of all the Kingdom's laws?" The commentary then bluntly justified the Parlement's opposition to Turgot's abolition of the corvée in 1776 as having been an opposition to "arbitrary authority" and even more bluntly accused Necker and the other ministers of callous disregard for the present woes of the corvéables.[98] It is hardly surprising that Versailles never saw this undiplomatic language. At about the same time, however, the ever-resourceful President Joly de Fleury came forward with a draft *règlement* for the reform of the corvée. This project came down particularly hard upon the abuse of *solidarité* in the countryside. *Solidarité* meant that peasants who had performed their own assigned tasks could be held responsible for the work not completed by others and that whole communities could be worked or taxed at frightening rates to compensate for the supervisory failures of lazy and unscrupulous contractors.[99] Though nothing came of Joly de Fleury's project, it illustrates (among other things) the judges' concern with the issue of taxation regardless of the social rank of the taxpayers involved.

No doubt the Parlement's detractors were highly skeptical about the professed humanitarianism of magistrates who had led the fight against Turgot's abolition of the corvée in 1776. Certainly the men of the Paris Parlement betrayed a complex motivation on this issue as on all issues. But it is important to note that the intendants themselves were split on the question of how best to administer the corvée.[100] Although a clear majority of them opted at one time or another for the corvée par adjudication, several resisted the new system as being more oppressive than the corvée en nature. The dissidents included Guéau de Reverseaux, intendant for Moulins from 1777 to 1781 and for La Rochelle after 1781, and Bertier de Sauvigny, intendant for Paris from 1776 until the Revolution. Both men, "remarkable administrators," were widely known for the humanitarian measures they introduced into their généralités, and both men felt that having the people perform their own tasks on the roads under strict supervision would cause them less hardship in the long run than would a tax additional to the taille to finance the work of hired laborers.[101]

Another intendant who maintained the traditional corvée, at least until 1780, was Jean Claude François Perrin de Cypierre, responsible for the généralité of Orléans from 1760 to 1785. In August 1777 Cypierre obtained a *mandement* from the government authorizing and describing in minute detail the traditional corvée. Lefebvre d'Amécourt acquired a copy of this *mandement* and contrasted it favorably to an authorization for parishes to adopt the corvée par adjudication in the généralité of Alençon.[102] The intendant for Alençon, Antoine Jean Baptiste Jullien, had formerly been d'Amécourt's colleague in the Enquêtes of the Parlement; he had left the court in 1765 and had become intendant for Alençon the following year.[103] When, in 1777, complaints reached the Parlement from communities in Normandy affected by Jullien's policies, d'Amécourt endeavored to persuade his one-time colleague to return to the corvée of personal labor. The resultant correspondence between the judge and the full-time administrator illuminates the perspectives of both sides on this difficult question.

In a letter to Jullien dated 16 November 1777, d'Amécourt complained that the corvée as administered in the Alençon généralité left everything to the discretion of the lower-level government agents, contractors, and engineers. Yet the machinations of these kinds of individuals, claimed d'Amécourt, so often discredited the regime of the intendants themselves. Why had Jullien not taken care to specify how far the corvéables electing to perform their own tasks would have to go from their homes? Why was nothing said about the duration of their work? Would those parishes that had fulfilled their obligation be liable to additional labors? It also seemed, pursued d'Amécourt, that these communities had to choose between the corvée en nature and the corvée par adjudication without knowing what the labor assigned to them for the coming year really involved. Besides, even if the communities opted for performing their own tasks, what was to prevent Jullien's subordinates from saying they were badly done and forcing the luckless peasants to repeat their labors? "It is, however, a principle, Monsieur, that a corvéable is not obligated to bring to his work anything but his own arms and his carts and wagons: he is not at all obligated to be a good ditchdigger; his work must be directed by a specialist: he cannot be held accountable for defective work, much less for unpredictable accidents such as a caving-in of earth, which however . . . your ordinance lays to his account." Moreover, if for some reason a community had not completed half its work within half the total time allotted, the ordinance authorized unspecified "entrepreneurs" to take over, evicting the original workers, completing the work as they best saw fit, and charging the parishes for their expenses. Indeed, it seemed as though the purpose of Jullien's ordinance was to make the traditional corvée so unpalatable to the parishes that they would in effect be forced to accept the newer system. But this would necessitate "a new impost that will be collected without registration of any edict." It would, claimed d'Amécourt, amount to six additional deniers per livre on the cash payment that the five wealthiest commoners in each community would be compelled to advance to the contractors to finance their operations. D'Amécourt concluded by recommending that Jullien adopt the wise measures implemented by Cypierre in his généralité of Orléans.[104]

In replying to this influential parlementaire three days later, Jullien stressed that he had given the communities under his jurisdiction the chance to pay an additional tax in place of performing personal labor because the vast majority of them preferred it that way. He assured his correspondent that each community was allowed to view its tasks before having to decide between personal labor and additional taxation. As for the requirement that half the assigned work be completed in half the allotted time, experience had shown this to be necessary: otherwise, the corvéables who opted for personal labor would lag behind and so have to face a double burden the following year. Jullien expressed surprise at the intimation that he wished to force an additional tax upon the people: why should he care how the work was performed, just so it was well executed and completed in time? In any case, most of his peasants preferred the tax, which was less inconvenient for them than were the required six days of unpaid labor for the peasants in Cypierre's généralité of Orléans. Jullien frankly saw no other way to encourage contractors to fix the roads than to guarantee them an advance payment from the pockets of the five wealthiest commoners in the affected parishes. He defended his subordinates, assured d'Amécourt that the "entrepreneurs" and supervisors were not allowed to abuse the corvéables on the roads, and concluded by stating that each intendant must adapt his policies to the character of his particular province.[105]

If on the one hand this correspondence illuminates some of the problems encountered by the king's administrators in eighteenth-century France, problems not always appreciated by the parlementaires, on the other hand it shows how one influential magistrate could respond to popular plaints by means other than the usual protest to Versailles.

Lefebvre d'Amécourt and his colleagues continued to interest themselves in the problem of the corvée during the waning years of the old regime. Thus, in 1780 the rapporteur d'Espagnac announced with satisfaction that "because the Court had deigned to occupy itself with the plaints of the corvéables," the tax levied upon many of them to subsidize work on the roads and bridges had been "moderated." At the same time, however, he counseled watchfulness to his associates: "the impost will have no limit from the moment that those assessing it and profiting from it think that they have nothing further to fear."[106] The Parlement continued to receive complaints from corvéables from time to time and sent them along to those in authority. Thus, during the summer of 1783 the intendant of the bridges and roads, Chaumont de la Millière, wrote to d'Aligre and d'Amécourt acknowledging receipt of the petitions they had sent along to him from the corvéables of the parish of Mareuil in lower Poitou. He promised to consult Blossac, intendant for that region, on the problem.[107]

The last spate of parlementary activity on the corvée issue came in 1785, probably in reaction to the consultations Calonne was having with the intendants in an effort to devise a plan for abolition of this duty.[108] Apparently in anticipation of legislation to this effect, President Joly de Fleury concocted a "compromise" edict that would have allowed parishes in the *pays d'élection* to convert their labor obligation (*corvée à bras*) but not their horses-and-vehicles obligation (*corvée de voiture*) to a money payment additional to the taille for the provisional period of one year.[109] He submitted two drafts along these lines to Lefebvre d'Amécourt during the summer, and the two men later planned in collaboration with First President d'Aligre to submit the project to the full Parlement and/or the government.[110] At least one government official who learned about the project, Chaumont de la Millière, described it derisively in a letter to an acquaintance as a "fine work" whose "substance came from M. Bertier [de Sauvigny] and whose style smacks of the First President." Not only was it an absurdity, he commented, but a pointless absurdity, because the corvée par adjudication was already established in most areas.[111] The proposed edict might indeed have been as impractical as Chaumont de la Millière suggested, but the very provisions he derided reflected unalterable parlementary concerns.[112] The corvée à bras would be temporarily replaced by a tax on all taillables, but a strict ceiling was to be placed upon the tax, and all commoners assessed ordinarily for less than ten deniers of taille or capitation were to be exempted. Strict limits were to be set upon how many wagons and horses the corvéables owed for the labor done by others, how far they would have to take their horses and wagons from home, and so on. Above all, the preamble to the second draft condemned administrative experiments that left communities at the mercy of greedy individuals in their midst or outside contractors, "entrepreneurs involved in all types of operations" who, uncontrolled by the wise measures of a uniform law, exploited the helplessness or simple-mindedness of the country parishioners.

Whether or not Chaumont de la Millière had been correct in attributing a role in this proposal to the intendant Bertier de Sauvigny, the parlementaires themselves let it drop after the vacations, and it was not until nearly the end of the following year that Calonne revived the troublesome issue of the corvée.[113] Still, President Joly de Fleury's abortive proposal in 1785 exposed concerns that the Parisian parlementaires had been articulating for nearly a decade. The magistrates' defense of the corvéable never extended during this period to a willingness to see the corvée itself abolished; yet their sympathy for those laboring on the kingdom's highways was sincere within limits imposed by a traditional view of ranks and obligations in society. Furthermore, the judges' very rejection of the principle of abolition of the corvée stemmed in part from their distrust of government operations and their animus against the taxation that always seemed to result from those operations. On this vital point, the parlementaires were espousing virtually everyone's cause in eighteenth-century France—to mention only one country in one period of time.

In summation, parlementary attitudes toward the middle and lower ranks of French society were as complicated as was the internal striation of the third estate itself. Whether championing the patrimonies of booksellers, pharmacists, and lemonade makers in the capital, remonstrating against unreasonable labors and novel taxes in the countryside, or defending consumers of all ranks everywhere, the men of the Parlement evinced a variety of concerns. They were judicial policemen of the ancien régime, obsessed with the danger of insubordination and riot. They were privileged proprietors defending the property of all Frenchmen. They were jurists who thought in terms of *corps et communautés* as well as in terms of individuals. They were parlementaires who would brook no challenge to their company's prerogatives. They were old-fashioned regulators who could not help but harbor suspicions of gens d'affaires and innovating government agents. And, last but probably not least, they were paternalistic humanitarians who prided themselves upon the role they played in articulating popular interests just as they prided themselves upon their championship of privilégiés and privileged institutions. It seems all too obvious to the modern eye that the magistrates' conception of popular interests was woefully inadequate, but the limited attention they devoted to those interests was nevertheless sincere. The parlementaires were tribunes of a myriad of conflicting interests that composed the ancien régime, and they were able to maintain that role until the fateful last years of the 1780s.

CHAPTER SIX

The Parlement and the "Pre-Revolution,"
1787–1788

On 29 May 1788 a Parisian barrister named Godard, in writing to an acquaintance, alluded to the emergence of three political factions at the capital and throughout the kingdom: the "Royalists," the "Parlementarians," and the "Nationals." He claimed that the latter two parties "were making common cause" and that the Nationals were hoping that the Paris Parlement, once triumphant over Keeper of the Seals Lamoignon, "would maintain the right principles."[1] Precisely what Godard's "right principles" amounted to is unclear; still, his reference to three factions and to an alliance between Parlementarians and Nationals could have characterized, and indeed may have mirrored, the internal politics of the Paris Parlement itself. While it would be exaggerating to say that the court's consensus on most public issues dissolved during 1787–88 under the pressures generated by the crown's financial crisis, there were undeniable strains within the company during this so-called pre-Revolution.[2] The leaders of the Grand' Chambre strove, as in the past, to justify the government's actions to the majority of their colleagues, while the latter, especially in the tumultuous assemblages of the Enquêtes and Requêtes, flaunted extreme parlementary pretensions or the Nationals' themes of public welfare and national regeneration. The disharmony previously limited to questions of judicial reform now plagued the Parlement in its consideration of most public issues; the final years of Bourbon absolutism were as troubled for the magistrates as for the sovereign whom they served.

There was a certain shift of energy and initiative from the older to the younger parlementaires during 1787–88. The guiding hand of the Grand' Chambre was weakened somewhat by death, retirement, and the unassertiveness of some of its members. Although Avocat-Général Séguier carried on as forcefully as ever, Procureur-Général Joly de Fleury died in December 1787 at the age of seventy-eight. His successor, his nephew Armand Guillaume Marie Joseph Joly de Fleury, was by all accounts undistinguished.[3] First President d'Aligre, already at odds with the government over his personal finances (see above, chapter 1), resigned late in 1788 and was replaced by the respected but ailing Lefevre d'Ormesson, who died early the following year. As for the other presidents à mortier on the Grand Banc, the youthful judge Etienne-Denis Pasquier noticed (and he later recalled) that they had "no striking merit and in particular no talent for oratory."[4] A similar situation prevailed among the regular counselors of the senior chamber. The king's rapporteur, the abbé Tandeau, joined on occasion with Lefebvre d'Amécourt, Ferrand, Outremont de Minière, and other grand' chambriers in support of government policy, but most of the court's veterans either sympathized with the vociferous opposition of the junior chambers or had a difficult time overawing it in the tempestuous debates of the tribunal's plenary sessions.[5] Moreover, contemporaries never tired of indicating judges of the senior chamber as well as members of the Enquêtes and Requêtes who were always ready to raise the standard of revolt against the government during this period. In this respect, grand' chambriers such as Robert de Saint-Vincent, Fréteau de Saint-Just, Abbé Le Coigneux de Bélabre, and Abbé Sabatier de Cabre resembled junior parlementaires such as Duval d'Eprémesnil, Huguet de Sémonville, Goislard de Montsabert, and Adrien Duport. In addition, the great majority of judges entering the lower chambers during the years after 1774 were extremely young, and there was an especially great influx of judicial novices during 1787–89.[6] These factors may well have complicated matters for the senior grand' chambriers as they strove to steer their company through the political storms of those years.

Yet, despite the stresses and strains within the Parlement during the last several years of its existence, there were strong underlying continuities as well. Indeed, the most inflammatory messages of the parlementary remonstrances, decrees, and oratory during 1787 and 1788 had either been enunciated as forthrightly in statements of the preceding thirteen years or at the very least had been implied in earlier statements. The following pages will argue that the leading grand' chambriers, and some of the most important antigovernment incorrigibles of the lower chambers such as Duval d'Eprémesnil, continued to hold traditional and therefore ambivalent views of the monarchy and the three estates and continued to patronize certain popular interests. The discussion will then focus upon two forms of parlementary extremism during 1787–88 and suggest that, even in these areas, the judges, young and old, were marking no sharp break with their recent past.

Monarchism, Raison d'Etat, and Property

Ambition as well as professionalism continued to orient some of the most influential parlementaires toward the monarchy. The best-documented example of the ambitious "royalist" in this period was Lefebvre d'Amécourt, who by 1789 had become fourth in seniority among the regular counselors of the Grand' Chambre.[7] D'Amécourt was one of the few magistrates who supported the abbé Tandeau's attempt to secure a fair hearing at the plenary session of 30 July 1787 for the proposed *sub-vention territoriale*, or tax on the lands of all three estates.[8] Soon after, according to a reliable witness, d'Amécourt joined several presidents of the Grand' Chambre in negotiating for the return of the Parlement from its exile at Troyes and in arranging for the extension of vingtième taxation in return for the government's withdrawal of the subvention territoriale. As part of the compromise, the indefatigible d'Amécourt once again became king's rapporteur in the Parlement![9] He was not alone in his ambitions, however. During April 1789 d'Amécourt was reportedly leagued with his long-time confidant, President Joly de Fleury, in an attempt to use the aging ex-minister Machault d'Arnouville to enter the government.[10] As late as the summer of 1789 the ambition of the two men was still a subject for Parisian gossip.[11]

But ambition was clearly not all. The parlementaires, especially those of the senior chamber, retained a strong professional identification with the monarchy. The aging and ailing procureur-général, Guillaume François Louis Joly de Fleury, demonstrated this remarkably when, in speaking at the Assembly of Notables in early 1787, he assailed Calonne's proposal to parcel out the royal domain in fiefs to be exploited under a feudal regime.[12] Joly de Fleury saw in such an arrangement disturbing principles "that could tend to weaken or pervert the maxim, immutable in France, that the king's domain is inalienable." In his accustomed fashion, Joly de Fleury asserted that it was his duty as the king's lieutenant in the Parlement to draw a line between the royal and feudal regimes and champion what belonged to the former. This meant, above all, declaring that the king's lands could under no circumstances be alienated as they might conceivably be under feudal contract. The procureur-général and his associates of the Grand' Chambre had enunciated much the same doctrine at the time of the dispute at Rheims eight years earlier. The complementary theme of a monarchical continuum in French history also reappeared here in the speaker's reference to the ancient collection of legal titles of royal domain. The chief of the king's men in the Parlement proclaimed in part that such legal titles had existed "under the first and second races" of French kings; that these titles had been scattered and lost during the troubles and usurpations of feudal times; and that in more modern times the French monarchs "had taken greater care of these titles, and had had them placed above the treasury of the Sainte Chapelle of the Palace [of Justice] at Paris that St. Louis had built." Although this sacred treasure of royal documents, titles, and charters had subsequently been moved to another stronghold within the Palais de Justice, continued Joly de Fleury, it had remained and would always remain under the protection of the Paris Parlement and in particular the procureur-général. Joly de Fleury and his successors would maintain that trust as they maintained their watch over the "rights of the Crown." The seasoned magistrate's identification with the crown could be stated in no more forceful a fashion.

Of course, professional self-interest was also very much at work here. The parlementaires who most ardently championed the centrality of monarchy in France were precisely those most aware of the company's utter dependence upon the continuation of monarchy. This awareness had in the late 1770s fathered parlementary misgivings about Necker's provincial assemblies; ten years later, Calonne's pending legislation on a more comprehensive network of provincial, district, and municipal assemblies aroused similar fears.[13] Here was the procureur-général discussing Calonne's reform at the Assembly of Notables early in 1787: "But can one in good conscience propose to the King that he renounce that exercise of the right of administering these provinces by his direct authority and give that function to a multitude of persons, who despite the best intentions, the most acute intelligence, the most active zeal, can never secure from their fellow provincials the most entire confidence, being in reality neither their mandatories nor their representatives, contrary to apparent insinuations?"[14]

Actually, Calonne's legislation firmly subordinated the projected provincial, district, and municipal assemblies to the intendants, but Joly de Fleury opposed even the most judicious administrative innovation. The traditional administrative arrangements had institutionalized Bourbon authority in the provinces by developing the regime of the intendants and enhancing the political role of the parlements, and that was what counted in Joly de Fleury's eyes.

Most of his associates shared his attitude, in 1787 as in the late 1770s. When Calonne's edict on the provincial assemblies was submitted by his successor Loménie de Brienne to the Parlement on 22 June 1787, several judges immediately objected to the vagueness of the terms of implementation of the new assemblies. On the recommendation of the young counselor Ferrand, who retold the story years later, the court registered the edict with the proviso "that the King would be most humbly implored to complete his good work and insure its stability by sending to his courts the promised regulations to be verified in the ordinary manner." This arrêté, which according to Ferrand passed "by an immense majority," reflected the old parlementary concern that, without strict control over the personnel, operations, and powers of such bodies, administrative innovation in the provinces might get out of hand—to the detriment of king, intendants, and parlements.[15]

It is only logical that the more seasoned jurists of the Grand' Chambre should have betrayed a similar conservatism with regard to the question of the Estates General. When several turbulent parlementaires accompanied their condemnation of "ministerial despotism" with a demand for the Estates General in 1787, the young magistrate Pasquier noted the pre-dominant reaction among the court's seniors: "The sober heads of the Grand' Chambre were troubled at the prospect. I could never forget what one of these old judges said to me then as he passed behind my bench and saw how enthused I was: 'Young man, a similar idea was often brought forward during your grandfather's time; this is what he always said to us then: "Messieurs, this is not a game for children; the first time that France sees the Estates General, she will also see a terrible revolution."'"[16] Such misgivings were perfectly consistent with what we already know about the senior judges' deeply rooted royalism.

What is less well known is that, even at this late hour, the court as a whole could distinguish explicitly between the old bugbear of ministerial despotism and the legitimate authority of the king. The most dramatic example in point was the Parlement's behavior at the tumultuous plenary session of 5 May 1788, which so closely preceded Lamoignon's judicial coup de force. One of the magistrates denounced to his fellows a clandestine publication that had the Parlement censuring "the enterprises of His Majesty upon the Magistracy rather than "the enterprises of the Ministers upon the Magistracy" in a decree of 3 May.[17] This incendiary squib was immediately referred to the parquet, and minutes later the court, upon the advice of Séguier, condemned it to be ceremoniously "torn and burned" at the foot of the Grand Staircase of the Palais de Justice. The parlementaires censured the work as "containing an insidious falsehood contrary to the respect due to the King, and designed to impute to the Court sentiments and expressions incompatible with its eternal and profound respect for the sacred person of the King." At the same session, Séguier denounced and demanded the suppression of another anonymous piece imputing disloyalty to the court; the suppression of this squib was accompanied by reiterated professions of loyalty to Louis XVI. Skeptical contemporaries might view such actions as last-minute politics designed to head off the heavy blows of the government, and as reflecting in addition the judges' hatred of their one-time colleague Lamoignon. The judges' action was assuredly both of these things, but it just as surely signified their desperate wish to stay in Louis's good graces and thus restore their old relationship with the crown.

As the preceding suggests, royalism in the Parlement was not confined to the Grand' Chambre. Indeed, it held sway among some of the most violent leaders of rebellion in the lower chambers, who shared their seniors' determination to distinguish between "ministerial despotism" and the legitimate authority of Louis XVI. If there was any acknowledged spokesman of the junior parlementaires throughout the late 1770s and 1780s, any standard bearer of revolt throughout the traumatic times of the "pre-Revolution" of 1787–88, it was surely Duval d'Eprémesnil. Yet, public and private papers alike make it absolutely clear that d'Eprémesnil's fundamental royalism remained as unshaken by events as did the royalism of the Joly de Fleurys and Lefebvre d'Amécourts and Séguiers of the Grand' Chambre. In a widely publicized pamphlet on the upcoming Estates General published in Paris toward the end of 1788, Duval d'Eprémesnil, though candidly confessing his attachment to the "just prerogatives of the Nobility and Clergy," just as forthrightly branded "ministerial despotism" as the "common enemy of the King and of the three orders." The king and the traditional social structure must remain; it was the perfidious innovations and arbitrariness of the king's ministers that must go.[18] Even more revealing, and convincing, is the unpublished correspondence from d'Eprémesnil to his wife during his Provençal exile in 1788. Over and over again in these letters the tribune of the parlementary opposition reiterated his fears that the king was being misled by his ministers and his hope that France could somehow return to an idealized situation in which there would be no despotic administrators between the sovereign and his subjects.[19] The subsequent collapse of the ancien régime only intensified d'Eprémesnil's allegiance to Louis XVI and to the monarchy. His parlementary colleague Ferrand later recalled d'Eprémesnil's anguish at "seeing the monarchy in flames" in 1789 and his vow to perish rather than see the crown utterly consumed.[20] As a matter of fact, this controversial parlementaire was to achieve a reputation as a zealous defender of the monarchy in the debates of the National Assembly that would eventually lead him to the revolutionary scaffold.[21]

A hardly less turbulent parlementaire of the Enquêtes was Huguet de Sémonville, and, in addressing his fellow judges on 16 July 1787 on the necessity of the Estates General, this ally of Duval d'Eprémesnil revealed a similar orientation.[22] He sought to allay the misgivings of many judges concerning the Estates General by reminding them how many times in past centuries this institution had supported French monarchs against the papacy, unruly provincial aristocrats, religious seditions, and other challenges to the crown and public tranquillity. The Estates General, he said, would enable the monarch to govern his realm with more efficiency and less abuse; surely it would not menace the monarchy itself. An anonymous work attributed to Huguet de Sémonville reinforced these sentiments by declaring that "France will remain a Monarchy, because that form of government is perhaps the sole form compatible with its wealth, its population, its extent, and the political system of Europe."[23] Something of the same orientation could be discerned in a long speech on the religious situation in France delivered in the Parlement on 9 February 1787 by another inveterate opponent of "ministerial despotism," Robert de Saint-Vincent.[24] An Adrien Duport, an Hérault de Séchelles, or a Le Peletier de Saint-Fargeau might cast off the claims and traditions of the ancien régime and enter wholeheartedly into a revolutionary career, but they seem to have been exceptions, at least among the articulate and influential judges. At the eleventh hour of the old regime, fidelity to the monarchist tradition continued to characterize parlementaires ranging from the cautious old men of the Grand' Chambre to some of the leading firebrands of the subordinate chambers.

Nevertheless, the parlementary advocacy of monarchy in France continued to be as ambivalent as ever. For one thing, it was predicated upon the distinction between the good, lawful sovereign (at this juncture, Louis XVI) and his evil and despotic ministers (Calonne, Brienne, and above all Lamoignon). All or nearly all of the judges subscribed to this distinction—as they showed on 9 May 1788 when every one of them signed collective and individual letters refusing service in Lamoignon's "Plenary Court" and condemning his comprehensive judicial reform.[25] These acts of collective and individual defiance climaxed months of rising tension between the ministers and the magistrates, months that had produced mounting frustration for Controller-General Loménie de Brienne and Keeper of the Seals Lamoignon and an outburst of increasingly radical decrees and proclamations from the pens of Duval d'Eprémesnil and other parlementaires.[26] On 3 May 1788, just six days before the magistrates' unanimous rejection of Lamoignon's judicial reform, the Parlement's propaganda on the kingdom's fiscal and constitutional crisis culminated in the famous arrêté purporting to list the "fundamental laws of the kingdom."[27]

It would have been manifestly impossible for Louis XVI and his ministers, steeped in the traditions of the French monarchy, to accept a constitutional catechism guaranteeing absolute tenure to magistrates, the absolute right of all sovereign courts in Paris and the provinces to reject "illegal" legislation, the periodicity of Estates General freely according (or refusing?) tax revenue to the government, all rights and liberties of the provinces, and rights of habeas corpus for all subjects. Louis XVI (let alone Henri IV, Richelieu, or Louis XIV) could not have accepted such a catechism in the spring of 1788, and the king responded swiftly enough with Lamoignon's coup de force two days later. As far as Louis was concerned, the Parlement's distinction between the lawful monarch and his despotic ministers made no sense. From the perspective of the Palais de Justice, however, it made all the sense in the world, mirroring though it did a nostalgic and hopelessly outdated vision of what monarchy in France should be.

And so Louis and Lamoignon in May 1788 launched their last attack upon the fractious parlementaires. That they ultimately failed was due to several things, none of which was more important than the government's continuing insolvency. But the question of royal finances brings us back to the other crucial element in the ambivalence with which the men of the Paris Parlement viewed the monarchy. If the parlementaires were officers of the crown trained to champion monarchy, they were also privileged landowners and tribunes of all other proprietors in their jurisdiction. It made no difference whether a seasoned veteran of the Grand' Chambre such as the procureur-général or an ardent rebel of the lower chambers such as Duval d'Eprémesnil or Goislard de Montsabert was speaking on the issue of taxation: the parlementaires as always opposed new forms and higher levels of taxation, or at the very least felt that new monetary tributes from the king's subjects necessitated constitutional concessions from the king.

Both Second President Lefevre d'Ormesson and Procureur-Général Joly de Fleury signaled the consistency of parlementary attitudes on this issue when they spoke out against Calonne's subvention territoriale at the first Assembly of Notables in early 1787. Joly de Fleury, after referring in his address to d'Ormesson's rejection of the proposed impost at an earlier session of the Assembly, seconded his colleague's opposition:

> I will be satisfied simply with having the honor to observe that . . . the privileges of the clergy and the nobility have merited in all times the greatest consideration because of their antiquity and that one has always had a similar consideration in matters of taxation for all the other privileged bodies of which the State is composed.
>
> Thus, as the new plan . . . would tend to destroy all privileges and prerogatives whatsoever since it would tax a portion of the fruits of all the lands . . . of all persons regardless of estate and quality . . .
>
> I think that the destruction of all these privileges and distinctions could have momentous consequences.[28]

The implications of such an attitude for the government were obvious to many, but apparently not to parlementaires such as Joly de Fleury. After all, he would have insisted, monarchical policies had so far been reconcilable with social hierarchy and privilege; why not, then, in the present and in the future? If monarchy meant everything to the judges, so, too, unfortunately for Louis and his ministers, did hierarchy, privilege, social order, property, and personal interest.

Calonne had not fixed the yield and duration of his subvention territoriale; when Loménie de Brienne took this impost over from his predecessor in the spring of 1787, he established its permanency but hoped to mollify the parlementaires and others by fixing its yield at an annual 80 million livres.[29] Yet, in addition to being permanent, Brienne's subvention territoriale would, like Calonne's tax, affect all classes of proprietors. It would also be levied as a lump sum on a given area, as was the taille upon commoners. This meant that rich proprietors might very well pay more than the poor, thus raising for the parlementaires the dread specter of the *contrainte solidaire*, which they had vainly tried to exorcise in so many past protests to the government.

Hence, the objections of Lefevre d'Ormesson and Joly de Fleury to

Calonne's tax were followed by a parlementary outcry against Brienne's proposal. The remonstrances of 26 July 1787 authored by the counselor Ferrand showed that nothing had changed since the controversy over Necker's readjustment of the vingtièmes:

> All taxation must be proportionate to need and must terminate with it. . . . the people must not increase their contribution except in the case where [government] expenses are reduced as much as possible. . . . as if such an impost was not already onerous enough in itself, its indefinite duration adds even more to its fearsomeness. Only too often have we seen taxes originally limited to a specified period extended because of State need or because of pretext; but we had never before seen a permanent tax established at the very time that the final liquidation of State debt seemed to be in sight.[30]

All wealth not required as public revenue for urgent public needs belonged to the taxpayers, declared the Parlement. Furthermore, as far as the public revenues were concerned, the king himself was merely the public servant who "dispensed" them, not a universal proprietor who could withhold such revenues for personal purposes.

The same message came from the redoubtable Duval d'Eprémesnil of the Enquêtes. On 13 August 1787, a week after Brienne had forced the jurists to register his legislation at a lit de justice, d'Eprémesnil persuaded his associates to issue an arrêté condemning the fiscal legislation and declaring its publication to be "clandestine," "null," and "illegal."[31] D'Eprémesnil's arrêté also fulminated against the abusive principle of the contrainte solidaire: "it is no less contrary to the primitive constitutions of the Nation . . . to see the Clergy and the Nobility subjected to a solidary contribution for the *Subvention territoriale*. . . . it is only in our days that we have seen the hatching of a system to render the Nobility and Clergy *solidaires* for an imposition that each person owes on his own revenue after a deliberation and consent without which all demanded commitments constitute an attack on property."[32]

D'Eprémesnil sensed the government's intention that from now on even rich and noble proprietors, and not merely the luckless taillables, should be held responsible for the raising of a certain amount of revenue; and he rejected this design outright. The contrainte solidaire as imposed upon certain rich taillables incidental to the corvée par adjudication had been bad enough; but to make nobles and clerics as responsible as commoners of the third estate for the raising of a given quota of tax revenue would be insulting to all members of the first two estates and perhaps disastrous for the wealthiest landowners. The Parlement's defiant arrêté of 13 August led almost immediately to its exile to Troyes. Although this banishment was later terminated by a compromise between ministry and magistracy involving withdrawal of the new impost and the reimposition of the old vingtième taxation, the parlementaires remained dissatisfied.[33] The following April Goislard de Montsabert of the Enquêtes denounced in plenary session the Brienne ministry's administration of the vingtièmes, and the company issued a stinging decree repeating all the old arguments against abusive and ever-increasing taxation.[34] Nothing had changed at the Palais de Justice, and nothing would change before revolution succeeded prerevolution and ushered in more radical reforms than even the parlementaires could have feared possible.

Could the magistrates advance any practical alternative to greater and more equitable taxation? As First President d'Aligre demonstrated in his tedious addresses at the First Assembly of Notables, and as the rapporteur Tandeau showed in his discussion of royal policies at the so-called *séance royale* of 19 November 1787, the parlementaires could still suggest nothing but *économie*, or in other words reduction of government expense, streamlining of bureaucracy, and publication of the government's accounts.[35] These were all valid and significant suggestions, but even when taken together they could not offer Louis and his ministers an escape from their dilemma. Parlementary ambivalence toward the crown on fiscal and constitutional matters was one of the factors that would lead both Parlement and crown to a demise amidst the flames of revolution.

The Conservative Vision of Society

All surviving evidence suggests that the judges' attitudes toward the three estates remained throughout the prerevolutionary crisis as ambivalent as their conception of the monarchy—and not just on the famous matter of the Estates General in September 1788. This was as true for Duval d'Eprémesnil's coterie of rebellious jurists as it was for the more cautious veterans of the court's senior chamber.

To be sure, the parlementaires vociferously defended the clergy and nobility against increased taxation during 1787–88; but they had always done so, and they had always shown a considerable degree of solicitude for "common" taxpayers too. Again, the procureur-général inveighed in 1787 against a proposal submitted to the notables to abolish serfdom where it still existed in France; but this instinctive defense of a seigneurial right in no way contradicted Joly de Fleury's awareness of how such vestigial institutions were continuing to retreat before the advance of royal (and parlementary) authority.[36] In addition, the parlementaires as conservative jurists opposed Lamoignon's sharp curtailment of seigneurial justice in 1788; but they had always been the first to proclaim the subordination of seigneurial justice to royal justice in the hierarchy of tribunals.[37] Professional and personal considerations motivated the judges to champion the privileges of nobles and clerics (and of many commoners as well) but simultaneously precluded them from favoring any sweeping concession of power to any one of the estates in French society.

Certainly the veterans of the court, raised on the Gallican tradition, could not have countenanced any such concession to the first estate. Necker's administrative experiments in the provinces had already sparked parlementary protests against clerical pretensions, and so had the specter of reviving Jesuitism in 1777. Shortly after the Parlement's return from its exile at Troyes in September 1787, First President d'Aligre sent Louis XVI an indignant memorandum entitled "Motive of hatred against the Parlements," in which he listed the parties allegedly guilty of slandering the magistracy to discredit it in royal eyes.[38] Among these culpable parties were "the clergy whose pretensions are often beaten back, the Court of Rome whose enterprises have so frequently necessitated the protest of the Magistrates," and "a powerful order that [attempts] incessantly to reappear and that believes the Parlements to be the authors of its destruction and an obstacle to its return"—a transparent allusion to the Jesuits. These factions, d'Aligre assured the king, "had an equal interest in debasing the Parlements" but could not possibly do so as long as the courts "had the consideration of the Sovereign and the people." In an impassioned speech of 9 February 1787, Robert de Saint-Vincent, renowned Jansenist of the Grand' Chambre and confidant to Duval d'Eprémesnil, had already made an oblique attack upon the proscribed Society of Jesus.[39] The charges of the two men reflected a latent suspicion of clerical motives in their company that could very well have been fanned into open hostility by any striking revival of clerical influence in political and administrative affairs.

The parlementaires were similarly wary of the second and third estates—and they revealed this well before their fateful decree of September 1788 concerning the Estates General. For example, in the very process of decrying Calonne's intention to levy additional taxation upon the nobility, the Parlement's procureur-général Joly de Fleury early in 1787 voiced his fear that such a policy could conceivably touch off increased political activity in the provinces.[40] Was it not possible, asked Joly de Fleury of the Assembly of Notables, that the nobles would react by demanding that they be exempted as in earlier centuries from *all* compulsory taxation and that all "notables" would demand permission to assemble in the provinces to discuss the issue? And could the sovereign afford to permit such assemblages? In asking such questions, Joly de Fleury was betraying the same institutional conservatism that had moved him and his fellows of the Parlement in earlier years to portray Necker's provincial assemblies as potential vehicles of aristocratic or bourgeois ambition. Such conservatism led the jurists during June 1787 to seek guarantees from Louis XVI concerning the "stability" of the provincial, district, and municipal assemblies whose establishment they reluctantly endorsed.[41]

The comments of the Joly de Fleury brothers on the new bodies were particularly revelatory of unchanging social conservatism at the Palais de Justice. The procureur-général observed that, "in general, all assemblies of residents excite much fermentation in minds, which renders them constantly tumultuous." Clearly he was worried about the potential for subversion of the social order in such institutions, as at another point in his papers he saw such assemblies as producing a "dangerous confusion of ranks . . . regarded as contrary to the constitution of the Monarchy."[42] But this very concern led him to view the first two orders as stabilizing elements in a sacrosanct hierarchy and not as a resurgent political elite. The assemblies, he remarked, might detract from the respect "due to persons of the order of the clergy and the order of the nobility," and this would be most unfortunate because clerics and nobles "contributed eminently by their example toward containing the French people in the sentiments of love and submission they naturally show to their sovereigns."[43] Clerics and nobles who led the way by loving and submitting to their sovereign conformed very neatly to the parlementary vision of an upper class that would never dream of fomenting a revolution in the state.

But it was President Jean Omer Joly de Fleury who most clearly articulated this conservatism. In April 1787, with the question of the provincial assemblies once more in the air, the president obtained from an acquaintance information concerning the administration of three small *pays* in southeastern France: Bresse, Bugey, and Gex.[44] From this information, President Joly de Fleury fashioned a memorandum lauding the assemblies already established in these regions as models of provincial administration.[45] His comments upon the roles of the three estates in these bodies were particularly significant. On the one hand, he noted, "the third Estate is composed only of deputies of the cities and principal market towns." There was no separate contingent representing an "order of peasants," as in Sweden. "It would be dangerous for France to create a fourth order; such an innovation would be contrary to the constitution of the monarchy." On the other hand, the king's authority in these assemblies was preserved by utilization of the third estate contingent to neutralize the clerical and noble contingents. The vote of the third estate was doubled in the governing councils of these assemblies. Consequently, the "clergy and nobility could not dominate proceedings, because the third Estate has two [votes] against their two, resulting in tie votes. The king's authority is undiminished because it retains the power to decide issues." The president summed up his remarks in a manner strikingly reminiscent of past parlementary statements on the issue of the provincial assemblies. "What is principally to be feared is that the clergy and nobility might have too much influence, or that one day they might have none at all." Like his brother, Jean Omer Joly de Fleury was continuing to bear witness to the parlementary conceptions of balance among the three estates and undiminished royal authority.[46]

A question then naturally arises as to the court's motives in recommending, in the notorious decree of 25 September 1788, that the upcoming Estates General follow the precedent of 1614, implying equal contingents representing the three orders and voting by order rather than by head.[47] The decree was hugely unpopular and almost overnight cost the Parlement the adulation it had won by its opposition to ministerial despotism. Yet the impression that the judges on this occasion betrayed their solidarity with a resurgent and reactionary aristocracy seems untenable. For one thing, many of the seniors in the court had already expressed reservations regarding the various institutional innovations of the prerevolutionary crisis. At the first Assembly of Notables in early 1787, the procureur-général voiced fears not only about the establishment of a national network of provincial assemblies but also about the revival of provincial estates.[48] In June of the same year, the arrêté on the provincial assemblies moved by the counselor Ferrand and passed, according to him, by "an immense majority" bespoke the magistrates' fears of too much innovation in provincial administration. At about the same time, if we can believe the memoirs of another judge, Pasquier, the "sober heads of the Grand' Chambre" were profoundly troubled by calls from less judicious parlementaires for the Estates General. At least among the more cautious members of the court, there was little enthusiasm in 1787 for provincial assemblies, provincial estates, or that ultimate of ultimates, the Estates General.

It is undeniable that after the court's return from its exile at Troyes late in the year, and after the dramatic séance royale of 19 November that led to the arrest of the duc d'Orléans and two of the judges, the Parlement adopted a progressively more radical stance on constitutional matters and seemingly warmed to the idea of the Estates General.[49] Yet, again, in view of the reservations voiced by the more seasoned jurists the year before, it seems logical to believe that the court's increasing radicalism reflected the pressure of events (i.e., the intensifying confrontation with the crown) rather than sympathy for the political pretensions of the aristocracy.

As it turned out, the issue was taken out of the Parlement's hands altogether in 1788 by the government's decision to summon the Estates General the following year. The magistrates were now facing a fait accompli, and it was natural for them to rally to their company's conservatism by invoking the example of the last convocation of the estates in their fateful decree of 25 September. Two participants in the session of 25 September later attempted to explain the motivation behind the decree, and both underscored the conservative reflex of the court on that day. In an address at the opening session of the second Assembly of Notables on 6 November 1788, President Lefevre d'Ormesson had this to say: "Already, by examining certain historical documents in the archives of Justice, your Parlement, Sire, has noted these two characteristics [i.e., regularity and convenience] in the form utilized in 1614, and has resolved to call for it. It will merit all Your Majesty's attention, not only because of the legal formalities with which it is accompanied to preserve the rights of all and those of each person; but because its origin is ancient, and because . . . it seems to demonstrate the correct custom and habit of the Monarchy."[50]

"Regularity," "correct custom and habit," and antiquity itself were what had counted in the court's invocation of 1614, according to Lefevre d'Ormesson. It is perhaps even more telling that one of his junior colleagues of the turbulent Enquêtes, Guy Marie Sallier, should much later have recalled a similar motivation behind the decree of 25 September:

> The preceding ministry had imprudently stated that there was no sure rule for the convocation, composition, and constitution of the Estates General. . . . The parlement judged that all would be lost, if no one could refer to certainties on this very important point . . . and although it must certainly forfeit its popularity in pronouncing against democracy, it did not hesitate at this juncture to fulfill its duty by recalling the fundamental principles on the legal form of the Estates General; the last which had been convened, that of 1614, seemed . . . to be the appropriate model, having been perfectly regular.[51]

Again, that concept of "regularity." The magistrates' constitutional radicalism may have been one of the factors leading to the government's convocation of the Estates General in 1789, but when forced to regard this convocation as a certainty the Parlement's immediate response was to fall back upon what seemed to be the prescription of the past.

Yet the arrêté of 25 September 1788 was itself overturned a scant ten weeks later by a coalition of rebels in the Grand' Chambre and Enquêtes. This action raised the possibility for some contemporaries, and has for some later historians as well, that Duval d'Eprémesnil and his confidants were taking up the cudgels in defense and furtherance of an aristocratic "revolt" or "revolution" as the prerevolutionary crisis wore on. But once again, the available evidence points to quite a different interpretation.

To be sure, from the time of his entry into the Parlement in 1775, Duval d'Eprémesnil had (along with his seniors of the Grand' Chambre) ardently championed existing aristocratic privilege. But he had been equally quick (notably during the controversy involving the vicomte de Noé) to ridicule and reject novel aristocratic pretensions and to champion monarchy and magistracy. D'Eprémesnil maintained this orientation throughout the prerevolutionary crisis, though his royalism was often obscured by his fanatical opposition to ministerial despotism. He achieved notoriety in August 1787 with his arrêté condemning Brienne's fiscal edicts and the lit de justice of 6 August that had compelled their registration. But if this arrêté restated the Parlement's traditional opposition to heavier and demeaning taxation of aristocratic lands, it also drew the traditional picture of a passive provincial aristocracy. D'Eprémesnil's arrêté asserted, in part, "that the gentleman retired upon his domain, whom it is important for the State to cherish, finds himself virtually chased from his château or humble cottage, when he has to pay taxes upon the habitation that is only an object of continual expense and upkeep for him. . . . it is however that retreat that makes him love France, [it is] an asylum where, sheltered from ambition, he can practice virtue, in preserving for his posterity the inheritance that the preceding reigns did not at all begrudge his ancestors."[52] Like his seniors of the Grand' Chambre during the debate over Necker's provincial assemblies, Duval d'Eprémesnil in August 1787 idealized the country aristocrat as a quiescent soul wishing nothing more than to be left in peace to cultivate his lands and his rustic virtues. D'Eprémesnil, and the majority of judges who endorsed his statement, knew very well that to defend an aristocracy living off its lands and its privileges was in no way to jeopardize the influence wielded in judicial and political affairs by the sovereign courts.

D'Eprémesnil established himself even more firmly in the government's bad books during the spring of 1788 when he sponsored a series of increasingly radical protests and decrees against governmental absolutism. The most famous of these, the arrêté of 3 May, which purported to list the "fundamental laws" of the kingdom, was speedily answered by Lamoignon's drastic reforms of justice and by d'Eprémesnil's own prolonged imprisonment. Ten weeks after the Parlement's triumphant reinstatement in the fall of 1788, the irrepressible d'Eprémesnil signaled his return to Paris by securing passage of the decree of 5 December over the scandalized opposition of the more mature parlementaires.[53] It was this *Arrêt sur la situation actuelle de la Nation* that overturned the decree of 25 September and signified to some the onset of aristocratic revolution within the king's foremost parlement.

The decree of 5 December 1788 attempted in part to restore the Paris Parlement's shattered popularity by disavowing the reference in the decree of 25 September to the 1614 Estates General.[54] It proclaimed the court's incompetence to determine the number of delegates speaking for the third estate, referred this matter to the wisdom of the king, and implored Louis to convene the Estates General as soon as possible. Furthermore, it accepted the equality of the three orders in matters pertaining to taxation. On the other hand, d'Eprémesnil's decree did not repudiate the principle of the "vote by order," thus leaving open the possibility of clerical and noble domination of the assembly. The decree also pointed toward a close cooperation between the sovereign lawcourts and the regularly convened Estates General in the future. The royal ministers, answerable to the Estates General and parlements for their actions, were to be judged by the latter for any malfeasance in office alleged against them by the former. Finally, the parlements would ratify no impost, indeed, no law of any kind that lacked the sanction of the Estates General.

A most eminent historian has characterized this decree as "the supreme expression of that project for an aristocratic revolution that Duval d'Eprémesnil, Huguet de Sémonville, Robert de Saint-Vincent, the abbé Lecoigneux had meditated during the entire crisis."[55] Yet in the pamphlet he had published on 7 December to explain his position on the Estates General, d'Eprémesnil revealed quite different intentions.[56] He conceded candidly that he still supported "the just prerogatives of the Nobility and the Clergy," but he just as candidly endorsed "the liberty of all, the property of all, the rights of all." However, the really crucial argument in his pamphlet was the argument for the traditional "vote by order" in the Estates General:

> Separate voting by the orders, each one so independent of the others that two of them cannot bind the third, that is the Constitution. . . .
> That having been stated . . . carefully preserve that vote by order, and preserve the orders' independence, and you will fortify them . . . against Ministerial enterprises, in giving affairs the time to ripen, individuals the time to become acquainted with each other, and Intrigues the time to betray themselves. . . .
> Oh! of course it is important that the Third Estate be fortified by number; but against whom? Against the Nobility and the Clergy? Not at all. . . . Against whom or what, then? It is essential to say it. Against Ministerial Despotism, common enemy of the King and of the three orders.[57]

Thus, went on d'Eprémesnil, let the nobility and clergy not take fright if the third estate should gain a more numerous representation in the upcoming assembly than ever before: the "general interest," the "interest of public liberty," required it. Clearly, d'Eprémesnil continued to be obsessed by ministerial despotism—he had, after all, just recently been incarcerated by the government—and he sought a balance and collaboration among the three orders that could preserve the monarchy and "public liberty" while defeating the purposes of despotic ministers. President Joly de Fleury had sought a similar balance and collaboration in his remarks upon the provincial administrations in Bresse, Bugey, and Gex; Avocat-Général Séguier voiced similar sentiments in a lengthy speech to the plenary session of 17 December 1788; and one of Duval d'Eprémesnil's alleged coconspirators, Huguet de Sémonville, had revealed the same brand of constitutional royalism as early as 16 July 1787 in urging a summons to the Estates General.[58] If there was a single parlementaire who voted for the decree of 5 December 1788 in the belief that he was helping to initiate or to further an aristocratic revolution, he has not left so much as an "anonymous" squib documenting that intention.

There undoubtedly was a certain kind of "revolution" harbored in the pronouncements of Duval d'Eprémesnil and the deans of the Grand' Chambre, and a different variety altogether in the rapturous enthusiasm of the youthful judges of the lower chambers who put the decree of 5 December 1788 over the top. Both varieties will be treated presently. For the moment it suffices to observe that parlementary radicalism during the prerevolutionary upheaval had little to do with the novel pretensions of any specific social order in French society.

The Patronization of Popular Interests

In between the remonstrances, decrees, lits de justice, séances royales, and banishments of the 1787–88 period, the men of the Parlement continued to dispense justice and enforce law and order within their jurisdiction. Toward the privileged associations and commoners of the third estate they evinced an unchanging paternalism and in so doing underscored the continuity of magisterial concerns.

To be sure, the court's response to the public had its expediential side as always. The decree of 5 December 1788, with which the majority of parlementaires tried in some measure to undo the damage wrought by the decree of 25 September, made it perfectly clear that some within the Parlement could court the public favor. Again, when the magistrates returned triumphantly from exile for the last time in September 1788, they immediately launched an inquiry into the public disorder then plaguing the capital. According to the young jurist Sallier, the inquiry sought to accuse the police, and not just the populace, of excessive behavior.[59] The court issued two decrees on 23 September: the first ordered a further investigation into complaints of excessive use of force by the police, and the second, though reverting to the familiar parlementary ban against seditious gatherings in the streets, also enjoined the municipal police to exercise their duties with moderation. Commented Sallier, "the people understood that decree so well, that the tumultuous mobs and merrymaking continued as before, and the Parisian guard was regularly insulted during the evenings."[60] Yet the Parlement's willingness to play politics during such a crisis was limited. The hugely unpopular decree of 25 September 1788 invoking the 1614 Estates General was passed almost unanimously, whereas the emendatory decree of 5 December could prevail only over the strenuous opposition of the more mature parlementaires. The magistrates were attuned to public opinion, but they were attuned to tradition and professionalism as well.

Nevertheless, tradition and professionalism dictated among other things the articulation of public grievances. The judges resumed their championship of specific interests when in August 1787 they protested Loménie de Brienne's stamp tax. The tax would affect daily transactions in commerce as well as litigation in the courts; predictably, the Parlement was pressured by interests ranging from the booksellers and printers to the consular justices (who dealt with lawsuits in business matters) to oppose the legislation.[61] Although the tribunal was forced to register the stamp tax along with the subvention territoriale at the lit de justice of 6 August, it struck back at both pieces of legislation a week later in Duval d'Eprémesnil's arrêté of 13 August. It is interesting that the arrêté stressed the abuse of solidarité even more in connection with individuals to be affected by the stamp tax than in connection with nobles and clerics to be affected by the new land tax. Brienne's stamp tax would assess fines against all those associated with documents discovered to have been left unstamped and hence untaxed, and in his arrêté d'Eprémesnil enlarged upon the hardship likely to result from such a provision:

> it is cruel to imagine that the lonely citizen living in the most profound solitude, the tranquil merchant working to increase the national commerce, by augmenting his personal trade, the wise practitioner consecrating his labors to the repose of families and to the service of his fellow citizens, all face the appalling prospect of finding themselves linked together in a common chain and subject, at the moment when they thought themselves least to be subject, to solidary fines, whose weight . . . would swallow up the totality of innocent as well as of guilty individuals.[62]

The arrêté also explained how the stamp tax would augment expenses in litigation through its levy upon documents used in justice. This polemic of 13 August 1787, taken in its entirety, points up once again the variety of interests in society championed by the parlementaires.

During these final years of its existence, the Parlement was especially active in its traditional role of surveillance over the supply of bread to Paris. The judges continued to be actuated in part by their unconquerable suspicion of gens d'affaires and their enterprises. It was all very well, in criticizing Brienne's stamp tax, to laud "the tranquil merchant working to increase the national commerce"; it was quite another thing to endure the fraudulent maneuvers of grain merchants that could affect the bread supply in the capital. Not that the bread issue had to reemerge before the court would resume its old assault against gens d'affaires. During the summer of 1787, several magistrates' denunciations of royal legislation according additional rights to the Compagnie des Indes and the Compagnie des Eaux de Paris spurred the Parlement to renew its attacks upon unnamed "speculators" and "capitalists" involved in the Indies trade and fire insurance operations at Paris.[63] Nonetheless, the judges were particularly concerned that there be sufficient provisions of grain in the marketplaces of the capital. Procureur-Général Joly de Fleury signaled this concern at the first Assembly of Notables by expressing some doubts about Calonne's proposed declaration reestablishing freedom in the grain commerce within the kingdom.[64] The Parlement eventually ratified this legislation under Brienne's ministry, on 25 June 1787, but the Parisian bookseller and diarist S.-P. Hardy reported the following day that the vote for registration had been close.[65] The judges, observed Hardy, remembered the troubles of 1776 only too well and feared that "rich and powerful persons" would once again profit from economic freedom to speculate upon the popular misery. The court's ratification of the act may have been facilitated by the fact that it authorized the provinces, upon request of their assemblies or estates, to suspend the export of grain in times of scarcity. However this may be, the following year was to see the court attentive once more to complaints from the marketplaces in the capital.

On 26 November 1788 the Parlement, reacting to the latest rise in the price of bread, ordered the officers of the parquet to determine the causes of the price increase. On 13 December, Séguier, speaking for the king's men, cited the meteorological disasters and poor harvests of the past two years but characteristically put the primary blame for the price increase upon the grain trade legislation and the cupidity of speculators and monopolists profiting from its provisions:

> It is not wheat that is lacking in France; the immoderate thirst for profit is making it disappear; insatiable avidity is monopolizing it; the opulent speculator still desires to enrich himself at the expense of the food of the poor and the indigent. . . . It is time to recognize the danger of a confidence that is too blind, to reestablish a legal surveillance, to order an . . . inspection in moments of crisis, and to avert through a wise and rigorous police the inconveniences and the abuses of an inhuman freedom that must every time victimize the people.[66]

A committee of judges was immediately appointed to recommend action on the matter, and five days later the court issued a decree reinforcing all existing regulations on the provisioning of grain to Paris.[67] The decree restated the familiar ban against "any fraudulent maneuvers tending to impede the provisioning of the markets," and it enjoined the suppliers of grain to the markets to follow all existing regulations set by the police, "so that the first hour of business in the markets will be for the small consumers . . . the second for the bakers, the third for the merchants." The jurists ordered their decree to be sent "wherever need required" and to be read out and published by all subordinate tribunals in the jurisdiction.

The court also instructed its newly created first president, Lefevre d'Ormesson, to raise the matter when he journeyed to Versailles to urge an expeditious convocation of the Estates General. Accordingly, on 21 December Lefevre d'Ormesson asked Louis XVI to devote special attention to "the subsistence of the People, at a time when the severity of the season has reinforced the other causes of the high price of grain and the other misfortunes that make the People suffer." The judges could only do so much in this vital area: "Your parlement, Sire, has done the most that it could do by issuing a decree that proscribes the schemes and intrigues employed to augment those high prices. The same decree establishes in the marketplaces the order of preference most favorable to poor persons unable to provide for themselves, but, Sire, there are insights of a superior order, resources more general and efficacious for the curing of such distressing ills."[68] In brief, the first president requested legislation to assure the poor their daily bread; but Louis, already under the shadow of the impending Estates General, put off Lefevre d'Ormesson and his colleagues with a noncommittal assurance of continued royal vigilance on the problem.

The magistrates, however, did not let the matter rest there. During February 1789 the syndics representing the Parisian bakers were called to the court to explain what they knew about the factors prolonging the economic crisis. In response, the syndics provided "some very curious information on wheat prices in France and in other countries and on the maneuvers employed to raise prices."[69] The parquet continued its own investigation of the problem, and as late as 4 April 1789 the Parlement approved reiterated protests on the bread issue to be delivered at Versailles. The matter was soon removed from the court's cognizance altogether with the convening of the Estates General and its transformation into the National Assembly. Nevertheless, it is evident that the parlementaires remained to the bitter end as faithful to their traditional defense of popular interests as to their advocacy of monarchy, hierarchy, and privilege.

A Revolution for Magistracy or for the Common Weal?

To say that the Parisian parlementaires championed a perplexing variety of special interests till the end of their professional days would be true. Yet the growing dynamic of constitutional radicalism in the parlementary viewpoint requires just as much attention, not only because of its implications for the magistrates' support of the Bourbon regime but also because it suggests a crucial subjectivity in attitudes at the Palais de Justice. The more the magistrates declaimed against ministerial despotism and trumpeted the rights of all Frenchmen, the more they seemed (or at least some of them seemed) to be elevating themselves and their institution and profession above the other individuals and institutions and professions of French society. Their public roles were so central and their zeal to fulfill them so great that by the time of the crisis of 1787–88 the parlementaires, already self-appointed censors of the monarchy, had almost become self-appointed oracles of a brave new world in France. The only question was, which new world would it be? Would it be, as some of the court's deans and prominent rebels seemed to augur, a world in which the magistracy fulfilled an unprecedented role? Or would it be, as the youthful idealists of the Enquêtes and Requêtes hoped, a world in which the public-spiritedness of all would somehow achieve the common weal?

Both visions arose from the Parlement's increasingly radical stance on constitutional questions. As this study has shown, that radicalism was no sudden offspring of the prerevolutionary crisis: it had been germinating for years prior to 1787. Thus, the judges had invoked the principle of taxation with representation in their protests of 1778 against Necker's policies on the vingtièmes. Thus, they had recommended the publication and, by implication, the public discussion of municipal and state financial records in the protests of the Calonne period. Thus, throughout the reign of Louis XVI, they had spoken of the king's subjects as "citizens" and of the king's realm as a "nation." Thus, Duval d'Eprémesnil had reportedly called as early as January 1777 for a convocation of the Estates General.[70] But it was only in the crucible of events attending the prerevolutionary crisis that the magistrates were driven to a systematic indictment of Bourbon absolutism. It was only then that they dignified the prerogatives of the three orders, the magistracy, and the provinces as "fundamental laws" of the kingdom. It was only then that they similarly exalted the rights of habeas corpus of all Frenchmen. And it was only then that they insisted not only upon the convocation of the Estates General but also upon the future periodicity of that assembly of the kingdom. The recognizable landmarks along the way of this incendiary propaganda were the court's protests against the séance royale of 19 November 1787, the statement of 3 May 1788 on the "fundamental laws," and the decrees of 25 September and 5 December 1788 on the upcoming Estates General.

From the chrysalis of this constitutional radicalism, formulated in response to the policies of Louis's ministers, issued the judges' visions of the future. On the one hand, there was the glorification of the magistracy's role in the state. This was reflected in the judges' tendency to apotheosize their profession as a sort of "fourth estate" in France. Here, for instance, was Séguier addressing his colleagues on 17 December 1788 on the matter of a "subversive" pamphlet favoring the third estate:

> That truly seditious work has only been so widely distributed in the present circumstances . . . to set the People in opposition to the Clergy, Nobility, and Magistracy, at the moment when the Clergy . . . is ready to honor itself by sacrificing its immunities; at the moment when the Nobility . . . seems to abandon its privileges and to retain only the honorific distinctions that constitute its essence; at the moment when the magistrates congratulate themselves for having been restored to their functions to exercise the worthiest ministry of the organs of the law, in inviting citizens of all ranks to occupy themselves with the misfortunes of the Fatherland.[71]

The clergy and nobility recommended themselves to Séguier by their apparent relinquishment of their useful "privileges" and "immunities," while the magistrates would continue to exercise critical duties. At about the same time that the Parlement's senior avocat-général was lauding his profession in the Palais de Justice, his colleague Lefevre d'Ormesson was lauding it even more extravagantly at the second Assembly of Notables:

> What would we be able to do for the Nation . . . if, around the Throne, and under the very shadow of the royal power, there had not been preserved that pure and free liberty of the Magistracy, which knows no fear other than that of being corrupted by flattery and complacency! . . .
> What happy security for Magistrates accustomed at all times to discerning the interests of the State through the least interests of the citizens . . . and to keeping constantly in view that long perspective through which one sees in advance . . . the public fortune extending with equal consistency through the most distant centuries![72]

The magistracy, declared the first president, "serves the Sovereign, defends the Fatherland, rules the citizens, and guards the sacred treasury of the Kingdom's Laws against all violation." The first president reiterated these sentiments on behalf of his company when, on 21 December, he urged Louis XVI to expedite the convening of the Estates General.[73]

The swelling pride and pretensions of the parlementaires appeared ever more strikingly in two crucial decrees of 1788. The arrêté of 3 May drafted by Duval d'Eprémesnil listed, as two of the "fundamental laws" of France, "the irremovability of the magistrates from office" and "the right of the courts to verify in each province the laws of the King and to order their registration only if they are reconcilable with the constituting laws of the province as well as with the fundamental laws of the State."[74] The two "fundamental laws" that immediately followed in d'Eprémesnil's litany of 3 May 1788 guaranteed all citizens the right to be brought immediately after arrest before "competent judges" and to be tried by "their natural judges." Here was an additional feather in the magisterial cap, as well as an essential right for all Frenchmen—though to Louis XVI and his ministers the arrêté of 3 May 1788 must have appeared to be parlementary pretension run wild.

But worse was yet to come. The d'Eprémesnil decree of 5 December 1788, in addition to wooing public opinion by disavowing the reference of 25 September to the 1614 Estates General, projected a future partnership between the regularly convened Estates General and the sovereign courts. Royal ministers accused of malfeasance in office "directly involving the entire Nation" would be judged in the courts, though such procedure must not "prejudice the rights of the Procureur-Général" of the Paris Parlement in such cases. Moreover, the sovereign courts would cooperate with the Estates General in legislating future taxation and indeed future ordinances of all kinds.[75] An increment in the judicial and political powers of the courts was obviously to accompany the new powers accorded the kingdom's future assemblies.

By this time the Parlement was past being able to provoke responses from Versailles, as the convocation of the Estates General was now occupying ministerial minds. But there was considerable indignation and concern within the Parlement itself as a result of d'Eprémesnil's decree of 5 December: the counselor Ferrand later recalled it as "that arrêté which demonarchized France," and the marquis de Bouillé learned from his neighbor in the country, Lefevre d'Ormesson, that the more moderate parlementaires had strenuously resisted its passage.[76] Yet most of the moderate judges who opposed the decree of 5 December had voted for the equally inflammatory arrêté of 3 May, and the more perceptive among them must have realized that their espousal of parlementary prerogatives and criticism of government actions had long been pointing in this direction. The first president himself, in declaring grandly to the Notables that the magistracy served the sovereign, defended the Fatherland, and ruled the citizens, had testified arrestingly to magisterial pride and pretension on the eve of revolution in France.

But there was also the other vision to be found among the parlementaires, that heady expectation of national regeneration and that conviction that the judges should help achieve it by subordinating their narrow interests to the common weal. This was a nebulous vision; indeed, it was more a mood of euphoric idealism than a program for the future. Its main adherents were the youthful jurists of the Enquêtes and Requêtes, urged on by the unemployed barristers, lawyers' clerks, and law students of the court's *basoche.* One of these enfants terribles of the Parlement, Guy Marie Sallier, later recalled their mood and activities during 1787–88:

> The young men of the enquêtes came to the assemblies of the chambers as if they were going into combat, and everything assured them victory in a contest that was too unequal. Besides the advantage of number, they had greater unity than those whom they assailed. They even had some partisans in the Grand' Chambre. Their orators pleaded a cause susceptible to those eloquent moments that always produce a great effect upon large assemblies. They seemed to be defending the rights and interests of the nation. Their courage could not fail to win over ardent youths who passionately embraced generous sentiments and did not bother to open their eyes to dangers.[77]

Or, as Sallier's confrere Pasquier said of himself and his fellows, "as soon as our interest was clearly put in the balance, we thought that the most glorious thing we could possibly do would be to sacrifice that interest to what we regarded as the public welfare."[78] Both men also recalled the contempt in which they and their comrades had held their seniors of the Grand' Chambre: they had ridiculed them as old men still slavishly obedient to tradition and to the whims of arbitrary government.

The politics of 1787 and 1788 gave these precocious juniors of the Parlement repeated opportunities to resist Authority, whether they perceived it in the government or in the parti ministériel of the Grand' Chambre. They must have been putty in the hands of judges such as Duval d'Eprémesnil, Robert de Saint-Vincent, Huguet de Sémonville, and Adrien Duport who collaborated within and without the Parlement to raise opposition to the government.[79] They were the ones whose numbers in the court assured passage of the constitutional pronunciamentos of 1787 and 1788; they were the ones in particular who saw d'Eprémesnil's arrêté of 5 December 1788 as a chance, perhaps the last chance, for the Parlement to redeem itself in public opinion. They may have failed throughout to notice—or at least failed to point out—that d'Eprémesnil, Robert de Saint-Vincent, and some of the other veteran firebrands of the court had not yet jettisoned the old parlementary pretensions. They certainly could not prophesy that the gathering political storm would eventually sweep away their institution and bear them and their more conservative colleagues onto divergent paths, later to be labeled by some as "revolutionary" and "counterrevolutionary." They were aware only that they rejected the "despotism" of the government and advocated the rights and liberties of all Frenchmen. And in this they were not totally different from their older or less ardent associates. Nearly all the justices of the Parlement shared to one degree or another a rejection—a momentous rejection—of arbitrary government.

In concluding this analysis of parlementary attitudes during the pre-revolutionary crisis of 1787–88, it is well to stress again how little those attitudes differed from the outlook of preceding years. The traditional leaders of the Grand' Chambre, and apparently most of the court's prominent "rebels" as well, attempted as always to reconcile their deeply rooted royalism with their·advocacy of all other interests in the state. Consequently, their stance toward the crown continued to be as ambivalent as their stance toward the three estates in French society. The judges also continued to suspect gens d'affaires of trafficking in the vital foodstuffs of the lower classes and until the very end displayed a genuine if limited concern for Frenchmen of humble station. Their protracted confrontation with the crown during most of 1787 and 1788 tempted the more reckless parlementaires, and at times even the seasoned veterans of the Grand' Chambre, to espouse a constitutional radicalism. Under the increasing pressure of events, such a radicalism was all too likely to flourish and to engender in turn extreme claims for the judiciary and for an idealized public interest. Nevertheless, such radical tendencies had long been foreshadowed in parlementary pronouncements upon public issues. Their slow germination through the years from 1774 to 1786 and sudden maturation during 1787 and 1788 suggested, as did many other developments of those years, that the French sovereign must soon be called to a revolutionary reckoning with his subjects.

The Parlement in History

When the winds of revolution blew in France, they scattered the Parisian parlementaires far and wide.[1] Certainly, the fates of some of the better-known judges suggest such a dispersion.[2] President Joly de Fleury, Avocat-Général Séguier, the former first president d'Aligre, and counselor Lefebvre d'Amécourt emigrated and refused to have anything to do with the new France. Other parlementaires absented themselves from France during the dangerous 1790s but made their peace with postrevolutionary regimes and carved out new careers under their aegis: the young counselor Ferrand, for instance, served as a minister of state under the Restoration. Among the younger jurists of the Enquêtes, perhaps Etienne-Denis Pasquier savored the greatest success after the revolutionary 1790s: he held high office under Napoleon and Louis XVIII, became the duc de Pasquier under Louis-Philippe, and died in 1862 at ninety-five, three-quarters of a century after his brief but unforgettable tenure in the tumultuous Enquêtes of the Paris Parlement. Yet other parlementaires decided, for better or worse, to weather the storm in France. Probably the majority of judges survived the political vicissitudes of the Revolution, as did the majority in the nobility to which they nearly all belonged, by simply lying low in the country through most or all of the period. Still, there were notable exceptions: the decision to follow a revolutionary career brought some fame to Adrien Duport, execution to Hérault de Sechelles, and a revolutionary's martyrdom to Le Peletier de Saint-Fargeau, while the decision to champion the ancien régime brought a conservative's martyrdom to that inveterate leader of the parlementary opposition, Duval d'Eprémesnil.

Thus, the maelstrom of the 1790s held a variety of fates in store for the erstwhile members of the most prestigious lawcourt of the old regime. What they would always share in common, however, was precisely their past service in an institution that had contributed signally to the unleashing of the revolutionary upheaval in France. This fact necessitates some final observations concerning the outlook of the Parisian parlementaires during the years from 1774 to 1789 and their role in the onset of the French Revolution.

For one thing, a careful study of what the judges were saying and doing during those years yields the impression of a group of conservative professionals trying resolutely to dispense the same justice and to articulate the same plethora of interests as always. Thus, the judges fought to preserve corporate prerogatives and petty judicial perquisites and remained faithful to the mechanistic and at times cruel ways of French justice; yet, they conscientiously dispensed that flawed justice year in and year out and revealed on occasion a genuine sympathy for Frenchmen caught in the toils of litigation or ministerial power. Thus, the judges championed the centrality of the monarchy in French history, law, and administration; yet, simultaneously, they championed property and individual rights and privilège in such a fashion as to challenge the practical continuation of that monarchy. Thus, the judges defended social hierarchy and order: but their very allegiance to that hierarchy and order meant that, although they would endorse existing privilege, they would in no wise endorse aristocratic, middle-class, or popular pretensions that could upset the traditional balance of institutional forces composing the old regime. Such consistent conservatism with regard to justice, governance, and the social order may have frustrated spokesmen of the king and of the three estates at times; yet, in maintaining this posture the parlementaires claimed that they were according satisfaction to all legitimate interests—even to the lowly consumers, corvéables, and taillables of their jurisdiction. The judges' conservatism was consistent both in that it embraced all interests in France and in that it extended through the 1770s and 1780s to the very hour of revolution in 1789.

And yet, not entirely consistent. The magistrates' pronouncements harbored a germ of constitutional and corporate radicalism from the earliest days of Louis XVI's reign, and that radicalism blossomed spectacularly during the "prerevolutionary crisis" of 1787–88. On the one hand, the men of the Parlement differentiated between what they regarded as the king's legitimate authority and what they continually censured as ministerial despotism. In opposing various government policies of the period, which they portrayed as manifestations of the latter phenomenon, the judges invoked the principles of individual freedom and of national consultation prior to taxation and in so doing advanced an ideal of constitutional government well-nigh irreconcilable with monarchy as practiced in France. On the other hand, the parlementaires, in their exercise of critical judicial and political functions and in their pride at fulfilling those functions, acted and spoke at times as if their company and profession were exempt from the restraints supposedly operating upon all estates and institutions (including the crown) in France. Parlementary pretensions were so hardened by the court's unremitting strife with rival tribunals and with the government that by the time of the crisis of 1787–88 the more ambitious judges saw the public weal as contingent upon an even greater role for their company in public affairs. The more responsible grand' chambriers were also moving in this direction, though probably unwillingly and only in response to the inexorably growing pressure of events. They must have sensed that their company's defiance on public issues was sapping the king's government, and their awareness of their own dependence upon the crown may have surfaced when that unnamed veteran of the senior chamber supposedly warned the youthful Pasquier about the perils of revolution in France. However, as long as the Parlement remained loyal to its defense of conflicting interests in state and society, and as long as it remained loyal to its sense of its own importance, its defiance of a government seeking always to increase revenues would continue to harden.

These conclusions regarding the parlementaires seem to suggest several things about the magistrates' impact upon France at this critical time. First, the parlementaires most likely had a "social" impact in spite of their own social conservatism. Insofar as the Parlement continued to the bitter end to apotheosize its own role and defend the concept of privilège that had always helped justify that role, it probably encouraged *all* estates and institutions to flaunt their ambitions before the weakening crown. In a more specific sense, the Parlement's invocation of the Estates General of 1614 may have had its "social" effect in 1788 by crystallizing latent tensions between conservative and reactionary nobles and clerics, on the one hand, and liberal nobles and clerics and the third estate, on the other.[3] The overall effect of the judges' invocation of privilege, magisterial prerogative, and constitutional precedent, therefore, was to testify to the ruinous proliferation and harsh dissonance of special interests in France.

Yet all these "social" dynamics pointed ultimately to a constitutional problem, the increasing isolation of the French monarchy from its more articulate upper- and middle-class subjects. For the special interests and pretensions (including parlementary pretensions) that were rotting eighteenth-century France had been especially able to flourish in the absence of a national consensus upon common rights, obligations, and purposes that only representative government could provide. The jurists of the Paris Parlement came to define this constitutional issue and proclaimed it to all who would listen. They did so by admitting the rhetoric of representative government into their protests, by celebrating individual liberty as a fundamental law of the kingdom, and by inveighing against lits de justice and lettres de cachet. The indictment of absolutism returned by the parlementaires acquired a national resonance during 1788, brought Louis XVI to his knees, and made the Revolution of the following years possible.

The conclusions of this study will provide small reassurance to those accustomed to viewing the men of the Paris Parlement merely as irresponsible critics of the crown, or as sponsors of an aristocratic resurgence, or as politicians hypocritically mouthing popular propaganda. Moreover, those interpretations of the Revolution's origins stressing "class" revolts—or at least stressing an initial aristocratic revolt led by the Parisian judges—now must seem somewhat less credible than before. Perhaps the provincial judges could be more easily worked into such a causal construct; but their attitudes have yet to be explored. Admittedly, the present study cannot by itself supply an alternative explanation of the coming of the French Revolution. Yet it would counsel perhaps a greater emphasis upon the constitutional breakdown of the 1780s as defined in the preceding paragraphs. It would, in other words, suggest that the king's alienation from his most articulate subjects and their lack of consensus among themselves were at bottom the factors most responsible for the crisis of the late 1780s and would present the greatest challenge to French statesmen as they and their country stumbled into an era of unprecedented change.

The Paris Parlement would not long survive in these new times. Nonetheless, it unquestionably served as witness to the past and augured something of the future as the Great Revolution got underway. The Parlement had marched hand in hand with the monarchy out of the troubles of the Middle Ages, and in its very last years of existence it was still reaffirming the centrality of the monarchy to French life. However, in those same last years the parlementaires were also conjuring up the new rights of the nation and the individual as well as the old rights of estates, provinces, and corporations as they opposed what they and many other Frenchmen regarded as arbitrary government. In doing so, they unwittingly helped sound their own death knell and that of the ancien régime in general; but they were also helping to ring in a new regime. Consequently, as flawed as the Parlement was by its inheritance from the past, it contributed to the evolution of public life in France, and some of the concerns it voiced have long survived that traditional society that many of its members never really wanted to abandon.

Notes

INTRODUCTION

1. Marcel Marion, *Histoire financière de la France depuis 1715*, vol. 1, passim; idem, *Le Garde des Sceaux Lamoignon et la réforme judiciaire de 1788*.
2. Pierre Gaxotte, *La Révolution française*, p. 81.
3. Michel Antoine, ed., *"Le Mémoire" de Gilbert de Voisins "sur les cassations,"* introduction; idem, *Le Conseil du roi sous le règne de Louis XV* (Geneva: Droz, 1970), pp. 271–73, 571–97.
4. Alfred Cobban, *A History of Modern France*, 1:67.
5. William O. Doyle, "The Parlements of France and the Breakdown of the Old Regime, 1771–1788," pp. 415–58.
6. John Gagliardo, *Enlightened Despotism* (New York: Thomas Y. Crowell, 1967), pp. 33–34, 52–53, 64.
7. Alexis de Tocqueville, *The Old Regime and the French Revolution*, pp. 54–55, 59.
8. Jules Flammermont, *Les Remontrances du Parlement de Paris au XVIIIᵉ siècle*, 3:xlvi–xlvii.
9. Jules Flammermont, *Le Chancelier Maupeou et les Parlements*, pp. 289, 394.
10. Hippolyte Monin, *L'Etat de Paris en 1789*, pp. 88–89, 103–104.
11. Henri Carré, "Turgot et le rappel des Parlements."
12. Henri Carré, *La Fin des Parlements, 1788–1790*, pp. 17–19.
13. Elie Carcassonne, *Montesquieu et le problème de la constitution française au XVIIIᵉ siècle*, esp. chap. 6.
14. Roger Bickart, *Les Parlements et la notion de souveraineté nationale au XVIIIᵉ siècle*; Daniel Mornet, *Les Origines intellectuelles de la Révolution française, 1715–1787* (Paris: Armand Colin, 1933), esp. pp. 433–35.
15. Jean Egret, *Louis XV et l'opposition parlementaire, 1715–1774*, esp. pp. 182–228.
16. Jean Egret, *La Pré-révolution française, 1787–1788*, pp. 325–37, 351–61.
17. Jules Michelet, *Histoire de la Révolution française*, vol. 1, introduction.
18. Albert Mathiez, *The French Revolution*, trans. Catherine Alison Phillips (New York: Russell and Russell, 1962), pp. 7–8, 24, 31.
19. Georges Lefebvre, *The French Revolution*, 1:88.
20. Albert Soboul, *The French Revolution, 1787–1799*, trans. Alan Forrest and Colin Jones (New York: Vintage Books, 1975), pp. 28, 37, 91, 111.
21. Franklin L. Ford, *Robe and Sword*, esp. pp. 246, 251.
22. R. R. Palmer, *The Age of the Democratic Revolution: A Political History of Europe and America, 1760–1800*, 2 vols. (Princeton, N.J.: Princeton University Press, 1959), 1:458–65.
23. J. François Bluche, *L'Origine des magistrats du Parlement de Paris au XVIIIᵉ siècle*. Bluche followed up his genealogical dictionary with a general discussion of the Parisian magistrates, *Les Magistrats du Parlement de Paris au XVIIIᵉ siècle*.
24. Jean Egret, "L'Aristocratie parlementaire française à la fin de l'ancien régime," pp. 1–14.

25. These citations are from Bluche, *Les Magistrats*, pp. 138, 288–89, 382.
26. J. H. Shennan, *The Parlement of Paris*, esp. pp. 110–48.
27. The question of the magistrates' ultraprivileged status is taken up at greater length in chaps. 1 and 4, herein.
28. Chap. 4, herein, discusses manifestations of this attitude in the eighteenth century.
29. Shennan, *Parlement of Paris*, p. 147.
30. For some of the leading salvos in this assault, see: Alfred Cobban, *The Social Interpretation of the French Revolution*; George V. Taylor, "Noncapitalist Wealth and the Origins of the French Revolution," *American Historical Review* 72 (January 1967):469–96; Denis Richet, "Autour des origines idéologiques lointaines de la Révolution française," pp. 1–23; William O. Doyle, "Was There an Aristocratic Reaction in Prerevolutionary France?" pp. 97–122; and Colin Lucas, "Nobles, Bourgeois, and the Origins of the French Revolution," pp. 84–126.

CHAPTER I

1. These remarks on the origins and competence of the Parlement are based on Marcel Marion, *Dictionnaire des institutions de la France aux XVIIe et XVIIIe siècles*, pp. 422–33, and J. H. Shennan, *The Parlement of Paris*, pp. 9–28, 78–85.
2. Shennan, *Parlement of Paris*, p. 79.
3. On the social and professional privileges of the Parisian parlementaires, consult Franklin L. Ford, *Robe and Sword*, pp. 27–29, 66–67.
4. J. François Bluche, *Les Magistrats du Parlement de Paris au XVIIIe siécle*.
5. These payments are discussed at greater length in chap. 3, herein, in connection with the parlementary debates over reform of the judicial system.
6. The development of specialized chambers within the Parlement is discussed thoroughly by Shennan, *Parlement of Paris*, pp. 14–28.
7. Thus, the term Grand' Chambre designated both the court's central chamber in the Palais de Justice and the senior personnel dispensing justice in that chamber. Plenary sessions held in the Grand' Chambre included the solemn convocations of the Cour des Pairs; in addition, the princes of the blood, peers of the realm, "honorary" magistrates, and other illustrious personages might be present when one of their number was party to a lawsuit.
8. The court's official records at the Archives nationales reveal that during these years the first president usually chose sixteen judges to serve on these committees: twelve grand' chambriers and the four deans of the four chambers of Enquêtes and Requêtes (Arch. nat., X^{1B} 8965–89, passim).
9. Bibl. nat., MS Nouv. acq. fr. 945, p. 238.
10. See, for example, Henri Carré, *La Fin des Parlements, 1788–1790*, pp. 11–12.
11. In this period, at least, the court's ten *présidents à mortier* in the senior chamber succeeded to the first presidency in order of seniority. The *mortier* was the cap or bonnet worn by these judges in court.
12. For d'Aligre's ancestry and career, refer to J. François Bluche, *L'Origine des magistrats du Parlement de Paris au XVIIIe siècle*, pp. 58–59.
13. See, for example, A. M. de Lescure, ed., *Correspondance secrète inédite sur Louis XVI, Marie-Antoinette, la cour, et la ville, de 1777 à 1792*, 1:296. For further substantiation of this point, see below, n. 38.
14. Comte Jacques-Claude Beugnot, *Mémoires, 1793–1815*, 1:117. For a corroborating opinion, see Abbé Jean-François Georgel, *Mémoires pour servir à l'histoire des événements de la fin du XVIIIe siècle*, 2:129.
15. Carré, *La fin des Parlements*, p. 11. The first president might have to entertain the king or distinguished foreign guests at his own *hôtel* and his own expense. He was also expected to receive his colleagues of the Parlement

lavishly on Saint Martin's night every November following the return of the full company from the annual vacations.

16. *Etat nominatif des pensions sur le trésor royal, imprimé par ordre de l'Assemblée nationale*, 1:5, 36.
17. For the ancestry and professional career of this parlementaire, consult Bluche, *L'Origine des magistrats*, pp. 259–61.
18. Lescure, *Correspondance secrète*, 2:295–96. See also Jacob-Nicholas Moreau, *Mes Souvenirs*, 2:375.
19. Carré, *La Fin des Parlements*, p. 12.
20. On the Joly de Fleurys in the eighteenth century, consult Bluche, *L'Origine des magistrats*, pp. 220–21.
21. *Etat nominatif*, 1:98.
22. Georgel, *Mémoires*, 2:130–31.
23. According to Jacob-Nicholas Moreau, usually a trustworthy source, President Joly de Fleury and his intimate from the Grand' Chambre, Lefebvre d'Amécourt, unsuccessfully urged the aged ex-minister Machault d'Arnouville to emerge from retirement and form another ministry—which would presumably have included these two parlementaires. Moreau, *Mes Souvenirs*, 2:381–83.
24. The careers of several members of this famous eighteenth-century robe family are treated at length in Paul Bisson de Barthélémy, *L'Activité d'un procureur général au Parlement de Paris à la fin de l'ancien régime*.
25. The judges were also assisted by a small army of clerks, notaries, ushers, etc. For information on Séguier's parentage and career, refer to Bluche, *L'Origine des magistrats*, pp. 386–87.
26. Examples of such unfavorable commentary are Georgel, *Mémoires*, 2:130–31, and Beugnot, *Mémoires*, 1:61. However, a more positive assessment of Guillaume François Louis Joly de Fleury's career in the parquet of the court is given in Barthélémy, *L'Activité d'un procureur général*, pp. 36–38, 81–82.
27. Even Beugnot, who, for one, was loath to concede oratorical brilliance to Séguier, admitted the common admiration of "his erudition and the soundness of his judgment" and the assertion of some that "he was the ultimate model of the good, old school of oratory." *Mémoires*, 1:59–60.
28. *Etat nominatif*, 1:144.
29. On the careers and lineage of these three magistrates, see Bluche, *L'Origine des magistrats*, pp. 382–83, 254, 393, respectively. The king's rapporteur, a kind of political agent in the court, should not be confused with the judicial rapporteurs who were appointed in litigation to evaluate the evidence of the litigants and suggest judgments to their fellow magistrates.
30. Georgel, *Mémoires*, 2, pp. 129–30.
31. Alexandre-Marie-Léonor de Saint-Mauris, prince de Montbarey, *Mémoires autographes*, 3:272–73.
32. In his *Souvenirs*, 2:381–82, Moreau referred to d'Amécourt's cooperation with Bertin in 1761 to help avert a confrontation between the crown and several parlements. Moreau, (2:90) described him as "friend and confidant of M. de Maurepas" and claimed that the latter had given the former advance news of the reinstatement of the old magistracy in 1774; Lefebvre d'Amécourt flatteringly chronicled Maurepas's long career in his own papers: Bibl. nat., MS Nouv. acq. fr. 22111, fols. 7–13. See Jean-Louis Giraud Soulavie, *Mémoires historiques et politiques du règne de Louis XVI*, 3:137–38, for d'Amécourt's alleged circulation of a pamphlet attacking Turgot during the latter's ministry, in the hope of obtaining a ministerial portfolio for himself. For letters detailing Lefebvre d'Amécourt's intrigues against Necker and alleging his political ambitions, see Lescure, *Correspondance secrète*, 1:319, 377; although this source alone would be suspect, its portrayal of d'Amécourt's ambitions agreed with all other contemporary accounts. And see above, n. 23.
33. Indeed, subsequent chapters will point up occasions upon which Lefebvre

d'Amécourt more or less authored his company's remonstrances himself. Preliminary drafts of these formal protests are preserved among his papers at the Bibliothèque nationale.

34. *Etat nominatif*, 1:404.
35. On Pasquier, see Bluche, *L'Origine des magistrats*, pp. 339–40, and Carré, *La Fin des Parlements*, p. 12.
36. On Sauveur, see Bluche, *L'Origine des magistrats*, p. 385, and Carré, *La Fin des Parlements*, p. 12. Pensions also went at times to the substitutes of the *gens du roi* and younger offspring of illustrious robe families, but the lion's share of royal gratuities fell to the leading grand' chambriers.
37. This memorandum, and the controversy prompting it, are discussed in chap. 2, herein.
38. Indeed, relations between the first president and the government were strained during the 1780s by d'Aligre's refusal to reimburse the crown for a *rente viagère* and a judicial post for his son, both of which had been granted earlier by the government. Under the threat of forfeiture of his office, d'Aligre finally honored his debts to the government in 1786. Arch. nat., K 163, letters of 5 and 11 August 1786 between d'Aligre and Keeper of the Seals Miromesnil; Louis Petit de Bachaumont, *Mémoires secrets pour servir à l'histoire de la république des lettres en France, depuis 1762 jusqu'à nos jours*, 23:255, 257. See also Beugnot, *Mémoires*, 1:117.
39. On this magistrate's social origins and career, see Bluche, *L'Origine des magistrats*, pp. 234–36, and Marcel Marion, *Le Garde des Sceaux Lamoignon et la réforme judiciaire de 1788*, passim.
40. In 1768, for instance, Lamoignon wrote secretly to Louis XV, complaining of "corruption" in his company and pledging his absolute fidelity to the interests of the crown. For this letter, dated 28 February 1768, see Bibl. nat., MS Fonds fr. 6877, fols. 1–2. See also Jacques-Mathieu Augeard, *Mémoires secrets de J.-M. Augeard*, pp. 76, 85, and Marion, *Le Garde des Sceaux Lamoignon*, pp. 10–12.
41. On Robert de Saint-Vincent, refer to Bluche, *L'Origine des magistrats*, p. 372; on Fréteau de Saint-Just, p. 187. The latter was to be one of Lamoignon's allies in the judicial reform controversy of 1783–84. On Abbé Le Coigneux de Bélabre, see Siméon-Prosper Hardy, *Mes Loisirs*, 7:854 (Bibl. nat., MS Fonds fr. 6686); see also Bachaumont, *Mémoires secrets*, 28:260. On Abbé Sabatier de Cabre, see Antoine François Claude, comte de Ferrand, *Mémoires*, p. 33.
42. Sources for these statistics: Bluche, *L'Origine des magistrats*, passim, and the *Almanach royal* for the years 1770 and 1776.
43. On the Enquêtes and Requêtes, consult Marion, *Dictionnaire des institutions*, p. 425, and Shennan, *Parlement of Paris*, pp. 14–28, 65–66.
44. It was known, officially and technically, as the Chambre des Requêtes du Palais. Its members long insisted that they were simultaneously parlementaires and holders of special commissions to dispense the civil justice associated with royal letters of *committimus*.
45. Bibl. nat., MS Nouv. acq. fr. 945, p. 238.
46. *Almanach royal* for 1776; A. de Roton, *Les Arrêts du Grand Conseil portant dispense du marc d'or de noblesse*; and Jean Egret, "L'Aristocratie parlementaire française à la fin de l'ancien régime," pp. 1–14.
47. On Duval d'Eprémesnil, refer to Henri Carré, "Un Précurseur inconscient de la Révolution," pp. 349–73.
48. Moreau, *Mes Souvenirs*, 2:416–17.
49. For example, he figured prominently in the mesmerism craze that swept the capital in the 1780s. See Robert Darnton, *Mesmerism and the End of the Enlightenment in France* (Cambridge, Mass.: Harvard University, 1968).
50. According to de Roton, *Les Arrêts du Grand Conseil*, p. 469, he was of very recent nobility; according to Carré, *La Fin des Parlements*, p. 3, he was seigneur of extensive lands near Le Havre.

51. For a sample of conflicting contemporary opinions on Duval d'Eprémesnil, see Bon-Pierre-Victoire, baron de Bésenval, *Mémoires*, 1:336, 2:317; and Paul Filleul, *Le Duc de Montmorency-Luxembourg*, p. 273.
52. Filleul, *Le Duc de Montmorency-Luxembourg*, p. 272.
53. On Goislard de Montsabert, see de Roton, *Les Arrêts du Grand Conseil*, pp. 368–69, and Carré, *La Fin des Parlements*, p. 271.
54. His *Mémoires*, referred to above in n. 41, appeared in 1897; his *Testament politique* was published at Paris (like the *Mémoires*) much earlier, in 1830.
55. See Georges Michon, *Essai sur l'histoire du parti feuillant: Adrien Duport* (Paris: 1924); and de Roton, *Les Arrêts du Grand Conseil*, p. 207.
56. See Louis-Philippe, comte de Ségur, *Mémoires ou souvenirs et anecdotes*, 1:371.
57. For this testimony by the duc de Montmorency-Luxembourg, see Filleul, *Le Duc de Montmorency-Luxembourg*, p. 292.

CHAPTER 2

1. See Bibl. nat., MS Nouv. acq. fr. 22110, fols. 2–4. Quoted from d'Amécourt's unpublished "Journal des principales époques du règne de Louis XVI."
2. Bibl. nat., MS Joly de Fleury 1028, fol. 268.
3. Arch. nat., X¹ᴮ 8965, session of 12 November 1774. Most of the proceedings are reproduced in Jules Flammermont, *Les Remontrances du Parlement de Paris au XVIIIᵉ siècle*, 3:232–55. The following citations are from the latter source.
4. Ibid., pp. 236–37.
5. Ibid., p. 239.
6. Ibid., pp. 239–40.
7. On the presidial courts, see E. Laurain, *Essai sur les Présidiaux*, and Edouard Everat, *La Sénéchaussée d'Auvergne et siège présidial de Riom aux XVIIIᵉ siècle*. The crown's chronic need for revenue had been one obvious motive for this creation of new judicial offices and honors.
8. For the history and specific judicial competence of this tribunal, consult Marcel Marion, *Dictionnaire des institutions de la France aux XVIIᵉ et XVIIIᵉ siècles*, pp. 265–66.
9. Flammermont, *Remontrances*, 3:252.
10. Ibid., pp. 252–53.
11. Ibid., p. 249. On other occasions, however, the Parlement, in assailing the rival tribunal, failed to mention the Estates General and characterized the Grand Conseil as a mere tool of ministerial policies.
12. Ibid., p. 250. The Cour des Aides judged lawsuits involving the assessment and collection of royal taxes such as the *taille*, the *aides*, and the *gabelle*. It judged such cases in last resort.
13. The comte de Provence had sounded this warning in a memorandum submitted to the government earlier in 1774. The memorandum had argued against the recall of the old magistracy. Jean-Louis Soulavie reproduced it in his *Mémoires historiques et politiques du règne de Louis XVI*, 2:207–208. The young Louis XVI, however, influenced by Maurepas and others and desirous of popularity, had ignored his brother's advice.
14. Arch. nat., X¹ᴮ 8965, sessions of December 1774 and January 1775.
15. *Ordonnance du Roi*, November 1774. For the full text, see François André Isambert et al., eds., *Recueil général des anciennes lois françaises*, 23:50–57.
16. According to Pidansat de Mairobert in his *Journal historique du rétablissement de la magistrature*. The two volumes of this work are numbered 6 and 7: they follow five earlier volumes of commentary on Maupeou's judicial coup de force put out by the same author. Pidansat de Mairobert's rendition of events in the parlementary sessions of this period is confirmed in part by

the court's records in the Archives nationales and is thus cited several times in this chapter. On the plenary session of 2 December, see 6:358–59.

17. These representations can be most easily consulted in Flammermont, *Remontrances*, 3:255–64.

18. Ibid., p. 258.

19. Ibid., p. 260.

20. Mairobert, *Journal historique*, 7:69–71. The official minutes of this session state that the assembly, by a vote of 102 to 42, rejected Orléans's proposed response to the king—probably because it was deemed too provocative. Arch. nat., X[1B] 8965, session of 20 January 1775.

21. For this arrêté, see Flammermont, *Remontrances*, 3:266–67.

22. For instance, individual parlementaires (especially Duval d'Eprémesnil) continued to raise controversial issues in the court's plenary sessions, and the Parlement several times registered legislation only after making reiterated protests to the king.

23. Bibl. nat., MS Joly de Fleury 488, fol. 84.

24. It was clear that the Grand Conseil as a sovereign court could and indeed must register whatever royal acts were germane to its functions. It was less clear, however, that this tribunal could upon its own initiative compel all presidial courts in the kingdom to register and publish such acts. Hence, the friction between the Grand Conseil and some of the presidials in 1775.

25. For examples of these complaints and charges, see Bibl. nat., MSS Joly de Fleury 480, fols. 176 ff., and 486, fols. 245–84. On the relationships among the provincial tribunals in this period, see also Philip Dawson, *Provincial Magistrates and Revolutionary Politics in France, 1789–1795*, pp. 63–65.

26. Bibl. nat., MS Joly de Fleury 480, fol. 178[2].

27. See the *Gazette de Leyde* during this period; see also Bibl. nat., MS Joly de Fleury 1064, fol. 263 ff.

28. Laurain, *Essai sur les Présidiaux*, p. 90.

29. A. M. de Lescure, *Correspondance secrète inédite sur Louis XVI, Marie-Antoinette, la cour, et la ville*, 1:90, 111.

30. *Gazette de Leyde*, 12 August 1777.

31. *Edit du Roi, portant règlement pour la jurisdiction des Présidiaux* (Versailles, August 1777). The full text is given in Isambert et al., *Recueil*, 25:84–92.

32. The Grand Conseil discerned in this legislation a "system that [gives] to the Parlements an unqualified superiority over the Bailliages, the Sénéchaussées, and the Presidials and forges among these courts and tribunals an indissoluble chain of power and subordination." Arrêté of 20 August 1777, Bibl. nat., MS Joly de Fleury 486, fols. 145–46. It was ironic that the presidials, having refused (at least in several cases) to register royal acts upon the order of the Grand Conseil, now found themselves forbidden to make a similar demand of inferior courts within their own jurisdictions!

33. *Lettres patentes du Roi, concernant les appels des causes à l'audience de la Grand' Chambre du Parlement* (Versailles, 11 December 1780). See Isambert et al., eds., *Recueil*, 26:398–402.

34. Bibl. nat., MS Joly de Fleury 522, fols. 352 ff.

35. For d'Amécourt's reflections on this matter, see Bibl. nat., MS Nouv. acq. fr. 22108, fols. 20–21.

36. For a copy of this polemic, entitled *Monsieur Neker à Monsieur d'Aligre*, see Bibl. nat., MS Joly de Fleury 522, fols. 360–60[5].

37. At least, the Parisian bookseller and diarist S.-P. Hardy was to report several years later that the younger judges of the Enquêtes had been aroused over the issue. Disappointingly, no direct evidence from the junior parlementaires themselves seems to have survived. On the comments of Hardy, a generally reliable source for parlementary matters, see below, pp. 46–47.

38. For this excerpt, and the entire text of the Joly de Fleury commentary, see Bibl. nat., MS Joly de Fleury 522, fols. 334–35.

39. Ibid., fol. 335.
40. Ibid.
41. J. François Bluche estimated that during the three years from 1758 to 1760, the average grand' chambrier earned, through gages and service in the Tournelle, 1,550 livres but lost 1,595 livres due to capitation and dixième over the same period. This resulted in an actual deficit of 45 livres. The situation twenty years later could not have markedly improved, given the continuing bite of royal taxation. But of course this calculation, as Bluche pointed out, ignored two factors of importance for the fortunes of the senior magistrates: the fees they received from daily activity in the Grand' Chambre and their handsome revenues from rentes and estates. Bluche, *Les Magistrats du Parlement de Paris au XVIIIe siècle*, pp. 168–72. *Vacances* are not to be confused with the *vacances* or annual recess of the court during September and October or with the Chambre des Vacations that administered justice in the absence of the full personnel during those months.
42. Whereas the vacations were evaluated strictly in the Enquêtes and Requêtes upon the number of hours employed in special professional services, the grand' chambriers tended to calculate their vacations on the basis of arbitrary estimates of how long their consideration of appointements "should" take. D'Aligre as first president considered himself present at all conferences compensated by vacations and so drew large fees from this source. Furthermore, he and the other members of the parti ministériel were in a position to arrogate the choicest plums among judicial assignments to themselves.
43. On this particular episode, see Bailey Stone, "The Old Regime in Decay: Judicial Reform and the Senior *Parlementaires* at Paris, 1783–84," *Studies in Burke and His Time* 16 (Spring 1975): 245–59.
44. See Félix Faulcon, *Correspondance*, 1:175–76, 290.
45. Mairobert, *Journal historique*, 6:395, 7:79.
46. See S.-P. Hardy, *Mes Loisirs*, 3:20 (Bibl. nat., MS Fonds fr. 6682), for a report of 23 January 1775 on the debates within the Parlement.
47. See Bon-Pierre-Victoire, baron de Bésenval, *Mémoires*, 3:1–52, for the most complete contemporary account of the parlementary debate over judicial reform during 1783–84. Bésenval, a prominent officer in the French army and the Swiss Guards, had long been close to Lamoignon and to Lamoignon's father before him.
48. Henri Carré alleged, without specifying his source, that Lepeletier de Rosambo, Bochard de Saron, and Le Peletier de Saint-Fargeau allied themselves with Lamoignon but that the other presidents of the Grand Banc supported the court's leadership. *La Fin des Parlements, 1788–1790*, p. 29.
49. Arch. nat., X^{1B} 8979, session of 11 March 1783.
50. Hardy, *Mes Loisirs*, 5:281 (Bibl. nat., MS Fonds fr. 6684); Louis Petit de Bachaumont, *Mémoires secrets pour servir à l'histoire de la république des lettres en France*, 22:186–88.
51. This pamphlet, the *Conversation familière de M. l'abbé Sauveur . . . avec Mlle Sauveur, sa très-honorée soeur*, dated April 1783, may be read in Bibl. nat., Lb^{39}, 320. See also Marcel Marion, *Le Garde des Sceaux Lamoignon et la réforme judiciaire de 1788*, pp. 19–21.
52. A scurrilous *Vie de M. d'Aligre* was reported in Bachaumont, *Mémoires secrets*, 22:251–52. Another pamphlet, entitled *Agonie des treize Parlements*, was cited by Carré, *La Fin des Parlements*, p. 29.
53. This polemic, the *Lettre d'un conseiller au Parlement de Paris à un ancien conseiller au Parlement, retiré dans ses terres*, dated 2 May 1783, may be consulted in Bibl. nat., Lb^{39}, 321.
54. The court's official records do not provide these names. They were mentioned by Hardy, *Mes Loisirs*, 5:284 (Bibl. nat., MS Fonds fr. 6684), and by Carré, *La Fin des Parlements*, p. 29. Given the prominence of all these magistrates, there can be little doubt that they were indeed on this commission.
55. Marion, *Le Garde des Sceaux Lamoignon*, p. 22.

56. Bachaumont, *Mémoires secrets*, 23:106–108.
57. For the king's exchange with d'Aligre, see Flammermont, *Remontrances*, 3:544–45.
58. Bachaumont, *Mémoires secrets*, 23:106–108.
59. The manuscripts of the proposals for reform can be consulted in Bibl. nat., MS Joly de Fleury 1028, passim. See also, at the Bibliothèque du Sénat, MS 81.
60. Significantly, however, Bésenval also recorded Lamoignon's apprehension that Calonne, eyeing the royal finances, might not long enthuse about any comprehensive judicial reform that could reduce or eliminate royal taxation levied in litigation. *Mémoires*, 3:2–6, 13 ff. The procureur-général made the same shrewd observation to his brother, President Joly de Fleury, in a letter of May 1784. Bibl. nat., MS Joly de Fleury 1028, fol. 9. Indeed, the court's leaders very cleverly played upon this issue in their negotiations with the government.
61. For this exchange of letters between the two men, refer to Arch. nat., K 695, docs. 26, 27. Doc. 25 is Lamoignon's letter to the king; his memorandum, enclosed with the letter, is doc. 28.
62. Reproductions of the memoir can be consulted in Bibl. nat., MS Joly de Fleury 1028, fols. 222–28, and in Bésenval, *Mémoires*, 3:29–42.
63. For this polemic, see Bibl. nat., MS Joly de Fleury 1028, fols. 268–85.
64. Ibid., fols. 268–69.
65. Ibid., fol. 276.
66. Ibid., fol. 292.
67. This commission of parlementaires had been designated in April to review the work of the reform conferences that had been meeting for over a year. First President d'Aligre insured the customary majority of grand' chambriers upon this commission. Arch. nat., X¹ᴮ 8980, session of 2 April 1784; X¹ᴮ 8981, session of 4 May 1784.
68. For contemporary accounts of this session, see Bachaumont, *Mémoires secrets*, 25:337–38, 241–42, and Bésenval, *Mémoires*, 3:42 ff.
69. The d'Amécourt memoir can be most readily consulted in Flammermont, *Remontrances*, 3:545–56.
70. Bachaumont, *Mémoires secrets*, 25:340–41.
71. For this ingenious document, see Bibl. nat., MS Joly de Fleury 1028, fols. 295–97.
72. For Miromesnil's comments to Louis XVI, and the final version of the king's response to the parlementaires, see Arch. nat., K 695, docs. 29, 30. Miromesnil (probably aware of reports concerning Lamoignon's ambitions) referred to *quelques Particuliers* who were endeavoring to "stir up trouble" in the Parlement. He also mentioned that the "principal members of the Parlement" were or would soon be examining some of the king's "important legislation."
73. Flammermont, *Remontrances*, 3:557–58.
74. For this denunciation, see ibid., pp. 442–43.
75. Ibid., p. 433.
76. Ibid., p. 443.
77. For this affair, see ibid., pp. 444–48.
78. The Requêtes de l'Hôtel was a tribunal staffed by *maîtres des requêtes* and judged certain privileged persons (secretaries of the king, officers of the royal household, etc.) subject to appeal to the Paris Parlement. It could also judge, in last resort, lawsuits attributed to it by decrees of the King's Council—of which this particular lawsuit was apparently an example. See Marion, *Dictionnaire des institutions*, p. 485.
79. Flammermont, *Remontrances*, 3:447–48. Of course, the magistrates were probably also thinking at this time of their corporate rival, the Requêtes de l'Hôtel.
80. Indeed, Louis XV's reign saw an epic controversy involving the Parlement, the crown, and the latter's recurrence to evocations and decrees of cassation.

See Michel Antoine, ed., *"Le Mémoire" de Gilbert de Voisins "sur les cassations,"* introduction.

81. One of the court's seniors penned this commentary in a *Mémoire concernant le projet de loi pour l'administration de la justice dans la ville de Reims.* Bibl. nat., MS Nouv. acq. fr. 22108, fol. 57.
82. Ibid., fol. 59.
83. On this affair, see Flammermont, *Remontrances*, 3:386. The entrepreneurs reportedly included members of the Caisse de Poissy, a privileged concern dealing in the trade of livestock at Paris.
84. The magistrates often defended small consumers against what they saw as the capriciousness of economic freedom in the commerce of grain, wood, and other commodities. Chap. 5, herein, discusses this problem in detail.
85. President Lamoignon's papers provide information on this affair. See Bibl. nat., MS Fonds fr. 6877, fols. 158–62.
86. Ibid., fol. 158.
87. Ibid., fol. 161.
88. For Lamoignon's *Réflexions sur l'arrêt à intervenir relativement aux jeux,* see ibid., fols. 111–13. Séguier's fiery indictment of the banquiers and *jeux défendus* in the capital may be read in Flammermont, *Remontrances*, 3:469, 471–72. The Parlement passed an arrêt on the subject on 20 February 1781; a royal declaration cracking down upon these illicit pastimes followed soon after, on 1 March 1781.
89. On this affair, see the minutes of the court's plenary sessions of 7 March and 5 May 1786 in Arch. nat., X^{1B} 8984, and the minutes of the plenary session of 11 August 1786 in X^{1B} 8985. S.-P. Hardy also commented frequently upon this episode in the sixth and seventh volumes of his journal: see Bibl. nat., MSS Fonds fr. 6685, 6686, passim.
90. Arch. nat., X^{1B} 8985, session of 11 August 1786.
91. Hardy, *Mes Loisirs*, 7:337–38 (Bibl. nat., MS Fonds fr. 6686).
92. For these comments by the court's procureur-général, see Bibl. nat., MS Nouv. acq. fr. 22108, fols. 10–19.
93. *Arrêt de la cour du Parlement, portant règlement pour les appointements sommaires.* Bibl. nat., MS Joly de Fleury 522, fols. 361–61^3.
94. For the observations of the procureur-général upon this decree and the reasons for its promulgation, see Bibl. nat., MS Nouv. acq. fr. 945, pp. 93–96.
95. Bibl. nat., MS Joly de Fleury 519, fols. 292–95, 307.
96. The legislation in its final form was dated 24 August 1780 and was registered in the Parlement on 5 September. For the text of this *Déclaration du Roi, Concernant l'abolition de la question préparatoire,* refer to ibid., fols. 313–13^1. The associated and equally notorious form of torture known as the *question préalable,* occasionally utilized to extract from condemned criminals information concerning their accomplices, was only abolished eight years later under Lamoignon's judicial ministry.
97. Arch. nat., X^{1B} 8985, session of 11 August 1786.
98. Faulcon, *Correspondance*, 1:290.

CHAPTER 3

1. For this essay, see Bibl. nat., MS Joly de Fleury 608, fols. 398–406.
2. Ibid., fol. 397.
3. The first president of the Parlement had demanded and eventually won the right to address the peers, when they attended parlementary sessions, without doffing his official hat or *bonnet,* although he accorded this mark of respect to his fellow presidents in the court.
4. This series of essays is actually a compilation of various authorities' statements on the history and corporate status of the Gallican church, appearing in the papers of Lefebvre d'Amécourt under the title: *Droit des souverains*

touchant l'administration de l'église: En deux parties. The author of the essays is referred to as "a Counselor of the Grand' Chambre"—presumably d'Amécourt himself, or a like-minded colleague. Bibl. nat., MS Nouv. acq. fr. 22106, fols. 54–135. The invocation of the "prerogative of the sovereigns" in the title is significant.

5. Ibid., fol. 69.
6. Ibid., fols. 82, 84. J. H. Shennan, *The Parlement of Paris*, pp. 222–40, discusses the Parlement's conduct in the religious and political troubles of those years.
7. Refer to Jean Egret, "Le Procès des Jésuites devant les Parlements de France," pp. 1–27.
8. The anonymous pro-Jesuit piece was entitled *Plan de l'apocalypse.* See the *Gazette de Leyde*, supplement to edition of 2 May 1777.
9. Ibid.
10. Ibid., 23 May 1777.
11. *Edit concernant les sujets du roi qui étaient engagés dans la société et compagnie des jésuites* (Versailles, May 1777). François André Isambert et al., eds., *Recueil général des anciennes lois françaises*, 25:1–4.
12. At least, so the *Gazette de Leyde* reported on 3 June. But the journal also reported that several provincial parlements, concerned about the lack of competent teachers for the *collèges* in their jurisdictions, looked askance at the Parisian judges' renewed campaign against an order previously so crucial in French education.
13. The *Gazette de Leyde* reported on 20 June that the government might very well impose its will upon the judges through a lit de justice. This, however, proved unnecessary, as the Parlement had ratified on 10 June legislation that somewhat ameliorated the ex-Jesuits' situation while maintaining the proscription of their order.
14. For this affair, consult Jules Flammermont, *Les Remontrances du Parlement de Paris au XVIIIᵉ siècle*, 3:525–30.
15. For these reiterated protests, see ibid., pp. 527–30. They were no more successful than the first representations had been.
16. Douglas Dakin discusses the *Mémoire sur les municipalités* in his fine study, *Turgot and the Ancien Régime in France*, pp. 272–80. Turgot apparently never discussed his ideas with Louis. Jean Egret suggests that Turgot saw their implementation as politically difficult and potentially subversive of the monarchy over the long run—though as a private citizen he might have welcomed some degree of constitutional change. Egret, *Necker*, pp. 127, 132. On the general question of the provincial assemblies, see Léonce de Lavergne, *Les Assemblées provinciales sous Louis XVI*, and Pierre Renouvin, *Les Assemblées provinciales de 1787*.
17. *Arrêt du Conseil portant établissement d'une administration provinciale dans le Berri* (Versailles, 12 July 1778). The main body of this decree is found in Isambert et al., *Recueil*, 25:354–56.
18. The seventh article of the decree stated only that the intendant would acquaint himself with the assembly's deliberations in his effort to see that royal orders were executed in Berry. Ibid., p. 356.
19. Lefebvre d'Amécourt eventually secured a copy of this memorandum; see Bibl. nat., MS Nouv. acq. fr. 22103, fols. 105–33. Henri Carré argues that it was Cromot du Bourg, chief financial agent of the comte de Provence, who betrayed Necker by circulating his *Mémoire sur l'établissement des administrations provinciales.* Carré, "Le Mémoire de Necker sur les assemblées provinciales," *Bulletin de la Faculté des Lettres de Poitiers*, 1893. Egret, *Necker*, p. 174, states that Cromot relayed the *Mémoire* to the parlementaires during April 1781.
20. As quoted in Dakin, *Turgot and the Ancien Régime*, p. 279. Turgot also commented scornfully to Du Pont de Nemours that Necker's project re-

sembled his own earlier proposal "as a windmill resembles the moon." Marcel Marion, *Histoire financière de la France depuis 1715*, 1:p. 324, n. 2.
21. See Gerald J. Cavanaugh, "Turgot," pp. 31–58. Cavanaugh contends that Turgot rejected Necker's assemblies not so much because he saw the monarchy as a permanent necessity in France as because he felt that rapid, unmeasured change was likely to result from this innovation and would play into the hands of the privileged classes in the provinces. Cavanaugh infers from other comments by Turgot that he envisioned an evolution of institutions in France that might one day obviate the necessity for monarchy there.
22. See the observations of Jean-Louis Soulavie in his *Mémoires historiques et politiques du règne de Louis XVI*, 4:133–34.
23. For some of d'Amécourt's observations, see Bibl. nat., MS Nouv. acq. fr. 22103, passim. The Joly de Fleury brothers' commentary is found in Bibl. nat., MS Joly de Fleury 1037, passim. For relevant papers from d'Espagnac, see MS Joly de Fleury 2539, passim. President Lamoignon's observations on this question may be consulted in Bibl. nat., MS Fonds fr. 6879, passim.
24. Bibl. nat., MS Nouv. acq. fr. 22103, fols. 48–49.
25. Ibid.
26. Ibid., fols. 70–71. This apologia for the intendants likely reflected the amicable relations between the leading parlementaires and several of the intendants. Notable among the latter was Guéau de Reverseaux, intendant for Moulins from 1777 to 1781. His opposition to Necker's institution of an assembly in his généralité in 1780 made him a natural ally of the magistrates, and Lefebvre d'Amécourt transcribed some of Reverseaux's criticisms of the provincial assemblies. For examples, consult Bibl. nat., MS Fonds fr. 11388, passim. Reverseaux, like the judges, saw the innovation as prejudicial to royal authority—and to the activities of judges and intendants alike.
27. Indeed, the *Gazette de Leyde*, which had secured a copy of the confidential memoir, pointed out in its edition of 20 April 1781 how the memoir assailed the intendants as selfish and ambitious individuals.
28. Bibl. nat., MS Nouv. acq. fr. 22103, fol. 50.
29. The *vingtièmes* and *corvée royale* receive a full treatment later in this chapter and in succeeding chapters.
30. For this memorandum to the king, consult Bibl. nat., MS Joly de Fleury 1037, fols. 54–57.
31. The magistrates' plan provided for the appointment of *syndics* to represent the three estates in the Moulins assembly and to work with the intendant (Reverseaux) and his agents to fulfill the tasks assigned to the assembly. In practice, such an arrangement would (and obviously was intended to) leave most power in the hands of a few royal bureaucrats and local proprietors and thus curb the activities of the assembly.
32. The grand' chambriers sent another memorandum to Louis, once again suggesting the appointment of syndics for the Moulins assembly. Bibl. nat., MS Joly de Fleury 1037, fols. 65–69. Their proposal was adopted by the government in an *arrêt du Conseil* of 29 July 1781. See Isambert, et al., eds., *Recueil*, 27:61–62.
33. Flammermont, *Remontrances*, 3:239–40.
34. On this matter, refer again to Michel Antoine, *"Le Mémoire" de Gilbert de Voisins "sur les cassations,"* introduction, pp. 1–20.
35. Flammermont, *Remontrances*, 2:714–808.
36. Joly de Fleury did this in his polemic against Lamoignon and the reformist faction in March of that year. Bibl. nat., MS Joly de Fleury 1028, fol. 280. On the career of Gilbert de Voisins, see J. François Bluche, *L'Origine des magistrats du Parlement de Paris au XVIIIe siècle*, p. 195.
37. I recently discovered d'Amécourt's copy of the work in Bibl. nat., MS Nouv. acq. fr. 22108, fols. 1–38. Its full title is *Vues sur les cassations d'arrêts et de jugements en dernier ressort*. Michel Antoine first unearthed the essay at

the Archives nationales (K 147, no. 8 bis). For purposes of convenience, I am citing from the essay as published by M. Antoine in *"Le Mémoire" de Gilbert de Voisins*. It is also known that Jean François Joly de Fleury wrote his own memoir on this controversy, but the memoir does not seem to have survived.

38. Antoine, *"Le Mémoire" de Gilbert de Voisins*, p. 20.
39. Ibid., p. 21.
40. Ibid., p. 23.
41. Ibid., pp. 23–24.
42. Ibid., p. 33.
43. Bibl. nat., MS Nouv. acq. fr. 960, p. 4. D'Amécourt's text went on, more forcefully: "cassation . . . is an extraordinary procedure to which recourse must not be had until all other possibilities have been exhausted." Antoine, *"Le Mémoire" de Gilbert de Voisins*, p. 5.
44. This episode was discussed above in chapter 2, pp. 54–55. Also, refer again to Flammermont, *Remontrances*, 3:444–48.
45. Ibid., p. 448.
46. Ibid., pp. 443–44.
47. Abbé Jean-François Georgel, *Mémoires pour servir à l'histoire des événements de la fin du XVIIIe siècle*, 2:172; his account (pp. 1–217) was the most thorough contemporary treatment of this celebrated affair. For subsequent scholarship, see Frantz Funck-Brentano, *The Diamond Necklace* (London: J. MacQueen, 1901); Louis Hastier, *La Vérité sur l'affaire du collier* (Paris, 1955); and Frances Mossiker, *The Queen's Necklace* (New York: Simon and Schuster, 1961).
48. Louis Petit de Bachaumont, *Mémoires secrets pour servir à l'histoire de la république des lettres en France*, 32:85. This version of the session of 31 May seems trustworthy, for it is supported by other commentators such as Georgel and Jacques-Mathieu Augeard. Moreover, Bachaumont soon published some private parlementary correspondence on the affair. He clearly had access to the court's internal proceedings.
49. For the judgment of the Grand' Chambre and Tournelle, embodied in the arrêt of 31 May, see Bibl. nat., MS Joly de Fleury 2089, fols. 116–31. On d'Amécourt's reported discourse, see Georgel, *Mémoires*, 2:199.
50. Bachaumont, *Mémoires secrets*, 32:87. Duval d'Eprémesnil politely criticized the procureur-général for not having immediately ordered the release of Cagliostro, who like the cardinal de Rohan had been involved but then acquitted in the affair. For this correspondence, see either Bibl. nat., MS Joly de Fleury 2089, fols. 166 ff., or Bachaumont, *Mémoires secrets*, 32:259–63.
51. The historical background to the dispute between the archiepiscopal and royal jurisdictions at Rheims is provided by M. Vanier, *Les Anciennes juridictions de Reims*.
52. *Mémoire concernant le projet de loi pour l'administration de la justice dans la ville de Reims*. Bibl. nat., MS Nouv. acq. fr. 22108, fols. 56–59. The memorandum resides in d'Amécourt's papers and is written in his hand; still, d'Espagnac, as the king's rapporteur, may have taken the initiative in a matter of considerable consequence for the king's justice.
53. Ibid., fol. 59.
54. *Réflexions sur la difficulté qui a été opposée par M. le Procureur-Général au projet qui lui a été présenté*. Identical copies of this tract, written, again, in d'Amécourt's hand, appear in his papers (ibid., fols. 4–8) and in the d'Espagnac papers (Bibl. nat., MS Joly de Fleury 2539, fols. 114–18).
55. Bibl. nat., MS Joly de Fleury 2539, fols. 116–17.
56. Vanier, *Les Anciennes juridictions de Reims*, p. 58.
57. As *rentiers* themselves, the magistrates continued to protest whenever the government "temporarily" withheld rentes from Parisian *officiers* and rentiers. This was not, however, a major issue in these last years of the old

regime. Of greater importance was the matter of the taille. Although the government traditionally could and did increase the taille and associated imposts without the issuance of registered edicts, there was a point beyond which it could not go without incurring opposition from the Parlement. As chap. 5 will show, the court was to protest arbitrary increases in the tailles in certain généralités starting in 1777. The Parlement would be reassured in 1780 that the government would promulgate no further increases without approval of the sovereign courts.

58. Bibl. nat., MS Nouv. acq. fr. 22103, fols. 71–72.
59. Necker's policy on the vingtièmes is treated at length later in this chapter.
60. Bibl. nat., MS Nouv. acq. fr. 22103, fols. 77 ff.
61. Bibl. nat., MS Joly de Fleury 1037, fols. 54–55.
62. *Arrêt du Conseil concernant la répartition des vingtièmes; et portant suppression des vingtièmes d'industrie dans les bourgs, les villages et les campagnes* (Paris, 4 November 1777). For the complete text, see Isambert et al., *Recueil*, 25:146–51. At this time, lands subject to the vingtièmes were those held by members of the second and third estates; the clergy was exempt.
63. Ibid., p. 147.
64. Flammermont, *Remontrances*, 3:394–95.
65. Actually, the court's investigation delved into two areas of complaint, one involving the assessment of lands subject to the vingtièmes and the other concerning the administration of the corvées and the taxation of *corvéables*. Both matters will be taken up later in connection with the judges' social attitudes.
66. Bibl. nat., MS Nouv. acq. fr. 22104, fols. 74–75.
67. That the Parlement had always to give way before a united and resolute government is stressed by William O. Doyle, "The Parlements of France and the Breakdown of the Old Regime, 1771–1788," pp. 415–58. Yet, would the government remain united and resolute as it became increasingly isolated from the governed?
68. Bibl. nat., MS Nouv. acq. fr. 22104, fols. 86–87. As of 1777, there were two vingtièmes: the duration of the first had not been fixed, and the second was supposed to expire in 1781. In their remonstrances of January 1778 the magistrates insisted that the first vingtième, like the second, be accounted a temporary rather than "perpetual" impost. Flammermont, *Remontrances*, 3:408–409.
69. Bibl. nat., MS Nouv. acq. fr. 22104, fol. 87.
70. Flammermont, *Remontrances*, 3:394–422.
71. On the administrative reforms achieved temporarily under the first ministry of Necker, see J. F. Bosher, *French Finances 1770–1795*; esp. pp. 142–65. The magistrates briefly protested the loan of January 1777 but no others during Necker's first ministry.
72. The confusion on this crucial matter was suggested by the protracted quarrel between Calonne and Necker over the royal finances during the 1780s. This is discussed anew by Egret, *Necker*, pp. 161–212.
73. Flammermont, *Remontrances*, 3:404; significantly, this was the first assertion in these protests rebutted in the royal response of 7 February (pp. 414–15).
74. This legislation (of 1780) is mentioned again in chap. 5.
75. Flammermont, *Remontrances*, 3:422–39. The court briefly protested in March 1780 against Necker's extension of the second vingtième beyond 1781 and proffered the standard parlementary advice: greater "economy" in government administration.
76. For instance, on 16 May 1781, S.-P. Hardy reported rumors that Necker was on the way out and mentioned four men, including d'Amécourt, as possible replacements. *Mes Loisirs*, vol. 4 (Bibl. nat., MS Fonds fr. 6683, pp. 457–58).

77. See Bachaumont, *Mémoires secrets*, 17:333, and Hardy, *Mes Loisirs*, 5:1 (Bibl. nat., MS Fonds fr. 6684). Yet, at times the government seems to have let the first president and his closest associates designate the king's rapporteur. Such was the case, ironically, when d'Amécourt was himself replaced by the abbé Tandeau at the start of 1786.
78. On Jean François Joly de Fleury's career, consult Bluche, *L'Origine des magistrats*, p. 221.
79. On this point, see Alexandre-Marie-Léonor de Saint-Mauris, prince de Montbarey, *Mémoires autographes*, 3:272.
80. *Edit portant établissement d'un troisième vingtième sur tous les objets assujettis aux deux premiers vingtièmes, à l'exception de l'industrie, des offices, et des droits* (Versailles, July 1782). The text utilized here is found in Bibl. nat., MS Nouv. acq. fr. 22104, fol. 215.
81. Ibid., fol. 222, offers these considerations.
82. Flammermont, *Remontrances*, 3:480. Of course, the principal magistrates themselves pocketed royal pensions.
83. Bibl. nat., MS Nouv. acq. fr. 22104, fols. 223–28. These sentiments were toned down in the court's formal protests.
84. For Finance Minister Joly de Fleury's comments upon this session, see Bibl. nat., MS Joly de Fleury 1438, fol. 208.
85. This speech is referred to in a minute written by one of the Joly de Fleury brothers. Bibl. nat., MS Joly de Fleury 1450, fol. 279. For d'Amécourt's draft of his remarks, see Bibl. nat., MS Nouv. acq. fr. 22104, fols. 366–75.
86. Bosher, *French Finances*, pp. 44–45, points out that these were nebulous terms without fixed meanings in the old regime; they did not at all designate budgetary categories and indeed could not, given the lack of any "budget" in the modern sense.
87. And, in fact, the edict stated that the new impost would expire at the end of the third year after the conclusion of the war. The peace was concluded in 1783, and the third vingtième accordingly expired at the end of December 1786.
88. Bibl. nat., MS Nouv. acq. fr. 22104, fol. 375.
89. Yet there is no hard evidence that the judges received such assurances. It is difficult to see how over the long run the government could have avoided increased taxation, most likely through root-and-branch reform resulting in the wealthier proprietors (regardless of estate) paying a greater share of such imposts. Interestingly, the minister of finances left among his papers computations pointing up fallacies in Necker's *Compte rendu*. Bibl. nat., MS Joly de Fleury 1438, fols. 214–24. There is no sign that any of these pessimistic calculations were communicated by Jean François Joly de Fleury to the Parlement.
90. Bibl. nat., MS Nouv. acq. fr. 22104, fols. 372–73.
91. For d'Aligre's comments, see Bibl. nat., MS Joly de Fleury 1450, fols. 270–71. For the court's initial protests over the new tax, delivered to Louis on 11 July, consult Flammermont, *Remontrances*, 3:477–78.
92. Flammermont, *Remontrances*, 3:479–82.
93. Calonne had been the procureur-général of the commission established in Brittany in 1765 to judge La Chalotais as the leader of the rebellious Breton parlementaires.
94. Calonne's most recent biographer does not attempt to dispel the rumors cited at the time by Augeard, Sallier, Moreau, and others alleging his involvement in the financial manipulations during the summer and autumn of 1783 that helped to abbreviate the ministry of Lefevre d'Ormesson. See Robert Lacour-Gayet, *Calonne*, pp. 56–60, 64.
95. For proof of this, see Lefebvre d'Amécourt's scathingly critical commentary upon Calonne's ministerial intrigues and policies, in Bibl. nat., MS Nouv. acq. fr. 22111, fols. 53–79.

96. Bachaumont, *Mémoires secrets*, 22:253, 25:87–90.
97. Flammermont, *Remontrances*, 3:514–15.
98. On this matter, see C. B. A. Behrens, "Nobles, Privileges, and Taxes in France at the End of the Ancien Régime," pp. 451–75. As Behrens notes, many lords also had to help their peasants meet the exaction of the tailles.
99. Flammermont, *Remontrances*, 3:601–602.
100. *Edit du Roi, portant création de quatre millions de rentes héréditaires, remboursables en dix ans* (Versailles, December 1785). Bibl. nat., MS Joly de Fleury 607, fols. 66–66⁵.
101. A. M. de Lescure, *Correspondance secrète inédite sur Louis XVI, Marie-Antoinette, la cour, et la ville*, 1:613.
102. For details, see Bibl. nat., MS Joly de Fleury 607, fol. 76.
103. For this memorandum, consult ibid., fol. 117–32.
104. D'Amécourt observed to his associate that a recent polemic against the controller-general contained "some good things" and might be of use. Ibid., fol. 111; Hardy, *Mes Loisirs*, 6:255 (Bibl. nat., MS Fonds fr. 6685).
105. Arch. nat., X¹ᴮ 8983, session of 13 December 1785.
106. Flammermont, *Remontrances*, 3:640–43. Inevitably, the jurists also reminded Louis of their patriotic response to the fiscal needs of the government during the last war and voiced their astonishment that now, in peacetime, the ministry was pressing for new loans.
107. Ibid., p. 647.
108. D'Amécourt described the scene in his own "Journal." See Bibl. nat., MS Nouv. acq. fr. 22111, fol. 79. Contemporary memorialists dramatized it as well. Hardy, among others, reported the strong reaction in parlementary ranks against the king's move, which was widely seen as Calonne's handiwork. *Mes Loisirs*, 6:264 (Bibl. nat., MS Fonds fr. 6685). A clerical grand' chambrier, the abbé Tandeau, eventually took the post—until Lefebvre d'Amécourt reassumed it a year later.
109. Bibl. nat., MS Joly de Fleury 607, fols. 99, 95; for the correspondence between the procureur-général and the ministry, see fols. 87–88, letters of 26 and 27 December 1785.
110. Ibid., fols. 89–90. D'Amécourt also alluded in this letter to a conference proposed to reconcile the two sides, but it would seem that such a colloquy, if ever seriously mooted, never materialized.
111. Refer again to d'Amécourt's scathing commentary in Bibl. nat., MS Nouv. acq. fr. 22111, fols. 53–79.
112. Bachaumont, *Mémoires secrets*, 31:32–33; Flammermont, *Remontrances*, 3:649–61.

CHAPTER 4

1. The journals, correspondence, and gossip sheets of contemporaries such as Bachaumont, Lescure, and Hardy abounded with descriptions of such liaisons between robe and sword. On the personal ties between Lefebvre d'Amécourt and certain seigneurs and courtiers, for instance, see A. M. de Lescure, *Correspondance secrète inédite sur Louis XVI, Marie-Antoinette, la cour, et la ville*, 1:319.
2. For a discussion of some of these special privileges, refer to the first section of chap. 1, herein.
3. *Edit portant suppression de la corvée* (Versailles, February 1776). The complete text of this edict is found in François André Isambert et al., eds., *Recueil général des anciennes lois françaises*, 23:358–70.
4. On 11 March S.-P. Hardy reported the Parlement's satisfaction at having learned that, when Malesherbes, stung by the first president's hostility to Turgot's edicts, had reminded d'Aligre that he was addressing a minister of

the king, d'Aligre had retorted that Malesherbes should himself remember that he was addressing the first president of the Parlement of Paris. Hardy, *Mes Loisirs*, 3:186–87 (Bibl. nat., MS Fonds fr. 6682).

5. Bibl. nat., MS Nouv. acq. fr. 22105, fols. 342–43.
6. Ibid., fols. 345–46.
7. Ibid., fol. 342.
8. According to Séguier, the clergy and nobility, along with other institutions in France, were "living bodies that can be regarded as the links in a great chain . . . held in the hands of Your Majesty, who is chief and sovereign administrator." By such means, the king could "maintain good order" in France. Jules Flammermont, *Les Remontrances du Parlement de Paris au XVIIIᵉ siècle*, 3:345–46.
9. Ibid., p. 283. The specific duty under discussion here was known as the *corvée des voitures*.
10. C. B. A. Behrens presents some of this evidence in "Nobles, Privileges, and Taxes in France at the End of the Ancien Régime," esp. on pp. 458–75.
11. Flammermont, *Remontrances*, 3:290–91. The economic status of the eighteenth-century French nobility is still a controversial subject. For evidence that the nobility, at least in certain areas, was thriftier, more businesslike in estate management, and generally better off than the popularly conceived *hobereau*, see Robert Forster, "The Provincial Noble: A Reappraisal," *American Historical Review* 68 (April 1963): 681–91. Yet Behrens, in "Nobles, Privileges, and Taxes in France," pp. 458 ff., argues from eighteenth-century testimony and subsequent research that the *hobereau* phenomenon was widespread. So, to some extent, does John McManners in his essay on the French nobility in Albert Goodwin, ed., *The European Nobility in the Eighteenth Century* (London: A. and C. Black, Ltd., 1953).
12. Noblemen could cultivate a certain amount of land tax free, and the exemption often extended to their parks, vineyards, and pastures. Furthermore, their tenants paid only the *taille d'exploitation*, which was less onerous than the *taille de propriété* paid by the commoners working on their own lands.
13. See Georges Lardé, *Une Enquête sur les vingtièmes au temps de Necker*.
14. The material utilized by Lardé is found in Arch. nat., H 1657–58. Additional material, which he apparently did not consult, resides in Bibl. nat., MSS Joly de Fleury 1464–65. Complaints about the assessment and collection of the vingtièmes were often accompanied by denunciations of the administration of the corvée royale. The next chapter will take up the latter issue.
15. Bibl. nat., MS Joly de Fleury 1464, fols. 204–205.
16. Flammermont, *Remontrances*, 3:395–413.
17. Refer again to Isambert et al., *Recueil*, 25:149. The "notable proprietors" were to cooperate in overseeing the assessments with the established agents of the government and parishes.
18. Flammermont, *Remontrances*, 3:411.
19. It was also against such "notables" in the parish communities that the dread sanction of the *contrainte solidaire* had long been invoked by royal tax collectors in the old regime. This meant that the wealthiest peasants were often forced to pay that portion of the taille and other imposts that their less wealthy or less scrupulous neighbors had failed to pay. Turgot abolished this practice, at least nominally, in 1775, but harsh treatment continued to be meted out to those parishes failing to produce the revenues expected of them.
20. Flammermont, *Remontrances*, 3:420.
21. Ibid., pp. 422–36.
22. Ibid., p. 432.
23. Ibid.
24. Ibid., p. 437. The magistrates may not have seriously anticipated restoration

of "the original exemption of lands of the Nobility from taxation." They did, however, complain that nobles and commoners were being included on the same tax rolls—and thereby touched upon a traditional sore point with the French nobility.

25. *Arrêt du Conseil concernant la perception du vingtième* (Versailles, 26 April 1778). See Isambert et al, *Recueil*, 25:279–80.

26. As quoted in Jean Egret, *Louis XV et l'opposition parlementaire, 1715–1774*, p. 191.

27. Bon-Pierre-Victoire, baron de Bésenval, *Mémoires*, 3:13.

28. Ibid., pp. 21–22.

29. Refer again to d'Amécourt's notices on the ministries of Necker and his successors: Bibl. nat., MS Nouv. acq. fr. 22111, fols. 47–79.

30. Although the judges (thinking perhaps of their own gratuities from the king) usually distinguished between justifiable and unjustifiable pensions, they became increasingly insistent upon the need for the government to curb its generosity as the 1780s progressed. By December 1785 the Parlement was demanding that the government "reject all those pretensions that ceaseless badgering, on the basis of ancient pedigree, presents as valid rights and that, even if accepted on trust, may turn out to be groundless claims." Flammermont, *Remontrances*, 3:642. Such language could not have endeared the parlementaires to their aristocratic cousins at court.

31. Material pertinent to this affair is found in Bibl. nat., MS Joly de Fleury 605, fols. 98–112.

32. For this document, see ibid., fols. 109–109³.

33. This pleading by Moreton-Chabrillant at his interrogation was cited by Blondel, Duplessis's procureur, in his brief against the defendant. Blondel himself was apparently responsible for the emphasis of certain passages in the brief.

34. Bibl. nat., MS Joly de Fleury 605, fols. 101–108, for the argument of Moreton-Chabrillant.

35. Hardy, *Mes Loisirs*, 5:195, 198, 202–204 (Bibl. nat., MS Fonds fr. 6684).

36. *Arrêt de la Cour de Parlement, en la Tournelle Criminelle, entre M. Pernot, Procureur en la Cour, appellant, et le comte de Moreton-Chabrillant, intimé.* For this decree of judgment, consult Bibl. nat., MS Joly de Fleury 605, fols. 112–12². The judges' verdict was in no way influenced by letters from the father and wife of the defendant to President Joly de Fleury, imploring him to use his influence to incline the magistrates of the Tournelle toward leniency (fols. 111, 110—letters of 26 July and 18 August 1782). Hardy reported that for days after the affair Moreton-Chabrillant was mocked in popular verse as the Chat-Brillant and Chat-Terni. Hardy, *Mes Loisirs*, 5:203–204 (Bibl. nat., MS Fonds fr. 6684).

37. For material pertinent to this affair, consult Flammermont, *Remontrances*, 3:590–600.

38. Several memoirists referred to d'Eprémesnil's denunciation of the affair in the Parlement, and it was d'Eprémesnil who submitted an essay on the historical role of the marshals of France to the committee of judges that wrote the court's remonstrances on this occasion.

39. These comments are recorded in Arch. nat., X¹ᴮ 8981, plenary session of 6 July 1784.

40. This fascinating document is preserved in Arch. nat., 158 A.P. 3, doss. no. 5. According to d'Eprémesnil, this historical notice was written "by the order of the king" for the commission of parlementaires charged with drawing up the remonstrances.

41. These remonstrances may be consulted most easily in Flammermont, *Remontrances*, 3:590–600.

42. Ibid., p. 590.

43. Ibid., p. 591.

44. Ibid., p. 592.
45. Ibid. In alluding to "the person of a gentleman," the judges clearly had the vicomte de Noé in mind. Like any nobleman, they were implying, Noé was entitled to justice in first instance in the proper civil bailliage, or sénéchausée, and, upon appeal, to parlementary justice.
46. Ibid., pp. 593–94. In other words, Noé, as mayor at Bordeaux, was an *officier de robe* as well as a gentleman. This was another consideration entitling him to justice in the civil courts.
47. Ibid., pp. 594–95.
48. They had a very practical reason for doing so: their concern for law and order at Bordeaux, even though the city and the Bordelais in general did not fall within their jurisdiction. They asserted that the interference of the provincial governor at Bordeaux meant "that the state of the municipality was violent. In losing its prestige, it was losing its authority." Ibid., p. 595.
49. Hardy, *Mes Loisirs*, 5:480–81 (Bibl. nat., MS Fonds fr. 6684). The illegally published denunciation was hawked under the title *Récit de la conduite des maréchaux de France à l'égard du vicomte de Noé: Extrait du procés-verbal des Chambres assemblées le 6 de ce mois*. It would be interesting to know if Duval d'Eprémesnil played a role in publicizing what was most likely his own address. His associates failed to adopt the procedure that was customary in such circumstances: hunting down the author and publishers of a clandestine work.
50. Flammermont, *Remontrances*, 3:599–600.
51. *Recueil de différentes matières judiciaires: Procès, mémoires, factums, procédures, etc., formé par Lefebvre d'Amécourt, conseiller au Parlement de Paris*. Bibl. nat., MSS Nouv. acq. fr. 940–87.
52. Bibl. nat., MS Nouv. acq. fr. 960, fols. 233–34; emphasis apparently by d'Amécourt himself. Significantly, most of the Paris Parlement's vast jurisdiction fell within the region of customary law.
53. For instance, refer to the commentary in Bibl. nat., MS Nouv. acq. fr. 987, p. 310, which emphasized that many of the corvées had been founded "only upon the violence and force of seigneurs."
54. The registers and minutes of the eighteenth-century segment of these conclusions of the procureurs-généraux must actually be consulted in three separate series: Arch. nat., X^{1A} 8950–9041, X^{1B} 4392–96, and X^{1B} 610.
55. For this specific lawsuit, see Arch. nat., X^{1A} 9036, 31 July 1782.
56. Ibid., 17 March 1783.
57. Specifically, twenty-four lawsuits resulted in decisions favoring parties identified as "seigneurs," "gentlemen," or clerical aristocrats, and eighteen suits ended in victories for individual commoners or communities of commoners. In addition, a number of litigants with names preceded by the simple *Sieur* won cases against identifiable seigneurs or aristocrats. Determination of the rank and profession of all parties in these approximately two thousand cases would have required a prohibitive amount of research in other archives; yet this would seem unnecessary in light of all the other material documenting the judges' social attitudes. The sample was taken from one volume at the Archives nationales, X^{1A} 9036.
58. Refer again to the *Réflexions sur la difficulté qui a été opposée par M. le Procureur-Général au projet qui lui a été présenté*. Bibl. nat., MS Nouv. acq. fr. 22108, fols. 4–5.
59. Traditionally, only princes of the blood received such largesse from the royal domain; moreover, their lands would ordinarily revert to the crown should they lack male heirs.
60. Refer again to Bibl. nat., MS Joly de Fleury 608, fol. 406.
61. Ibid.
62. Flammermont, *Remontrances*, 3:257. The protests of 8 January 1775 were analyzed at length in chap. 2, herein.

63. Ibid.
64. Ibid., p. 258.
65. "Although the Grand Conseil developed originally from the king's Council, it has been totally cut off from it by its conversion into an extraordinary judicial bureau; it is absolutely foreign to the Court of France where all the major affairs of State must be considered." Ibid., p. 259.
66. Bibl. nat., MS Nouv. acq. fr. 976, fol. 75; MS Nouv. acq. fr. 22103, fols. 40–41. This may have been a bit alarmist: Necker had certainly not intended to establish a clerical domination of his assemblies.
67. Ibid., MS Nouv. acq. fr. 22103, fols. 41–42.
68. Ibid., fol. 44.
69. Ibid., fols. 96–97. The decree of July 1778 had stipulated that voting would be by head rather than by order in the Berry assembly.
70. This was discussed in the first section of chap. 3, herein. See again the *Gazette de Leyde*, supplement to edition of 2 May 1777, for a report on the grand' chambriers' continuing distrust of the Jesuits.
71. See the *Mémoire sur l'Assemblée provinciale de Moulins*, transcribed in his papers. Bibl. nat., MS Fonds fr. 6879, fols. 55–74.
72. These misgivings were expressed in some *Réflexions sur les administrations provinciales*, transcribed in Lamoignon's papers. Ibid., fols. 81–92.
73. For these comments, see Bibl. nat., MS Nouv. acq. fr. 22103, fols. 45–46.
74. These remarks are found in the Lamoignon papers. Bibl. nat., MS Fonds fr. 6879, fol. 58. Similar apprehensions were registered in the papers of the abbé d'Espagnac (Bibl. nat., MS Joly de Fleury 2539, passim) and throughout the papers of Lefebvre d'Amécourt.
75. Bibl. nat., MS Nouv. acq. fr. 22103, fol. 40.
76. Ibid., fols. 46–47.
77. These commendatory comments, by either the procureur-général or the president, are found upon the first folio in Bibl. nat., MS Joly de Fleury 1037. The brothers' styles are similar.
78. Ibid., fols. 9–10. These scathing comments were apparently written by one of the grand' chambriers themselves, for on fol. 16 one of the Joly de Fleury brothers implied that the essay of which they were a part had been submitted to Necker by the Parlement before the revelation of the director-general's surreptitious memorandum to Louis XVI. On fol. 15 the author characterized himself as a "magistrate . . . who would like to be something else." Was this Lefebvre d'Amécourt, or perhaps Lamoignon?
79. Ibid., fol. 8.
80. Bibl. nat., MS Nouv. acq. fr. 22103, fols. 51–52.
81. Bibl. nat., MS Joly de Fleury 1037, fol. 66.
82. Refer again to the discussion of these two official memorandums from the Parlement to the king in chap. 3, herein, and to the memorandums themselves: Bibl. nat., MS Joly de Fleury 1037, fols. 54–57, 65–69.
83. Ibid., fol. 56. Additional evidence of the senior magistrates' misgivings about the personnel (above all, the aristocratic personnel) of the provincial assemblies resides in Bibl. nat., MS Fonds fr. 11388. As indicated before, this volume contains a huge amount of administrative material transcribed by Lefebvre d'Amécourt. One large dossier contains the complaints of various people against the intendant of the généralité of Moulins but also against (in d'Amécourt's own words) "the abuses of authority by gentlemen" in that area (fol. 59).
84. As mentioned in chap. 3, the government adopted the essential elements of this plan for the Bourbonnais assembly in its decree of 29 July 1781. For the text, refer again to Isambert et al., *Recueil*, 27:61–62. The establishment of a nationwide system of provincial assemblies had to await Calonne's campaign of reform in 1787.
85. Bibl. nat., MS Joly de Fleury 1037, fol. 54.

CHAPTER 5

1. *Edit portant suppression des jurandes et communautés de commerce, arts et métiers* (Versailles, February 1776). For the complete text: François André Isambert et al., eds. *Recueil général des anciennes lois françaises*, 23:370–86.
2. Most of these petitions were addressed to Procureur-Général Joly de Fleury and can be consulted in Bibl. nat., MS Joly de Fleury 462, fols. 99–184.
3. Refer again to Jules Flammermont, *Les Remontrances du Parlement de Paris au XVIIIe siècle*, 3:345–46.
4. Ibid., pp. 346–47.
5. Ibid., p. 309. At another point, the remonstrances referred ominously to "those creatures born to trouble all societies, whose passions, relatively unrestrained by education, join to the brute energy of nature the force they acquire in the licentiousness of the cities." Such individuals were the very ones curbed by the guilds and courts of Paris, the judges claimed (pp. 309–10).
6. Ibid., pp. 314–15.
7. Ibid., p. 318.
8. Ibid., pp. 329–30.
9. Ibid., pp. 350–51. Yet the judges, despite their invocation of "urgent circumstances" justifying additional revenues to the government, were here contradicting their own counsel to the king on other occasions to reduce the "public revenues" of taxation.
10. For instance, the properties of the defunct associations, the *gages* of their officers, and the fees and tolls incidental to the business of the proscribed associations could be used to compensate those creditors validating their claims. See again Isambert et al., *Recueil*, 23:370–86. Furthermore, there was no reason why the government must reduce or abrogate the capitation upon merchants losing their privileges. Yet Séguier was perhaps correct in suggesting that the government itself would have to shoulder part of the burden of the debts of the proscribed guilds and communities. There were no guarantees against such a development—as the burgeoning public debts of the Revolution would soon show.
11. Refer again to the published text of the edict.
12. Flammermont, *Remontrances*, 3:311.
13. Ibid., pp. 351–52.
14. For these "reiterated" remonstrances, delivered at Versailles on 19 May, see ibid., pp. 369–74. The judges protested the imposition of a lit de justice as well as the substance of Turgot's edicts.
15. Their protectionist views outlasted the ancien régime, for that matter. It was not until 1791 that the revolutionaries terminated a bitter debate by finally dissolving the system of guilds and commercial-industrial protectionism within France.
16. *Arrêt du Conseil portant règlement sur la durée des privilèges en librairie* (Versailles, 30 August 1777). Isambert et al., *Recueil*, 25:108–12. The decree set limits upon booksellers' and printers' control over books they had produced, and opened the book trade to greater competition from the provinces.
17. For the Parlement's discussion of this matter during late 1777, 1778, and 1779, see Arch. nat., X^{1B} 8969–73, passim.
18. For d'Eprémesnil's own copy of his twenty-four-page *Récit*, see Arch. nat., 158 A.P. 3, doss. no. 4. See also (in the Archives nationales) X^{1B} 8971, session of 23 April 1779.
19. *Déclaration du Roi portant règlement pour le Collège d'Auxerre* (Fontainebleau, 31 October 1776). The text utilized here is found in Arch. nat., X^{1A} 8819, fols. 56–61.
20. See Flammermont, *Remontrances*, 3:389–94.
21. Ibid.

22. See the minutes of the court's plenary sessions during the summer months of 1783: Arch. nat., X^{1B} 8979.
23. Ibid., session of 29 July 1783. The court also launched its own review of the regulations governing the asylums and houses of detention in the capital, and continued in the following months to receive information on these establishments directly from the lieutenant-général and his agents.
24. For these proceedings, see Flammermont, *Remontrances*, 3:482–84.
25. This financial statement was to indicate the city's "ordinary" and "extraordinary" revenues, the capital owed to creditors and the arrears on repayments of that capital, the debt traceable to new construction projects, annual maintenance costs, and so on. As *rentiers*, many of the judges were creditors themselves, and this no doubt quickened their interest in municipal finances.
26. Flammermont, *Remontrances*, 3:484; see p. 523, for d'Aligre's appearance at Versailles in September 1783.
27. Ibid., pp. 524–25.
28. The frequency of severe winters in the Parisian area during the 1770s and 1780s is reflected periodically in the journal of the book seller S.-P. Hardy. Bibl. nat., MSS Fonds fr. 6680–87, passim.
29. For examples in the d'Amécourt papers, see Bibl. nat., MS Nouv. acq. fr. 974, pp. 4, 6, 7–8. In the last case, one Charles Jacques Pinguenet was condemned by decree of the court on 27 October 1781 to be tied to a stake in the place Maubert for two hours, then flogged and branded and sent to the galleys "for having abused the confidence of persons for whom he had been *homme d'affaires*." It is also worth recalling that one of the senior parlementaires, in commenting upon the jurisdictional dispute at Rheims in 1779, had censured the "pernicious art of gens d'affaires" who battened off the troubles of the litigants of that city. Refer again to Bibl. nat., MS Nouv. acq. fr. 22108, fol. 56.
30. For instance, on 28 November 1768, Séguier had branded the physiocrats as a "sect" that "claimed to know everything" and was endeavoring "to change all customs and morals." The physiocrats "shouted for liberty, and liberty had leveled everything from one end of the Kingdom to the other; the sciences, arts, commerce, and agriculture itself have seen their age-old foundations overthrown." Flammermont, *Remontrances*, 3:13. When, at the same session, the grand' chambrier de Chavannes had attempted to refute Séguier's arguments, his address had been "vehemently attacked by the présidents à mortier of the Parlement" (pp. 18–19).
31. Bibl. nat., MS Nouv. acq. fr. 22111, fols. 34–35.
32. *Arrêt du Conseil sur la liberté du commerce des grains dans le royaume* (Versailles, 13 September 1774); Isambert et al., *Recueil*, 23:30–39; *Lettres patentes du Roi, concernant le commerce des grains dans l'intérieur du royaume* (Fontainebleau, 2 November 1774). The text utilized here is found in Arch. nat., X^{1A} 8809, fols. 77–80. Turgot elaborated upon his physiocratic ideas in an *Extrait des Registres du Conseil d'Etat*. A copy is appended to the parlementary draft of the November 1774 letters patent on the grain trade in Arch. nat., X^{1B} 9060.
33. Flammermont, *Remontrances*, 3:267.
34. Bibl. nat., MS Joly de Fleury 462, fols. 36–37.
35. S.-P. Hardy reported on 20 December that the edict had passed by only two votes. *Mes Loisirs*, 2:484 (Bibl. nat., MS Fonds fr. 6681). Pidansat de Mairobert, *Journal historique du rétablissement de la magistrature*, 6:415, gave the vote as 68 to 34. Both accounts stated that the magistrates' approval of the legislation had come only after government assurances about forthcoming regulations to insure an adequate supply of bread to the people.
36. Hardy, *Mes Loisirs*, 2:484 (Bibl. nat., MS Fonds fr. 6681).
37. Flammermont, *Remontrances*, 3:267–68.
38. Bibl. nat., MS Nouv. acq. fr. 22111, fol. 35.

39. The full text of the arrêt of 4 May is published in Flammermont, *Remontrances*, 3:268–69.
40. Ibid., p. 271.
41. *Déclaration du Roi, par laquelle Sa Majesté . . . supprime tous les Droits établis dans la ville de Paris sur les Blés, Méteils, Seigles, Farines, Pois, Fèves, Lentilles, et Riz, et modère les Droits qui subsistent sur les autres Graines et Grenailles* (Versailles, 5 February 1776). Isambert et al., *Recueil*, 23:318–29.
42. So reported the marquis d'Albertas in his *Journal de nouvelles* (7 vols., Bibl. nat., MSS Nouv. acq. fr. 4386–92), 5:2387; (MS Nouv. acq. fr. 4390), entry of 1 February 1776.
43. Flammermont, *Remontrances*, 3:295, 305–306, 304–305. The magistrates were able to grasp the basic principles of supply-and-demand relationships, but some contemporary economic thinkers would have severely criticized their forays into the field of marketplace dynamics. For instance, the judges stated flatly that "it is always the first trader on the scene who determines the price of the commodity. The competition of several others can make it fall, but it will always remain comparable to the first price fixed" (p. 306). For the judges, this was an observation reflecting past experience; for their critics, these were speculations flawed by insufficient experimentation with a free market. Prices, the latter would insist, could be much more flexible, much more closely attuned to competition, than the parlementaires realized.
44. Ibid., pp. 298–99.
45. Ibid., pp. 300–301.
46. Ibid.
47. Ibid., pp. 311–12. Some of the threatened *corps et communautés* had predictably made this argument in their petitions to the Parlement. Refer again to Bibl. nat., MS Joly de Fleury 462, fols. 99–184.
48. For example, it is worth recalling that the edict on the guilds maintained the old regulations on the pharmacists, goldsmiths, and booksellers and printers. Furthermore, the edict did not, as the judges intimated, sweep away all of the traditional *police* in the other professions. Finally, the judges failed to acknowledge Turgot's efforts to maintain extra stocks of grain in the environs of the capital.
49. Hardy, *Mes Loisirs*, 5:266–67 (Bibl. nat., MS Fonds fr. 6684).
50. *Arrêt du parlement concernant les fourrages*, 19 July 1785. Isambert et al., *Recueil*, 28:67–68.
51. Hardy, *Mes Loisirs*, 6:152 (Bibl. nat., MS Fonds fr. 6685).
52. There is much interesting material pertaining to the commerce in wood in and around eighteenth-century Paris in Hippolyte Monin's *L'Etat de Paris en 1789*, passim.
53. *Arrêt du parlement concernant la vente et la livraison des bois dans les chantiers de la ville de Paris*, 6 July 1784. Isambert et al., *Recueil*, 27:431–36.
54. *Déclaration du Roi portant règlement pour le mesurage et la qualité des bois à brûler destinés à l'approvisionnement de Paris*, 8 July 1784. Isambert et al., *Recueil*, 27:437–38.
55. *Bois blanc* usually meant the softer fir or pine wood that was of less value than other types of wood as a source of heat, and hence cost less (before 1784) than did the bois flotté and bois neuf. The *bois neuf* was newly cut and had not yet been stripped of its bark; apparently the *bois flotté*, whatever its specific type, was, like the bois neuf, relatively hard and relatively valuable as an energy source. Firewood was sold by the *voie* or "cartload," equivalent to around two cubic meters. This is the unit of measure mentioned most often in eighteenth-century legislation on firewood.
56. Flammermont, *Remontrances*, 3:586–89.
57. On this declaration, consult Arch. nat., X[1B] 8983, session of 9 August 1785.

58. Flammermont, *Remontrances*, 3:626–30.
59. Ibid., p. 632.
60. Ibid., pp. 632–33. This arrêté is also found in Arch. nat., X¹ᴮ 8983, session of 9 August 1785.
61. Flammermont, *Remontrances*, 3:633.
62. Ibid., p. 634.
63. On the last point, Le Pelletier de Mortefontaine recommended not only that all the wood merchants be held strictly to account for the amounts of wood they had pledged to supply the city but also that they be *rendus solidaires*, that is, held responsible collectively for any amounts of this commodity that individual merchants failed to supply. He also directly linked the issues of wood and bread by suggesting that the Parlement make an exact calculation of "the increase in the price of bread that might be caused by the excessive price of wood." Ibid., pp. 637–38.
64. *Arrêt du Parlement pour la coupe et l'exportation des bois destinés à l'approvisionnement de la ville de Paris*, 30 December 1785. Articles 7 through 19 of the decree are published in Isambert et al., *Recueil*, 28:119–22.
65. S.-P. Hardy, *Mes Loisirs*, 6:207–208 (Bibl. nat., MS Fonds fr. 6685).
66. Bibl. nat., MS Nouv. acq. fr. 22105, fol. 1. The parlementaire in question was probably either the rapporteur d'Espagnac or Lefebvre d'Amécourt.
67. Ibid., fols. 1–2. The exact amount of money earmarked for work on the roads would first be determined. The involved funds would be put in the treasuries of the *receveurs* of provincial towns and could be removed only on orders of the chief municipal officers of the towns nearest the work to be done, as authorized by the intendant overseeing the given généralité. The money would go to engineers and overseers of the work, and at year's end these administrators would have to verify the practical uses of the funds entrusted to them. Such verifications would pass to the receveurs and other municipal officers and from them to the contrôleur-général des finances.
68. Refer again to Isambert et al., *Recueil*, 23:358–70. Articles 5 through 8, and 10–11, outlined measures for the collection, administration, and control of the funds deriving from the new imposition.
69. Bibl. nat., MS Nouv. acq. fr. 22105, fols. 95–96.
70. *Déclaration qui rétablit l'ancien usage observé pour les réparations des grands chemins* (Versailles, 11 August 1776). Isambert et al., *Recueil*, 24:68.
71. The text of the Parlement's registration is not given by Isambert, but Lefebvre d'Amécourt wrote it out in full. Bibl. nat., MS Nouv. acq. fr. 22105, fols. 146–47.
72. See S.-P. Hardy's report of 30 August 1776 in *Mes Loisirs*, 3:267 (Bibl. nat., MS Fonds fr. 6682). Hardy for the most part sympathized with parlementary opposition to the crown, but even he decried Clugny's legislation as compromising the moral authority of the young monarch and spreading unrest through the countryside.
73. For an excellent discussion of the problem of the corvée royale in the post-Turgot period, see André Lesort, "La Question de la corvée des grands chemins sous Louis XVI après la chute de Turgot (1776–1778)," pp. 49–95. On Necker's handling of the issue, see also Jean Egret, *Necker*, pp. 83–87.
74. Lesort, "La Question de la corvée," p. 62.
75. Ibid., p. 54.
76. Ibid., p. 56.
77. Bibl. nat., MS Joly de Fleury 463, fols. 90–91; MS Joly de Fleury 1450, fols. 117–122; MS Joly de Fleury 1464, fols. 87–88. Most of the parlementary material on the corvée royale is found in the papers of the Joly de Fleury brothers (MSS Joly de Fleury 1450, 1464–65), Abbé d'Espagnac (MS Joly de Fleury 2536), and Lefebvre d'Amécourt (MS Nouv. acq. fr. 22105). Additional material resides in the Archives nationales, H 1657–58.
78. Bibl. nat., MS Joly de Fleury 1464, fols. 190–91. In response to a letter from

the parlementaires, Cypierre, the intendant for the Orléans region, removed this individual from the list of corvéables (fol. 193, letter of January 1778). On the other hand, the Parlement's eagerness to track down and eliminate abuses in this area could be neutralized by consideration of other interests. Thus, an undated memorandum dealing with an alleged abuse in the Parisian region warned that the intendant for Paris "could be compromised in that affair" and counseled inaction on the matter (MS Joly de Fleury 1465, fol. 43). The intendant in question was Bertier de Sauvigny, long an ally of the court's leaders.

79. Bibl. nat., MS Joly de Fleury 1450, fols. 74–75. See also Flammermont, *Remontrances*, 3 : 440–42.

80. For this second, more peremptory letter, dated 13 November, see Bibl. nat., MS Joly de Fleury 1450, fol. 101.

81. Ibid., fols. 105, 154.

82. Bibl. nat., MS Joly de Fleury 1464, fols. 108 ff.

83. See, for example, the memorandum from the judicial officers at Mâcon dated April 1778. Bibl. nat., MS Joly de Fleury 1465, fols. 24–25.

84. For the findings of the parquet's investigation, consult Arch. nat., H 1657, fols. 1–465, and, in Lefebvre d'Amécourt's papers, Bibl. nat., MS Nouv. acq. fr. 22105, fols. 23–43. The records in the Archives nationales indicate the généralités of Alençon, Amiens, Dijon, La Rochelle, Limoges, Lyons, Moulins, Nancy, Orléans, Paris, Poitiers, Riom, Rouen, Soissons, and Tours. For some reason, the d'Amécourt papers omit Lyons and Rouen but supplement the records in the Archives nationales by presenting information from Bourges and Châlons. Some of the correspondence from the officers of the bailliages and sénéchaussées of these généralités still survives in these dossiers; in the majority of cases, however, only the parquet's summation of this correspondence remains. All of the bailliages and sénéchaussées in seven of the généralités, and nearly all in the other généralités (except for those généralités shared with other parlements) sent reports in to the Parisian parlementaires.

85. Lefebvre d'Amécourt made these favorable comments upon Cypierre's encouragement of the traditional corvée. Bibl. nat., MS Nouv. acq. fr. 22105, fol. 33.

86. Ibid., fol. 23.

87. Ibid., fol. 34.

88. Ibid., fols. 37–41.

89. Ibid., fol. 43.

90. Flammermont, *Remontrances*, 3 : 440.

91. This *Résumé*, drawn up by the parquet, signed by d'Aligre, and dated 30 March 1778, is preserved in Arch. nat., H 1658, fol. 3.

92. Ibid. The first president, in his conversations at Versailles, may also have utilized protests formulated by his associate d'Amécourt. The critique by Lefebvre d'Amécourt came down hard upon the malfeasance of unnamed administrators of the corvée in various provinces. In particular, it denounced the intendants for "pronouncing *solidarité*" against the peasants, that is, forcing those corvéables who had acquitted their tasks to complete the work of less conscientious peasants. Bibl. nat., MS Nouv. acq. fr. 22105, fols. 60–65.

93. Flammermont, *Remontrances*, 3 : 440–41.

94. Ibid., p. 441.

95. Ibid., pp. 441–42.

96. Actually, Miromesnil, who was probably acting for Necker, wrote twice, first on 28 August and again the following day, at which time he announced the royal summons to Versailles. Bibl. nat., MS Joly de Fleury 1464, fols. 66 and 74, letters of 28 and 29 August 1778.

97. Ibid., fols. 69–70, 78, for the letters of the first president and procureur-général, respectively.

98. Bibl. nat., MS Nouv. acq. fr. 22105, fols. 108–10.
99. Ibid., fols. 201–204. President Joly de Fleury's proposed règlement was in twelve articles and was preceded by a long memoir denouncing instances of solidarité pronounced against corvéables and demanding strict controls upon the amount and duration of labor upon the roads (for the memoir, see fols. 205–12).
100. For the reaction of the intendants, refer again to Lesort, "La Question de la corvée," and to Egret, *Necker*, p. 85. Of twenty-four intendants responding to queries from Necker concerning the corvée in September 1777, eighteen supported the corvée par adjudication and six preferred the corvée en nature.
101. Lesort, "La Question de la corvée," pp. 60, n. 1, and 65. Bertier de Sauvigny in particular was known for his attempts to establish a more equitable assessment of taxes in his area. He had long objected to the very principle of the corvée and established it in the généralité of Paris only in 1783, upon the more traditional footing. Reverseaux had experimented with the corvée par adjudication while intendant for Moulins; at La Rochelle, after 1781, he favored the more traditional corvée en nature.
102. On Cypierre, see Louis Guerin, *L'Intendant de Cypierre et la vie économique de l'Orléanais, 1760–1785* (Orléans, 1938). For Cypierre's *mandement*, see Bibl. nat., MS Nouv. acq. fr. 22105, fols. 197–99; for the Alençon authorization, see fols. 195–96. In 1780, Cypierre was to adopt a policy allowing the communities of his généralité much more freedom to choose the corvée par adjudication. Lefebvre d'Amécourt left a copy of the mandement effecting this change among his papers (fols. 126–31) but failed to comment upon it.
103. Vivian R. Gruder, *The Royal Provincial Intendants*, p. 90. Jullien had been in the Parlement for fourteen years.
104. For d'Amécourt's letter, see Bibl. nat., MS Nouv. acq. fr. 22105, fols. 267–71; for the list of grievances from Alençon that provoked d'Amécourt's correspondence, see fols. 124–25.
105. Ibid., fols. 251–65.
106. For d'Espagnac's comments, refer to Bibl. nat., MS Joly de Fleury 2536, fol. 172.
107. His letters to d'Aligre on 1 June 1783 and to d'Amécourt on 18 July 1783 are found in Bibl. nat., MS Nouv. acq. fr. 22105, fols. 115, 116. A memorandum from Mareuil, in Bas-Poitou, is found on fols. 119–22 of the same volume.
108. For the material on this affair, see Bibl. nat., MS Joly de Fleury 605, fols. 277–392. On Calonne's activities, see Lesort, "La Question de la corvée," pp. 64 ff.
109. Bibl. nat., MS Joly de Fleury 605, fols. 294–308.
110. The first draft, found on fols. 294–96, ibid., was dated 27 June; the second (fols. 300–308) was not dated. The collaboration and its purposes were indicated in a letter from d'Aligre to President Joly de Fleury dated 22 October. Ibid., fol. 350.
111. Lesort, "La Question de la corvée," p. 61. I have not been able to document the involvement of Bertier de Sauvigny in the project, but Chaumont de la Millière would have been aware of the former's amicable relations with the leading parlementaires at Paris.
112. The preamble to the second draft of Jean Omer Joly de Fleury's proposed edict was particularly revealing. Refer again to Bibl. nat., MS Joly de Fleury 605, fols. 305–308.
113. Calonne continued to meditate a reform of the corvée royale and replaced it provisionally throughout the kingdom with a tax additional to the taille in November 1786. This provisional reform became definitive with legislation of June 1787, though of course the Revolution was soon to do away with this imposition as well.

CHAPTER 6

1. As quoted in Henri Carré, "La Tactique et les idées de l'opposition parlementaire," p. 7.
2. Refer again to Jean Egret, *La Pré-révolution française*, pp. 149 ff.
3. For example, S.-P. Hardy on 18 December 1787 commented that the new procureur-général was "notoriously" unsuited for the position, "as much owing to ignorance and incapacity as to his dissipations of all kinds." Hardy, *Mes Loisirs*, 7:318 (Bibl. nat., MS Fonds fr. 6686). He was the younger son of President Jean Omer Joly de Fleury.
4. Etienne-Denis, duc de Pasquier, *Histoire de mon temps*, 1:24. Pasquier excluded from this characterization the future revolutionary Le Peletier de Saint-Fargeau, who, he said, had oratorical abilities but failed to utilize them in defense of the government.
5. Hardy characterized Outremont de Minière, a lay counselor of the Grand' Chambre, as particularly supportive of the government's legislation creating a network of provincial assemblies in 1787. Hardy, *Mes Loisirs*, 7:117 (Bibl. nat., MS Fonds fr. 6686). On the general passivity of the senior chamber, refer to Guy Marie Sallier-Chaumont de la Roche, *Annales françaises*, p. 80.
6. As noted in chap. 1, fifty-nine of the seventy-one lay counselors admitted during this period were less than thirty-five years of age in 1790, and some of the much smaller number of clerical judges must have been as youthful. According to the *Almanach royal* of 1790, nine of seventy-three counselors of the Enquêtes and seven of fourteen judges of the Requêtes entered the court during this period. Of the eighty-seven regular judges of Enquêtes and Requêtes all told in 1789, fully sixty had entered during the 1780s.
7. *Almanach royal* of 1790.
8. *Edit portant suppression des deux vingtièmes et quatre sous par livre du premier vingtième, et établissement d'une subvention territoriale dans tout le royaume* (Versailles, August 1787). François André Isambert et al., eds., *Recueil général des anciennes lois françaises*, 28:394–400. On d'Amécourt's support of Tandeau on 30 July 1787, see Egret, *La Pré-révolution française*, p. 167.
9. See Jacob-Nicholas Moreau, *Mes Souvenirs*, 2:356, and Hardy, *Mes Loisirs*, 8:102–103 (Bibl. nat., MS Fonds fr. 6687).
10. Refer again to Moreau, *Mes Souvenirs*, 2:381–83, for particulars on this maneuver by the two magistrates.
11. See, for example, A. M. de Lescure, *Correspondance secrète inédite sur Louis XVI, Marie-Antoinette, la cour, et la ville*, 2:364, for rumors concerning d'Amécourt; on President Joly de Fleury, see Hardy, *Mes Loisirs*, 8:215 (Bibl. nat., MS Fonds fr. 6687).
12. Calonne's proposal, however, was intended to introduce a more efficient exploitation of the royal domain and would have left it under the "direct lordship" of the king. For the comments of the procureur-général, consult Bibl. nat., MS Joly de Fleury 1038, fols. 26–27, and 1041, fols. 109–10. The Notables rejected the proposal for reasons similar to those adduced by Joly de Fleury.
13. *Edit portant création d'assemblées provinciales et municipales* (Versailles, June 1787). Isambert et al., *Recueil*, 28:364–66.
14. Bibl. nat., MS Joly de Fleury 1038, fol. 25; see also fol. 20 for more extensive remarks on this question.
15. Antoine François Claude, comte de Ferrand, *Mémoires*, p. 10. Also, refer again to Isambert et al., *Recueil*, 28:364–66.
16. Pasquier, *Histoire*, 1:27.
17. Arch. nat., X^{1B} 8988, session of 5 May 1788.
18. *Réflexions d'un magistrat sur la question du nombre et celle de l'opinion par ordre ou par tête*. The pamphlet was dated 7 December. For the full text,

see either Bibl. nat., Lb[39], 821, or Hardy, *Mes Loisirs*, 8:165–66 (Bibl. nat., MS Fonds fr. 6687).
19. Refer to Arch. nat., 158 A.P. 3, doss. no. 24, esp. letters 18, 19, 20.
20. Ferrand, *Mémoires*, p. 30.
21. D'Eprémesnil was elected to the Estates General as a delegate of the nobility and continued to serve in that body as an outspoken apologist for the old regime after its transformation into the National Assembly. On his defense of the king in the National Assembly, see: *Proposition inutilement faite par M. d'Eprémesnil à l'Assemblée (sur l'inviolabilité de la personne royale)* ... *le 28 mars 1791, suivie d'un aperçu de l'opinion qu'il aurait prononcée, s'il avait eu la liberté de parole*. Bibl. nat., 8° Le[29], 2094. For details on his subsequent career and execution, see again Henri Carré, "Un Précurseur inconscient de la Révolution."
22. *De la nécessité d'assembler les Etats-Généraux dans les circonstances actuelles, et de l'inadmission du timbre: Fragment du Discours de M. de Sémonville, conseiller au Parlement, dans la séance du 16*. Bibl. nat., 8° Lb[39], 377.
23. *Réflexions sur les pouvoirs et instructions à donner par les provinces à leurs députés aux Etats-Généraux*. Attributed to Huguet de Sémonville by the revolutionary and Napoleonic librarian and editor Antoine-Alexandre Barbier. Bibl. nat., Lb[39], 11117.
24. Refer to Arch. nat., X[1B] 8986, session of 9 February 1787; Jules Flammermont, *Les Remontrances du Parlement de Paris au XVIIIᵉ siècle*, 3:694–95.
25. The original letters are found in Arch. nat., KK 1327, fols. 118–19. See also Hardy, *Mes Loisirs*, 7:433 (Bibl. nat., MS Fonds fr. 6686), for details on the session of 9 May 1788.
26. On these developments, see Egret, *La Pré-révolution française*, pp. 325–37, 351–61. See also Robert Darnton, "Trends in Radical Propaganda on the Eve of the French Revolution" (Ph.D. diss., Oxford University, 1964), pp. 270–315.
27. The arrêté is published in Flammermont, *Remontrances*, 3:745–46.
28. For these remarks, consult Bibl. nat., MS Joly de Fleury 1040, fols. 253–54.
29. Refer again to the provisions of this legislation: Isambert et al., *Recueil*, 28:394–400.
30. Flammermont, *Remontrances*, 3:671–73. These protests also declared the Parlement's inadequacy to legitimize permanent taxation and asserted that only the Estates General could fulfill this function. On Ferrand's authorship of these remonstrances, see Ferrand, *Mémoires*, p. 12, and Sallier, *Annales françaises*, p. 94.
31. The lit de justice of 6 August 1787 had been staged for the registration of both the land tax and a comprehensive stamp tax. For the arrêté, see Flammermont, *Remontrances*, 3:692.
32. Flammermont, *Remontrances*, 3:690.
33. Although the magistrates would probably have preferred this kind of tax to the subvention territoriale (because the vingtième obviously could not exceed a level of 5 percent), they continued to see it as liable to administrative abuse.
34. See on this episode: *Discours de M. Goislard de Montsabert, conseiller au Parlement de Paris ... le ... 29 avril 1788, à M. le premier président, sur les vérifications ministérielles entreprises pour accroître la masse des vingtièmes*. Bibl. nat., 8° Lb[39], 6383 or 6385. See also Arch. nat., X[1B] 8988, session of 29 April 1788.
35. For d'Aligre's addresses, see *Procès-verbal de l'assemblée de notables, tenue à Versailles, en l'année 1787*, pp. 82, 312 (sessions of 22 February and 25 May 1788). For Tandeau's speech, see Arch. nat., either KK 1326, fols. 317–34, or X[1B] 8987, session of 19 November 1787.
36. For these comments by Guillaume François Louis Joly de Fleury, see Bibl. nat., MS Joly de Fleury 1040, fol. 321.

37. On the subordination of the seigneurial courts in the Paris Parlement's jurisdiction to the eighteenth-century procureurs-généraux, see again Paul Bisson de Barthélémy, *L'Activité d'un procureur général au Parlement de Paris à la fin de l'ancien régime*, p. 227, n. 1.
38. Bibl. nat., MS Joly de Fleury 2114, fols. 308–309.
39. Refer again to Flammermont, *Remontrances*, 3:694–95. In his speech, Robert de Saint-Vincent had linked the traditional persecutors of Protestants with "those who destroyed Port-Royal."
40. For these observations, see Bibl. nat., MS Joly de Fleury 1040, fols. 275–76.
41. Refer again to Ferrand, *Mémoires*, p. 10.
42. Bibl. nat., MS Joly de Fleury 1040, fols. 231, 233.
43. Bibl. nat., MS Joly de Fleury 1038, fol. 20.
44. For the correspondence between President Joly de Fleury and the acquaintance, named Varenne, see Bibl. nat., MS Joly de Fleury 1042, fols. 76, 77–78.
45. *Administration des pays de Bresse, Bugey, et Gex.* The memoir, dated April 1787, is found in Bibl. nat., MS Joly de Fleury 1037, fols. 104–108.
46. Even more striking indications of the president's social conservatism in 1787 are to be found in the series of dissertations on French constitutional history that Jean Omer Joly de Fleury left among his manuscripts. See especially the excursus entitled *Résultat de plusieurs vérités qui se trouvent établies par les Monuments de la Première et Deuxième Race des Rois de France*, in Bibl. nat., MS Joly de Fleury 2116, fols. 42–89; and the president's own favorable reaction to this consistently royalist interpretation of French history, entitled *Réflections sur le mémoire intitulé résultat* (fols. 90–98). A primary theme throughout is the emergence and utility of the third estate as a counterweight to the clergy and nobility.
47. For the most important section of this decree, refer to Egret, *La Pré-révolution française*, p. 338.
48. For these observations, consult Bibl. nat., MS Joly de Fleury 1040, fols. 295–98.
49. The court's official pronouncements began to broach the possibility of the Estates General as early as 26 July 1787, when the remonstrances against Brienne's fiscal legislation, which the counselor Ferrand had drafted, were presented to Louis XVI. After the arrest of the duc d'Orléans and the two judges, however, the court's invocation of the Estates General became more frequent and insistent. Flammermont (*Remontrances*, vol. 3, passim) has published most of the pertinent protests and decrees of 1788.
50. *Procès-verbal de l'assemblée de notables, tenue à Versailles, en l'année 1788*, pp. 68–69 (session of 6 November 1788).
51. Sallier, *Annales françaises*, p. 209. He also remarked that the decree had passed by "a nearly unanimous vote."
52. Flammermont, *Remontrances*, 3:690.
53. On the opposition within the tribunal, see especially François-Claude-Amour, marquis de Bouillé, *Mémoires*, pp. 63–64; Sallier, *Annales françaises*, p. 229; and Ferrand, *Mémoires*, p. 29.
54. The full text of the decree is given in Flammermont, *Remontrances*, 3:780–82.
55. Egret, *La Pré-révolution française*, p. 349.
56. Refer again to d'Eprémesnil's *Réflexions d'un magistrat*. It is interesting that both of the parlementaires who later recalled this decree in their memoirs claimed that d'Eprémesnil had been encouraged in his course of action by individuals outside the Parlement. Sallier, in his *Annales françaises*, pp. 227–28, claimed that encouragement came from Necker, in a letter here quoted in full. Ferrand alluded in his *Mémoires*, pp. 29–30, to the influence of Mme d'Eprémesnil, who was allegedly in touch with various "factions" in Paris. Yet d'Eprémesnil's correspondence with his wife in 1788 shows how determined he was that his company should play a leading role in defining constitutional issues at this critical juncture.

57. *Réflexions d'un magistrat,* pp. 4–6.
58. For Séguier's address, refer to Flammermont, *Remontrances,* 3:782–84. The senior avocat-général expressed similar thoughts in a pamphlet entitled *La Constitution renversée: Réflexions de M. Séguier, avocat général au Parlement à Paris.* Bibl. nat., 8° Lb³⁹, 5604. Also, refer again to *De la nécessité d'assembler les Etats-Généraux,* esp. pp. 2–6.
59. Sallier, *Annales françaises,* pp. 205–208. See also Flammermont, *Remontrances,* 3:777.
60. Sallier, *Annales françaises,* p. 208. However, it should be recalled that even in less tumultuous times the magistrates' obsession about law and order was partially balanced by their solicitude for the rights of suspects and inmates of prisons and hospitals.
61. *Déclaration concernant le timbre* (Versailles, 4 August 1787). Isambert et al., *Recueil,* 28:400–15. For the complaints of the booksellers and printers, see Bibl. nat., MS Joly de Fleury 2114, fols. 24–28. In general, they asserted that the new impost would make newspapers, almanacs, promissory notes, licenses of all kinds, and other printed material too expensive to print or buy. On the pressure exerted by the consular courts, see Egret, *La Pré-révolution française,* p. 162.
62. Flammermont, *Remontrances,* 3:690.
63. For information on this affair, see Arch. nat., X¹ᴮ 8986, session of 28 July 1787; and X¹ᴮ 8987, session of 4 August 1787. The court had no time to remonstrate on the matter, but it went so far as to decree unanimously on 4 August 1787 that a committee of judges study the problem of the alleged malfeasance in the Indies trade and fire insurance business.
64. For Joly de Fleury's remarks, see Bibl. nat., MS Joly de Fleury 1040, fol. 291.
65. *Déclaration pour la liberté du commerce des grains* (Versailles, 17 June 1787). Isambert et al., eds., *Recueil,* 28:361–64. Hardy reported a vote of 95 to 81 in favor of the legislation. *Mes Loisirs,* 7:123. (Bibl. nat., MS Fonds fr. 6686.)
66. Flammermont, *Remontrances,* 3:798.
67. This decree is found in *ibid.,* pp. 798–99.
68. Ibid., p. 797.
69. Ibid., p. 799.
70. He had done so, according to the marquis d'Albertas, in claiming at a plenary session of the court that a lottery in life annuities proposed by Necker was too important an affair for parlementary registration. Few of his colleagues had supported him on the issue. Marquis d'Albertas, *"Journal de nouvelles,"* 6:2653 (Bibl. nat., MS Nouv. acq. fr. 4391).
71. Flammermont, *Remontrances,* 3:784.
72. *Procés-verbal de l'assemblée de notables, 1788,* p. 485 (session of 12 December 1788).
73. Refer again to Flammermont, *Remontrances,* 3:796.
74. Ibid., pp. 745–46.
75. Specifically, the decree projected "collaboration between the Estates General and the sovereign courts so that the courts must not and will not suffer the levying of any impost not approved, nor consent to the execution of any law not requested or agreed to, by the Estates General." Ibid., p. 781. It is especially significant in this connection to recall d'Eprémesnil's support in his pamphlet of 7 December 1788 for "separate voting by the orders, each one so independent of the others that two of them cannot bind the third." Such an arrangement would preclude or at least work against the control of the assembly by either the aristocracy or the third estate.
76. Ferrand, *Mémoires,* p. 29; Bouillé, *Mémoires,* p. 64.
77. Sallier, *Annales françaises,* p. 80.
78. Pasquier, *Histoire,* 1:27–28. Ferrand in his *Mémoires,* pp. 8–9, sketched a similar picture of the young jurists of the Enquêtes and Requêtes.
79. In his *Mémoires,* pp. 63–64, the marquis de Bouillé claimed that the decree

of 5 December 1788 was prepared in the sessions of a so-called *club des enragés* formed by the duc d'Orléans and counting among its members d'Eprémesnil, Duport, de Sémonville, and Le Peletier de Saint-Fargeau. Another memorialist, the minister Barentin, saw the decree as "the product of seditious gatherings at the residence of M. Duport" and listed the "revolutionary" parlementaires who supposedly frequented those assemblages. C.-L.-F. de Paule de Barentin, *Mémoire autographe sur les derniers conseils du roi Louis XVI*, pp. 86–88. Yet, however this may be, Duval d'Eprémesnil would soon be coming to a parting of the ways with his erstwhile allies Duport and Le Peletier de Saint-Fargeau. Refer to the anonymous introduction to the *Discours et opinions de d'Eprémesnil, précédés d'une notice sur sa vie.*

CONCLUSION

1. The Parlement continued to hold its ordinary sessions and to dispense justice through most of 1789. By decree of the National Assembly, however, only a skeleton crew in the Chambre des Vacations remained on at the Palais de Justice after the vacations of September–October 1789 to administer essential justice. The Assembly abolished the entire parlementary system the following year.

2. This subject has not been exhaustively researched, but Henri Carré traced the post-1789 careers of some of the parlementaires in his book *La Fin des Parlements, 1788–1790*. The information in this paragraph is taken from that source.

3. On this point, refer again to Colin Lucas, "Nobles, Bourgeois, and the Origins of the French Revolution," and to Jean Egret's analysis of the political propaganda of late 1788 and early 1789 in *La Pré-révolution française.*

Bibliography

It has seemed most natural to divide the bibliography into the following five sections: (1) essential reference works, including almanacs, dictionaries, and edited documentary collections; (2) parlementary records and papers; (3) pamphlet literature from, or especially concerning, the Parisian parlementaires; (4) general memoirs and journals of the period; and (5) subsequent scholarship on parlementary affairs. In each section, only those sources proving immediately useful to the book are mentioned; readers desiring to cast their nets more widely for the immense wealth of eighteenth-century historical studies are advised to consult the bibliographies of more general works.

ESSENTIAL REFERENCE WORKS

Almanach royal. Paris: Debure, for the years from 1774 to 1789.

Bluche, J. François. *L'Origine des magistrats du Parlement de Paris au XVIIIᵉ siècle;* Paris: Fédération des Sociétés historiques et archéologiques de Paris et de l'Ile-de-France, 1956.

Etat nominatif des pensions sur le trésor royal, imprimé par ordre de l'Assemblée nationale. 3 vols. Paris: Imprimerie nationale, 1789–90.

Flammermont, Jules. *Les Remontrances du Parlement de Paris au XVIIIᵉ siècle.* 3 vols. Paris: Imprimerie nationale, 1888–98. Flammermont published in the third volume of this series all parlementary speeches and protests delivered to Louis XVI during the 1774–89 period, as well as certain deliberations within the court's plenary sessions. The complete minutes and registers of plenary sessions help comprise series X^{1A} and X^{1B} in the Archives nationales (see below, second section).

Isambert, François André, et al., eds. *Recueil général des anciennes lois françaises: Depuis l'an 420 jusqu'à la révolution de 1789.* 29 vols. Paris: Belin-LePrieur, 1822–33. The text of legislation pertinent to the Parisian parlementaires is not always found in this compilation of French law. When this is the case, the reader is directed to copies of the legislation left by the magistrates among their own papers or among their company's official records.

Marion, Marcel. *Dictionnaire des institutions de la France aux XVIIᵉ et XVIIIᵉ siècles.* Paris: A. Picard, 1923.

Monin, Hippolyte. *L'Etat de Paris en 1789: Etudes et documents sur l'ancien régime à Paris.* Paris: Jouaust, 1889.

Procès-verbal de l'assemblée de notables, tenue à Versailles, en l'année 1787. Paris, 1788.

Procès-verbal de l'assemblée de notables, tenue à Versailles, en l'année 1788. Paris, 1788.

Roton, A. de, *Les Arrêts du Grand Conseil portant dispense du marc d'or de noblesse. Commentés et complétés par J. de la Trollière et R. de Montmort.* Paris: S. G. A. F., 1951. The decrees in question were apparently issued by the Conseil des Dépêches rather than by the Grand Conseil during the 1770s and 1780s. The decrees excused young and noble parlementaires, among

Bibliography

other noblemen, from the obligation of paying the *marc d'or de noblesse,* upon assuming office, and they provide information about the social origins of the young jurists entering the court during this period. The vast majority of these judges were lay rather than clerical, and it is these lay jurists whose decrees of dispensation were published by de Roton and his collaborators.

PARLEMENTARY RECORDS AND PAPERS

The official records of the Paris Parlement make up the several X series in the Archives nationales. The judicial decrees, minutes, and registers found therein comprise one of the most imposing documentary collections surviving from the old regime in France. Other series in this national repository contain genealogical and administrative information germane to the membership and functions of the Parlement. However, most collections of personal papers surviving from the eighteenth-century parlementaires repose in the Bibliothèque nationale, including the copious holdings in the manuscript archive of the Joly de Fleury family. Although, for the years prior to 1774, there are abundant and valuable parlementary papers housed in other Parisian repositories, essential documents deriving from the 1774–89 period are wholly concentrated in the Archives nationales and Bibliothèque nationale. Duplications of parlementary registers, minutes of plenary sessions, decrees, and other documents may be found scattered throughout the following archives: Bibliothèque de l'Arsenal, Bibliothèque historique de la Ville de Paris, Bibliothèque Mazarine, Bibliothèque Sainte-Geneviève, Bibliothèque du Sénat, Société de l'Histoire du Protestantisme Français, Archives de Paris et de l'Ancien Département de la Seine, and Les Archives du Ministère des Affaires Etrangères. But, to repeat, all essential sources for the Paris Parlement of Louis XVI's reign are concentrated in the two principal repositories of historical records, the Archives nationales and Bibliothèque nationale.

Archives Nationales

158 A.P.   See especially cartons 3 and 9: Personal papers of Jean Jacques IV Duval d'Eprémesnil.

H 1657–58.   Administrative papers deriving from the Parlement's investigation of the corvée royale and vingtièmes during 1777–78.

K 695.   Correspondence between the government and the Parlement relating to the judicial reform controversy of 1783–84.

KK 1326–27.   *Troubles du Royaume de France au sujet des édits, déclarations, etc., enregistrés aux lits de justice de 1787 et 1788 par le Parlement de Paris et ensuite par les autres Cours du Royaume.*

X¹ᴬ 8562–601.   Registers of plenary sessions (Conseil secret) during the period 1774–89.

X¹ᴮ 8965–91.   Minutes of plenary sessions (Conseil secret) during the period 1774–89.

X¹ᴬ 8809, X¹ᴬ 8819, X¹ᴬ 8832, X¹ᴮ 9060, X¹ᴮ 9062.   Miscellaneous information on legislation and parlementary activities of the 1774–89 period.

X¹ᴬ 9036.   Conclusions of Procureur-Général Joly de Fleury in litigation, announcing parlementary judgments. (Sample for period July 1782–June 1783.)

X¹ᴬ 9041.   Conclusions of Procureur-Général Joly de Fleury in litigation, announcing parlementary judgments. (Sample for period October 1788–March 1789.)

Bibliography

Bibliothèque nationale

Fonds français 6877–79.   Personal papers of President Chrétien François II de Lamoignon de Basville.

Fonds français 11388.   *Mémoires divers relatifs à l'administration provinciale, en général, et à celle de la Généralité de Moulins, en particulier.*

Fonds français 11389.   *"Traité des Etats" et notes diverses sur l'administration provinciale, en particulier sur celle que des arrêts du Conseil établirent, en 1778 et 1779, dans le Berry et le Dauphiné.*

Nouvelles acquisitions françaises 940–87.   *Recueil de différentes matières judiciaires: Procès, mémoires, factums, procédures, etc.,* formé par Lefebvre d'Amécourt, conseiller au Parlement de Paris.

Nouvelles acquisitions françaises 22103–12.   *Papiers de Lefebvre d'Amécourt: Mémoires et documents sur l'histoire et l'administration de la France.*

Collection Joly de Fleury.   This series of over 2,500 volumes, a legacy of the famous family of the eighteenth-century robe in France, constitutes a cardinal source for information on the personnel and activities of the Parlement in that century. Volumes of special importance consulted for this study:

1028, 2125. Controversy over judicial reform during 1783–84.

1037. Provincial assemblies (1781–87).

1038–44, 1466, 2114–16.   Events and issues of the prerevolutionary crisis (1787–88).

1432–42.   Eleven-volume collection of papers deriving from the tenure of Jean François Joly de Fleury as minister of finances (1781–83).

1443–44, 1448–50.   Other financial matters invoking the Parlement's attention during the 1780s.

1464–65.   Parlementary investigation into the administration of the corvée royale (1776–81).

2088–89.   Diamond Necklace affair (1785–86).

2201.   Miscellaneous projects for reform of the French lawcourts during the 1780s.

2536–46.   Eleven-volume collection of the papers of the abbé Sahuguet d'Espagnac, rapporteur in the Parlement until his death in 1781. Two volumes in particular—2536 and 2539—provide much information on the controversies surrounding the corvée royale and provincial assemblies, respectively.

Other volumes utilized: 461–63, 466, 478, 480, 485–86, 488, 496, 498, 504–505, 507–508, 514, 516, 519–20, 522, 526, 528, 533, 539, 541, 548, 553, 555–56, 558–59, 605–608, 1051, 1064, 1682, 1729, and 2527.

PAMPHLET LITERATURE

Conversation familière de M. l'abbé Sauveur . . . avec Mlle Sauveur, sa très-honorée soeur. April 1783. Bibl. nat., Lb[39], 320.

Lettre d'un conseiller au Parlement de Paris à un ancien conseiller au Parlement, retiré dans ses terres. May 1783. Bibl. nat., Lb[39], 321.

Conférence entre un ministre d'Etat et un conseiller au Parlement. N.d. Bibl. nat., 8° Lb[39], 462.

Suite de la conférence du ministre avec le conseiller. N.d. Bibl. nat., 8° Lb[39], 463.

2e suite de la conférence du ministre avec le conseiller. N.d. Bibl. nat., 8° Lb[39], 464.

Bibliography

Rapport de M. l'abbé Tandeau, de l'édit d'emprunt enregistré à la séance du roi au Parlement, le 19 novembre 1787. N.d. Bibl. nat., Lb[39], 470.

Façon de voir d'une bonne vieille, qui ne radote pas encore. Attributed to Antoine Louis Séguier by revolutionary and imperial editor-librarian Antoine-Alexandre Barbier. N.d. Bibl. nat., Lb[39], 750.

Réflexions d'un magistrat sur la question du nombre et celle de l'opinion par ordre ou par tête. December 1788. By Duval d'Eprémesnil. Bibl. nat., Lb[39], 821.

Réflexions sur les pouvoirs et instructions à donner par les provinces à leurs députés aux Etats-Généraux. N.d. Attributed to Huguet de Sémonville by Barbier. Bibl. nat., Lb[39], 11117.

La Constitution renversée: Réflexions de M. Séguier, avocat général au Parlement à Paris. N.d. Bibl. nat., 8º Lb[39], 5604.

Discours de M. Goislard de Montsabert, conseiller au Parlement de Paris . . . le . . . 29 avril 1788, à M. le premier président, sur les vérifications ministérielles entreprises pour accroître la masse des vingtièmes. N.d. Bibl. nat., 8º Lb[39], 6383 or 6385.

Discours et opinions de d'Eprémesnil, précédés d'une notice sur sa vie. 1823. Bibl. nat., X 18835 bis.

Proposition inutilement faite par M. D'Eprémesnil à l'Assemblée (sur l'inviolabilité de la personne royale) . . . le 28 mars 1791, suivie d'un aperçu de l'opinion qu'il aurait prononcée, s'il avait eu la liberté de parole. N.d. Bibl. nat., 8º Le[29], 2094.

De la nécessité d'assembler les Etats-Généraux dans les circonstances actuelles, et de l'inadmission du timbre: Fragment du Discours de M. de Sémonville, conseiller au Parlement, dans la séance du 16. July 1787. Bibl. nat., 8º Lb[39], 377.

Déclaration de M. d'Eprémesnil, au sujet d'un imprimé faussement répandu sous son nom. 1789. Bibl. nat., 8º Lb[39], 6826.

Avertissement de M. d'Eprémesnil, à l'occasion de trois libelles anonymes qu'il a reçus de Beaucaire, par la poste. 1789. Bibl. nat., 8º Lb[39], 6957.

Observations sur une assertion de M. de Menou, au sujet des frais de l'ancienne administration judiciaire comparée à la nouvelle, proposées le 30 août 1790 à l'Assemblée nationale, par M. d'Eprémesnil. 1790. Bibl. nat., 8º Lb[39], 3980.

Discours de M. d'Eprémesnil à l'Assemblée nationale, au sujet de l'affaire des magistrats de Rennes. 1790. Bibl. nat., 8º Le[29], 423.

GENERAL MEMOIRS AND JOURNALS

d'Albertas, Marquis. *"Journal de nouvelles": Formé pour le marquis d'Albertas, premier président du Parlement de Provence (1770–1783).* 7 vols. Bibl. nat., MSS Nouv. acq. fr. 4386–92.

d'Allonville, Comte Armand. *Mémoires secrets, de 1770 à 1830.* 6 vols. Paris, 1838–45.

Augeard, Jacques-Mathieu. *Mémoires secrets de J.-M. Augeard . . . (1760 à 1800).* Paris, 1866.

Bachaumont, Louis Petit de, et al. *Mémoires secrets pour servir à l'histoire de la république des lettres en France depuis 1762 jusqu'à nos jours.* 36 vols. London, 1777–89.

Barentin, C.-L.-F. de Paule de. *Mémoire autographe sur les derniers conseils du roi Louis XVI.* Paris, 1844.

Bésenval, Bon-Pierre-Victoire, baron de. *Mémoires.* 3 vols. Paris, 1805.

Beugnot, Jacques-Claude, comte de. *Mémoires, 1783–1815.* 2 vols. Paris, 1867–68.

Bouillé, François-Claude-Amour, marquis de. *Mémoires.* Paris, 1821.

Choiseul, Etienne-François, duc de. *Mémoires.* Paris: Fernand Calmettes, 1904.

Bibliography

Croy, Emmanuel, maréchal duc de. *Mémoires . . . sur les cours de Louis XV et Louis XVI.* Paris, 1897.

Documents concernant le règne de Louis XVI, 1ᵉʳ janvier 1783–22 décembre 1792. Bulletins d'informations rédigés à Versailles et à Paris par un témoin, familier de la Cour. 3 vols. Bibl. nat., MSS Nouv. acq. fr. 13276–78.

Dufort, J.-N., comte de Cheverny. *Mémoires sur les règnes de Louis XV et Louis XVI et sur la Révolution.* 2 vols. Paris, 1886.

Faulcon, Félix, *Correspondance.* 2 vols. Poitiers: G. Debien, 1939–53.

Ferrand, Antoine François Claude, comte de. *Mémoires.* Paris, 1897.

Gazette de Leyde. Nouvelles politiques publiées à Leyde. 57 vols. Leiden, 1760–1810.

Georgel, Abbé Jean-François. *Mémoires pour servir à l'histoire des événements de la fin du XVIIIᵉ siècle, depuis 1760 jusqu'en 1806–1810, par un contemporain impartial.* 6 vols. Paris, 1817–18.

Hardy, Siméon-Prosper. *Mes Loisirs, ou, Journal d'événements tel qu'ils parviennent à ma connaissance (1764–1789).* 8 vols. Bibl. nat., MSS Fonds fr. 6680–87.

Lescure, A. M. de, ed. *Correspondance secrète inédite sur Louis XVI, Marie-Antoinette, la cour, et la ville, de 1777 à 1792.* 2 vols. Paris, 1866.

Mairobert, Pidansat de. *Journal historique du rétablissement de la magistrature.* 2 vols. London, 1774–76.

Montbarey, Alexandre-Marie-Léonor de Saint-Mauris, prince de. *Mémoires autographes.* 3 vols. Paris, 1826–27.

Montmorency-Luxembourg, duc de. Cited in Paul Filleul, *Le Duc de Montmorency-Luxembourg.* Paris, 1939.

Moreau, Jacob-Nicholas. *Mes Souvenirs.* 2 vols. Paris, 1898–1901.

Pasquier, Etienne-Denis, baron et duc de. *Histoire de mon temps: Mémoires du Chancelier Pasquier.* 6 vols. Paris, 1893–95.

Sallier-Chaumont de la Roche, Guy Marie. *Annales françaises: Depuis le commencement du règne de Louis XVI jusqu'aux Etats-Généraux, 1774–1789.* Paris, 1813.

————. *Essais pour servir d'introduction à l'histoire de la Révolution française, par un ancien magistrat du Parlement de Paris.* Paris, 1802.

Ségur, Louis-Philippe, comte de. *Mémoires ou souvenirs et anecdotes.* 2 vols. Paris, 1843.

Sémallé, Jean René Pierre, comte de. *Souvenirs.* Paris, 1898.

Soulavie, Jean-Louis Giraud. *Mémoires historiques et politiques du règne de Louis XVI.* 6 vols. Paris, 1801.

Talleyrand-Périgord, Charles-Maurice, duc de. *Mémoires.* 5 vols. Paris, 1891–92.

Vitrolles, Eugène François Auguste d'Arnaud, baron de. *Mémoires.* Paris: Farel, 1950.

SUBSEQUENT SCHOLARSHIP

Antoine, Michel, ed. *"Le Mémoire" de Gilbert de Voisins "sur les cassations": Un épisode des querelles entre Louis XV et les Parlements, 1767.* Paris: Sirey, 1958.

Barthélémy, Paul Bisson de. *L'Activité d'un procureur général au Parlement de Paris à la fin de l'ancien régime: Les Joly de Fleury.* Paris: Société d'édition d'enseignement supérieur, 1964.

Behrens, C. B. A. "Nobles, Privileges, and Taxes in France at the End of the Ancien Régime." *Economic History Review,* 2d ser., 15, no. 3 (April 1963): 451–75.

Bickart, Roger. *Les Parlements et la notion de souveraineté nationale au XVIIIᵉ siècle.* Paris: F. Alcan, 1932.

Bluche, J. François. *Les Magistrats du Parlement de Paris au XVIIIᵉ siècle (1715–1771).* Paris: Les Belles-Lettres, 1960.

Bibliography

Bosher, J. F. *French Finances, 1770–1795: From Business to Bureaucracy.* Cambridge: Cambridge University Press, 1970.

Carcassonne, Elie. *Montesquieu et le problème de la constitution française au XVIIIe siècle.* Paris: Presses Universitaires de France, 1926.

Carré, Henri. *La Fin des Parlements, 1788–1790.* Paris: Hachette, 1912.

———. "Un Précurseur inconscient de la Révolution: Le Conseiller du Val d'Eprésmesnil." *La Révolution française* 33 (July–December 1897): 349–73.

———. "La Réaction parlementaire de 1775 et le procureur général de Moydieu." *Revue d'histoire moderne et contemporaine* 11 (1908–February 1909): 349–58.

———. "La Tactique et les idées de l'opposition parlementaire." *La Révolution française* 29 (July–December 1895): 97–121.

———. "Turgot et le rappel des Parlements." *La Révolution française* 43 (July–December 1902).

Cavanaugh, Gerald J. "Turgot: The Rejection of Enlightened Despotism." *French Historical Studies* 6 (Spring 1969): 31–58.

Cobban, Alfred. *A History of Modern France.* Vol. 1: *Old Regime and Revolution, 1715–1799.* Baltimore: Penguin Books, 1968.

———. *The Social Interpretation of the French Revolution.* Cambridge: Cambridge University Press, 1964.

Crétineau-Joly, J.-A.-M. *Histoire religieuse, politique, et littéraire de la Compagnie de Jésus.* 6 vols. Paris: P. Mellier, 1845–46.

Dakin, Douglas. *Turgot and the Ancien Régime in France.* London: Methuen, 1939.

David, René, and de Vries, Henry P. *The French Legal System: An Introduction to Civil Law Systems.* New York: Oceana Publications, 1958.

Dawson, Philip. "The Bourgeoisie de Robe in 1789." *French Historical Studies* 4 (Spring 1965): 1–21.

———. *Provincial Magistrates and Revolutionary Politics in France, 1789–1795.* Cambridge: Harvard University Press, 1972.

Doyle, William O. "The Parlements of France and the Breakdown of the Old Regime, 1771–1788." *French Historical Studies* 6 (Fall 1970): 415–58.

———. "Was There an Aristocratic Reaction in Pre-revolutionary France?" *Past and Present* 57 (November 1972): 97–122.

Egret, Jean. "L'Aristocratie parlementaire française à la fin de l'ancien régime." *Revue historique* 208 (1952): 1–14.

———. *Louis XV et l'opposition parlementaire, 1715–1774.* Paris: Armand Colin, 1970.

———. *Necker: Ministre de Louis XVI, 1776–1790.* Paris: Honoré Champion, 1975.

———. *La Pré-révolution française, 1787–1788.* Paris: Presses Universitaires de France, 1962.

———. "Le Procès des Jésuites devant les Parlements de France." *Revue historique* 204 (1950): 1–27.

Eisenstein, Elizabeth. "Who Intervened in 1788? A Commentary on *The Coming of the French Revolution.*" *American Historical Review* 71 (October 1965): 77–103.

d'Estang, Bastard. *Les Parlements de France.* 2 vols. Paris: Didier, 1857.

Everat, Edouard. *La Sénéchaussée d'Auvergne et siège présidial de Riom au XVIIIe siècle: Etude historique.* Paris: E. Thorin, 1885.

Faure, Edgar. *La Disgrâce de Turgot.* Paris: Gallimard, 1961.

Flammermont, Jules. *Le Chancelier Maupeou et les Parlements.* Paris: A. Picard, 1883.

Ford, Franklin L. *Robe and Sword: The Regrouping of the French Aristocracy after Louis XIV.* Cambridge: Harvard University Press, 1953.

Galy, Germain. *Le Cadastre de la France, son intérêt juridique.* Paris: Sirey, 1942.

Gaxotte, Pierre. *La Révolution française.* Paris: Arthème Fayard et Cie, 1928.

Bibliography

Glasson, Ernst. *Le Parlement de Paris: Son rôle politique depuis le règne de Charles VII jusqu'à la Révolution*. 2 vols. Paris: Hachette, 1901.

———. "Le Parlement de Paris sous Louis XVI." *Revue parlementaire*, vols. 24–26 (1900).

Gomel, Charles. *Les Causes financières de la Révolution française*. 2 vols. Paris: Guillaumin 1892–93.

Goubert, Pierre. *L'Ancien Régime*. 2 vols. Paris: Armand Colin, 1969–73.

Gruder, Vivian R. *The Royal Provincial Intendants: A Governing Elite in Eighteenth-Century France*. Ithaca, N.Y.: Cornell University Press, 1968.

Herbin, René, and Pebereau, Alexandre. *Le Cadastre français*. Paris: F. Lefebvre, 1953.

Jacomet, Pierre. *Vicissitudes et chutes du Parlement de Paris*. Paris: Hachette, 1954.

Lacour-Gayet, Robert. *Calonne: Financier, réformateur, contre-révolutionnaire, 1734–1802*. Paris: Hachette, 1963.

Lardé, Georges. *Une Enquête sur les vingtièmes au temps de Necker: Histoire des remontrances du Parlement de Paris (1777–78)*. Paris: Letouzey et Ané, 1920.

Laurain, E. *Essai sur les Présidiaux*. Paris: L. Larose, 1896.

Lavergne, Léonce de. *Les Assemblées provinciales sous Louis XVI*. Paris: Michel Lévy Frères, 1864.

Lefebvre, Georges. *The French Revolution*, trans. Elizabeth M. Evanson. 2 vols. London: Routledge and Kegan Paul, 1969.

Lesort, André. "La Question de la corvée des grands chemins sous Louis XVI après la chute de Turgot (1776–1778)." In *Comité des travaux historiques et scientifiques: Section d'histoire moderne et contemporaine* 8 (1927): 49–95.

Lucas, Colin. "Nobles, Bourgeois, and the Origins of the French Revolution." *Past and Present*. 60 (August 1973): 84–126.

Madelin, Louis. *The French Revolution*. London: William Heinemann Ltd., 1925.

Mandrou, Robert. *La France aux XVIIe et XVIIIe siècles*. Paris: Presses Universitaires de France, 1970.

Marion, Marcel. *Le Garde des Sceaux Lamoignon et la réforme judiciaire de 1788*. Paris: Hachette, 1905.

———. *Histoire financière de la France depuis 1715*. Vol. 1: *1715–1789*. Paris: A. Rousseau, 1914.

Michelet, Jules. *Histoire de la Révolution française*. 10 vols. Paris: Calmann-Lévy, 1909–10.

Petot, Jean. *Histoire de l'administration des Ponts et Chaussées, 1599–1815*. Paris: M. Rivière, 1958.

Renouvin, Pierre. *Les Assemblées provinciales de 1787: Origines, développements, résultats*. Paris: A. Picard, 1921.

Richet, Denis. "Autour des origines idéologiques lointaines de la Révolution française: Elites et despotisme." *Annales, E.S.C.*, January–February 1969, pp. 1–23.

Shennan, J. H. *The Parlement of Paris*. London: Eyre and Spottiswoode, 1968.

Tocqueville, Alexis de. *The Old Regime and the French Revolution*, trans. Stuart Gilbert. New York: Doubleday, 1955.

Vanier, M. *Les Anciennes juridictions de Reims: Lectures faites à l'Académie de Reims, 1869–1870*. Rheims: P. DuBois et Cie, 1870.

Villers, Robert. *L'Organisation du Parlement de Paris et des Conseils Supérieurs d'après la réforme de Maupeou, 1771–74*. Paris: Jouve et Cie, 1937.

Index

Index

197 (n. 98), 198 (nn. 12, 19); considered by Parlement in connection with *corvée royale* after Turgot's disgrace, 82, 143–53, 162; considered by Parlement in connection with Turgot's reform of *corvée royale*, 94–95; as related to Necker's provincial assemblies, 115–16

Tandeau, abbé (parlementaire), 25, 155, 163, 196 (n. 77), 197 (n. 108)

Taxation populaire, 134. See also Grain and bread: issues considered in Parlement

Thèse nobiliaire, 9. See also Aristocratic resurgence and revolution

Titon de Villotran (parlementaire), 26

Tocqueville, Alexis de, 5–6

Toulouse Parlement, 41, 54–55, 73

Tournelle, 20, 29, 43, 102, 104, 189 (n. 41)

Toussac, chevalier de (rural seigneur), 97

Turgot, Anne-Robert-Jacques, baron de l'Aulne, 3, 25, 56, 185 (n. 32); suggests system of provincial assemblies during ministry, 67, 192 (n. 16); criticizes Necker's provincial assem-

blies, 68–69, 77, 192–93 (n. 20), 193 (n. 21); attempts reform of *corvée royale,* 93–97, 100, 135, 141–42, 149; attempts to abolish Parisian guilds, 121–26, 135; implements free grain trade, 131–33, 135, 203 (n. 32); abolishes *contrainte solidaire* against wealthy peasants, 198 (n. 19)

University of Paris: parlementary supervision over, 16, 20

Vacations, 18, 45–52, 58, 67, 74, 189 (nn. 41, 42). See also Chambre des Vacations

Vingtièmes, 23; during Necker's first ministry, 70, 77–82, 96–100, 116, 144–45, 147, 174, 195 (nn. 62, 68, 75); during Jean François II Joly de Fleury's ministry, 83–85, 196 (n. 87); during Calonne's ministry, 86–88; considered by Parlement during Turgot's ministry, 93–94; during "Pre-Revolution," 156, 162–63

Wood supplies to Paris. *See* Firewood supplies to Paris: investigated by Parlement

227